Date D

Inclusive
Cultural
Empathy

Inclusive Cultural Empathy

MAKING RELATIONSHIPS CENTRAL IN COUNSELING AND PSYCHOTHERAPY

Paul B. Pedersen

Hugh C. Crethar

Jon Carlson

AMERICAN PSYCHOLOGICAL ASSOCIATION
WASHINGTON, DC

Published by
American Psychological Association
750 First Street, NE
Washington, DC 20002
www.apa.org

To order
APA Order Department
P.O. Box 92984
Washington, DC 20090-2984
Tel: (800) 374-2721; Direct: (202) 336-5510
Fax: (202) 336-5502; TDD/TTY: (202) 336-6123
Online: www.apa.org/books/
E-mail: order@apa.org

In the U.K., Europe, Africa, and the Middle East, copies may be ordered from
American Psychological Association
3 Henrietta Street
Covent Garden, London
WC2E 8LU England

Typeset in Goudy by Circle Graphics, Columbia, MD

Printer: Edwards Brothers, Inc., Ann Arbor, MI
Cover Designer: Berg Design, Albany, NY
Technical/Production Editor: Tiffany L. Klaff

The opinions and statements published are the responsibility of the authors, and such opinions and statements do not necessarily represent the policies of the American Psychological Association.

Library of Congress Cataloging-in-Publication Data

Pedersen, Paul, 1936–
  Inclusive cultural empathy: making relationships central in counseling and psychotherapy / Paul B. Pedersen, Hugh C. Crethar, and Jon Carlson. — 1st ed.
      p. cm.
  Includes bibliographical references and index.
  ISBN-13: 978-0-9792125-1-2
  ISBN-10: 0-9792125-1-0
  1. Cross-cultural counseling. 2. Psychiatry, Transcultural. 3. Ethnopsychology. 4. Counselor and client. 5. Therapist and patient. I. Crethar, Hugh C. II. Carlson, Jon. III. Title.

  BF636.7.C76P43 2008
  158'.3—dc22
                                    2007033128

British Library Cataloguing-in-Publication Data
A CIP record is available from the British Library.

Printed in the United States of America
First Edition

The discovery by quantum physicists that matter is neither particle nor wave, but always simultaneously both, destroys the basis of the either/or approach that we have grown accustomed to using when we analyze something or define it. And so, in attempting to describe the workings of the web of inclusion, I will approach it both as a pattern, a model for coherently ordering people and their tasks; and as a process, a way of thinking and acting, of behaving and solving problems as they arise.

—Sally Helgesen, *The Web of Inclusion: A New Architecture for Building Great Organizations* (2005, p. 9)

CONTENTS

LIST OF TABLES, FIGURES, AND EXHIBITS

TABLES

FIGURES

EXHIBITS

PREFACE

Although there is widespread agreement that culture mediates all counseling relationships, there is no widespread agreement on exactly how culture—or multiculturalism—shapes the empathic relationship between client and counselor. This book is our attempt to describe how cultural similarities and differences influence empathic relationships in the counseling process. We set out to accomplish this through critique and exploration of the empathy construct. We ground our discussion in research but also base it on our own teaching and learning about multicultural counseling over the years. We believe that the expanded, or more inclusive, definition of empathy proposed in this book takes the multicultural movement to the next level of generic application.

We have seen counseling practices spread from industrialized countries where ideology tends toward individualism to other societies with different worldviews. With these changes in setting, the individualistic assumptions behind many counseling theories and practices have come to stand out as such, and it is clear that not all such theories and practices are universally appropriate. This book describes how empathy in counseling and other therapeutic and human service-oriented work can become less individualistic and more relationship centered, and therefore, more multicultural. This change has not occurred suddenly, and we document the research by others leading us beyond individualism in the search for empathic multicultural counseling relationships. Much of this research was produced outside the Euro-American envelope and has therefore not been given the attention it deserves in Euro-American publications, although even in conventional counseling textbooks the emphasis on relationship-centered models is increasingly evident (Clark, 2007). Each of the three authors has arrived at this insight—that inclusive counseling relationships make counseling more multicultural and more effective—by a different path.

Paul Pedersen taught university students for 3 years in Indonesia, 2 years in Malaysia, and 1 year in Taiwan, then returned to the University of Minnesota as a foreign student advisor for 8 years. He was a visiting professor in the Department of Psychology at the University of Hawaii for 4 years and the chair of counseling at Syracuse University for 14 years. He is now retired and is a visiting professor at the University of Hawaii in the Department of Psychology. He learned from his Asian clients and students about how counseling includes a contextual network of families, friends, and relationships. Each client brings with her or him to the counseling session a frame of reference determined by her or his own cultural milieu. Sometimes these "culture teachers" in the client's life take control of the client's decisions and become more important than the client her- or himself. To exclude these culture teachers in the counseling interview is to ignore the client's reality. An inclusive alternative more typically found in Asian and other non-Western cultures broadens the focus beyond the individual client to the whole cultural context.

Hugh Crethar was raised primarily in Hawaii, with a few years in southern Florida. His formative cultural learning occurred on the North Shore of Oahu, where his culture teachers were from Polynesian (Hawaiian, Samoan, Tongan, Fijian, and Maori) as well as Japanese and Chinese cultures. He was raised to value extended family networks ('ohana) and with a focus on the health of the community as a whole, instead of the family of origin. 'Ohana can be defined as a group of both closely and distantly related people who share nearly everything, from land and food to children and status. He also has close ties with Latinos and Latino culture, as he spent several years of his early adult life connecting with this portion of his heritage. He has long embraced collective and inclusive perspectives and encourages others to do so as well.

Jon Carlson studied in urban settings and has completed doctoral degrees in counseling (Detroit) and clinical psychology (Chicago). He, like Pedersen and Crethar, has lived and worked in Hawaii and was exposed to the myriad cultures found there. He has traveled in Asia, Africa, South America, and Europe. He and his wife Laura have five children, including Ben and Kali, who were adopted as babies from Korea. Experience and exposure have helped him to realize and appreciate the complexity of connecting with others.

This book brings together our combined experiences, insights, and perspectives that have been emerging over the years in our other publications, teaching, and research activities. In writing this book we discovered the heart and core of all our previous publications summarized in the concept of *inclusion*. We had been writing parts of this book in all our previous publications, but finally we have a comprehensive perspective into which all the previous writings fit together.

The intended audience for this book includes teachers and students of counseling and helping services in psychologically based professions. We assume that the competent professional never stops learning and, therefore, is a lifelong student even when that professional has become a teacher. To minimize our roles as both student and teacher is to endanger our professional competence in a world of growth and change. Sometimes the book refers to the reader as a student and/or teacher to emphasize the importance of these combined roles. This book presumes that we are all teachers and that we are all students at the same time in the transfer of knowledge from one person to another. This book can be used as a classroom text in courses that presume helper roles in multicultural contexts, or as a book for professional development and continuing education of current practitioners. The practical skills and implications of inclusive cultural empathy grow out from our literature review, theoretical discussion, and description of the awareness–knowledge–skills developmental framework, so we hope that readers will approach the book as a whole and read it from beginning to end. Although the term *counselor* is used throughout this book, we define that term broadly across disciplines to include human service providers, therapists, and others who provide formal and/or informal support in formal and/or informal contexts. In some cases the readers may well not perceive themselves as "counselors" even though they function as helping professionals.

Sometimes this book uses the term *non-Western* as a contrast to Western perspectives. We recognize the complexity and heterogeneity of within-group differences for both Western and non-Western identities. Our point of highlighting this contrast is simply to demonstrate contrasting alternative perspectives that different people from different backgrounds depend on in constructing their perspectives. Because we are especially familiar with Asian cultures as a result of our backgrounds, the book occasionally refers to Asian examples within the larger non-Western category.

Inclusive cultural empathy, the model for counseling and related professions that we describe in this book, has become a key to unlock the deeper meaning behind everything we have done so far in our careers. It is like a flash of insight that suddenly illuminates the dark corners of a room. We hope you the reader will likewise experience your own flash of insight that will reveal to you a truth that you already knew . . . but did not "know" that you knew.

Inclusive
Cultural
Empathy

INTRODUCTION

In this book we present a model for counseling and other professional human service relationships called *inclusive cultural empathy* (ICE). This model grew from our awareness that (a) the functions of counseling have a history of several thousand years and (b) the alternatives to talk therapy include many different means of restoring a healthy balance in the client's cultural context. Hence, our model of empathy is inclusive because it incorporates functions and modes of counseling that may fall outside conventional definitions of who a counselor is, what roles he or she plays, who a client is, and what her or his goals in help-seeking are. We include not only the relationship between a counselor and client but also the many relationships within the client's cultural context. We posit that the degree of inclusion can also be an outcome measure for empathic counseling (Pedersen, 1991; Pedersen & Ivey, 1993). Our model of empathy is cultural because it seeks to take the many facets of clients' cultural context—facets we will discuss at some length beginning in chapter 3—into account. The task of this book is not to introduce a new multicultural theory to compete with humanism, behaviorism, or psychodynamic approaches. The task is rather to infuse inclusion into whatever theory is being applied and to take multiculturalism to the next level of generic relevance.

We have found that non-Western perspectives provide a useful vocabulary for identifying the inclusive characteristics of ICE, but we do not intend our model only for use with clients whose ethnic or national cultures differ from the counselor's. Rather, we use Asian and other non-Western worldviews in the early part of the book to show one way among many possible ways that understandings of the empathy construct can be expanded. We expect that many readers approach this book with a working definition of culture to which an initial discussion of ethnocultural contrasts will be most immediately accessible.

The research literature about empathy demonstrates a consistent conclusion that relationship factors are a necessary—but perhaps not sufficient—condition for competent counseling. However, there is no consensus on how to develop successful counseling relationships. Part of the confusion in the literature about counseling relationships is the result of failing to distinguish between the two different definitions of empathy. The convergent definitions of empathy focus exclusively on knowing the individual in depth and excluding contextual factors that might distract from that subjective focus on the individual (Clark, 2007; Egan, 2002; Rogers, 1961). The divergent definitions of empathy focus inclusively on knowing the individual in the broadly defined cultural context in which that individual lives (Chung & Bemak, 2002; Ridley & Udipi, 2002). The divergent definition of empathy is acknowledged indirectly in the literature about empathy to the extent it influences the counselor–client relationship, but the primary conventional focus is on convergent empathy. Most of the research on empathy predicates the sharing of identical emotions in experiential, communication, and observational modes as best described by Carl Rogers (see Clark, 2007; Rogers, 1961).

Decety and Jackson (2004) demonstrated the most extreme form of individual-centered convergent empathy in their discussion of the architecture of human empathy from the perspective of neuroscience. Empathy is defined as an affective response to another person's emotional state, a cognitive capacity to take the other person's perspective, and a regulatory mechanism to keep track of self and other feelings. ICE makes the divergent definition of empathy a primary focus for understanding and building the counseling relationship. To some extent this change in salience turns the conventional findings about empathy upside down with implications that challenge the conventional perspective. ICE extends the empathy construct by applying a relationship-centered perspective to the client's larger cultural context.

What happens when a client's cultural context is ignored? What happens when the helper diminishes the differences between the client's culture teachers and the client? The counselor is likely to impose her or his own self-reference criteria about what is normal or appropriate client behavior without regard for the client's criteria. The counselor who assumes there is only one client in the room is already in trouble. Each "virtual" client brings many culture teachers with her or him into the counseling interview. These culture teachers may be more real to the client than the counselor.

This book is divided into 11 chapters. In chapter 1, we review the research literature describing empathy as an exclusive focus on knowing the individual as an entity separate from the context in which that individual exists. Psychology as a science has typically treated cultural differences as a distraction from the understanding of a universal/individual truth. This is in sharp contrast with anthropology, for example, where the emphasis is on the cultural differences and the total context. The network of literature describing empathy as having an inclusive focus is also reviewed in the first chapter. Readers will notice that the publications emphasizing inclusion and context frequently come from Asian and non-Western sources.

Chapter 2 plumbs the rich philosophical and religious worldviews embedded in the many cultures around the world for relationship-centered models. The purpose of this chapter is to provide an alternative vocabulary for translating empathy theories and models of the client's cultural context from an individualistic to a relationship-centered perspective. This alternative vocabulary includes key terms regarding the self, the function of relationships, expectations for development across the life span, definitions of health, and appropriate helping roles. We then focus the discussion of health and helping roles and a list of therapies that can be viewed as alternatives to conventional counseling as it is most often practiced in industrialized countries. Our inventory of therapies includes Asian as well as African and Native American therapies.

Chapter 3 introduces and defines ICE, the assumptions behind it, and some of its implications for practice. Even if the reader does not agree with the premise of ICE, we hope that the conversations between us and the reader will result in a better understanding of the generic counseling relationship.

Next follows a three-stage sequence for developing ICE. The sequence moves from awareness to knowledge to skill. Professionals who wish to practice ICE must first develop an awareness of culturally learned assumptions about the counseling process and the counselor her- or himself (chapters 4 and 5). Moving to the second stage involves acquiring knowledge and gathering information based on the earlier identified assumptions (chapters 6 and 7). In the third stage, specific skills based on accurate awareness and meaningful knowledge are discovered and honed (chapters 8 and 9). Because all behaviors are learned and displayed in a cultural context, accurate awareness, meaningful knowledge, and appropriate intervention skill need to be based on that cultural context.

Chapters 10 and 11 offer insight into the impact of ICE as it can be applied to advocacy and to enriching the field's definitions of counseling and psychotherapy. Several examples of client empowerment are found in chapter 10. Chapter 11 concludes by presenting a number of resources for deepening the awareness, knowledge, and skills needed to develop ICE. While we expect the activities, training models, simulation, and thinking exercises to be of particular interest to counselor educators and trainers, we do encourage other readers to try them out as well.

We use several related terms referring to culture and counseling in this book. *Cross-cultural* refers to the comparison across cultures of one perspective with another. It primarily refers to ethnocultural comparisons. This term was one of the original concepts used to describe culture and counseling (Pedersen, 2000a). The term *multicultural* refers to the multiple cultures in each context and even in each person, emphasizing not only the ethnic and national origins of our learned assumptions but also their age, gender, socioeconomic status, and other affiliational origins (Pedersen & Ivey, 1993). The term *culture-centered* is a new term, based on making culture central to understanding each context and providing an alternative to individualism for understanding the counseling process (Pedersen, 1991). Within this text you will encounter the terminology "her or his" and "he or she" in alphabetical order instead of the traditional order wherein the male gender is always listed first. We chose to do this in an effort to promote gender equity in language use which we feel is more representative of the message of ICE.

Our hope is to provoke some discussion about the importance of what Geertz (1975) called "thick descriptions" of culture and the immediate usefulness of a culture-centered perspective in counseling and the human services. We hope you will finish reading this book with more questions than you had before. We hope that reading this book will make the "easy answers" to complex problems less desirable to you. We hope that through reading this volume your relationships—both professional relationships with clients and personal relationships—will be made stronger than ever and your capacity for empathy with the diversity of cultures in our global society will become a permanent resource for you.

1

TRADITIONAL AND NONTRADITIONAL PERSPECTIVES ON EMPATHY, HELP-SEEKING, AND HEALTHY OUTCOMES

Although everyone agrees that empathy is important, there is much disagreement about how empathy is defined and how the condition of empathy is developed in counseling relationships. This first part of our book surveys the conventional definitions of empathy and empathy development and also devotes special attention to how empathy is defined across cultures. The more popular and conventional definitions of empathy are grounded in research in the European American cultural context in which individualism is often the preferred perspective. Clark (2007) provided a good review of the empathy literature showing how it emerged from Carl Rogers's work in the 1940s.

In addition, literature from Asia and other non-Western cultures is reviewed to show how empathy can be conceptualized more broadly in non-individualistic cultures. The collective social perspective tends to prefer a more inclusive definition of identity and therefore of empathy as well. The terms *Western* and *non-Western* are used to describe some cross-cultural contrasts. These labels are not intended to imply two monolithic perspectives but

Parts of chapter 1 are from *Culture-Centered Counseling Interventions*, by P. Pedersen, 1997, Thousand Oaks, CA: Sage. Copyright 1997 by Sage. Adapted with permission.

rather to demonstrate that there are many contrasting and complex perspectives about what we call empathy. Many people who live in Western geographical contexts prefer the perspective we are labeling non-Western and vice versa. The labels are used as a matter of convenience, recognizing the limitations of both labels in surveying the wide-ranging alternatives.

Inclusive cultural empathy (ICE) is defined as a social perspective to supplement the individualistic perspective as appropriate. ICE is presented as a stance from which to question other aspects of helping relationships as well, such as How do (and how should) humans develop and grow in their capacity for empathy, and how is growth measured? What is the meaning and importance of gender? What is the goal of help-seeking?

The concept of empathy in a therapeutic setting appears to have taken root with the work of Theodor Lipps, who focused on aesthetic responses to contemplation of works of art in the late 19th century (Szalita, 1976). Lipps used the German term *Einfühlung* to describe an aesthetic response to art, more specifically sculpture, as an inroad to understanding the inner being of the artist. He has been credited for moving the helping professions from a focus on *sympathy* to a focus on *empathy* (Jahoda, 2005). Occult artist and aesthetician Vernon Lee (1856–1935) is also credited for early use of the same term, referring to it as an aesthetic parallel to psychic processes (Hayward, 2005). The concept appears to have been introduced in English by Edward Titchener in the early 1900s (Peitchinis, 1990). In this chapter we introduce the construct of empathy and how it has evolved as part of Western psychology. We demonstrate that conventional empathy is a culture-bound construct and point to its limitations as such. We also open discussion on the possibilities a more inclusive model of empathy can offer.

THE HISTORICAL ROOTS OF EMPATHY

Most, if not all, the literature reviewed in defining conventional empathy originated in Europe and North America, reflecting the individualistic cultural preferences of that social context. The therapeutic relationship has long been acknowledged as a key component of change as a result of therapy (Watson, Goldman, & Vanaerschot, 1998). Likewise, empathy has long been considered a cornerstone of effective therapy and pivotal to the development of the therapeutic alliance (Bohart & Greenberg, 1997). The belief in the importance of empathy in psychotherapy and counseling began to make headway with theorists and practitioners throughout the early 1900s. For example, empathy was mentioned as an important factor in psychotherapy by early theorists such as Sigmund Freud, Gordon Allport, and Alfred Adler (see Peitchinis, 1990).

In his early work to promote the significance of empathy in the counseling relationship, Carl Rogers (1959) defined empathy as the ability "to perceive the internal frame of reference of another with accuracy and with the emotional components and meanings which pertain thereto as if one were the person without ever losing the as if condition" (pp. 210–211). Such empathy requires therapists to offer their own presence as professionals who hear, feel with, and validate the individual's basic experience consistently throughout the therapeutic relationship. Rogers (1975) later emphasized that the presentation of empathy is "temporarily entering the private perceptual world of the other and becoming thoroughly at home in it" (p. 4). In this way, empathy serves as a vital component in the provision of an optimal therapeutic environment in which clients' psychological health is improved. More recently, theorists have argued that empathy and unconditional positive regard are effectively opposite sides of the same coin. This is to say that therapists cannot have empathy for their clients if they do not also have unconditional positive regard (Bozarth, 1997).

A review of the literature yields evidence that the definitions of empathy break down to two main categories: empathy as cognitive skill or ability and empathy as an emotion or dimension of personality. When empathy is defined as a behavior or activity, the focus tends to be on the communication process in the relationship. Scholars have argued that there is a marked difference between the ability to cognitively grasp issues and take roles and the ability to experience empathy as an emotion (Feshback, 1975; Meharbian & Epstein, 1972). It has been argued by numerous scholars that both emotional and cognitive dimensions are necessary for accurate empathic responses (Bohart & Greenberg, 1997; Buie, 1981; Goldstein & Michaels, 1985; Ickes, 1997).

When empathy is perceived as an emotional response, the focus is generally on the affective components of the therapeutic relationship. From this perspective empathy is an emotional response that the therapist experiences wherein deeper connectivity with the client is the result. A basic presumption of this definition of empathy is that some individuals may have a more natural propensity to experience empathy than others. An example of this perspective is clarified with the statement that "empathy in its broadest sense refers to the responsiveness of an individual to the feelings of another person" (Iannotti, 1975, p. 22).

Empathy has been studied as a behavior or skill in which people can increase their accuracy. The presence of empathy in the therapeutic setting is often noted with simple and concise definitions, such as that given by Adlerian theorists Dinkmeyer and Sperry (2000), who noted that "empathy is best defined as the communication of understanding" (p. 78). Ickes (1997) reviewed the body of research on the measurement of empathic accuracy and concluded that it is currently most effectively measured in two approaches, which are clarified in detail in his text. A key issue of focus in assessing empathic accuracy is effectively measured when the focus is on matching criteria assessed in an interpersonal context based on objective standards of correctness. This is hypothesized to be carried out through a number of skills that are developed, including that of perspective production and perspective suppression (Hodges & Wegner, 1997).

Perspective production involves a number of efforts in combination. For example, a therapist who is trying to produce perspective will pay specific attention to and rehearse a variety of possible thoughts and feelings by doing such things as imagining her- or himself in the spatial standpoint of the other person. For example, sometimes this is referred to as "walking in the other person's shoes." This therapist will have greater success if he or she simultaneously attends to the goals of the client as well as to the changing contexts of the client (see Hodges & Wegner, 1997). This requires understanding why the client behaved in a particular way, not just what the client did from the therapist's perspective. This attention appears to require a great deal of cognitive ability and focus to be maintained and accurate.

To take the perspective of another person, therapists also need to develop the ability to suppress other perspectives, most importantly their own. This activity is called *perspective suppression*. Research has produced evidence that this second requirement to the development of empathy may be much more difficult than the production of perspective (e.g., Keysar, 1994). This may be due to the fact that many perspectives therapists consider enter their consciousness through automatic processes they cannot readily control. Nonetheless, it appears evident that efforts may be made to develop clearer and more effective empathy for those with whom therapists work. Barrett-Lennard (1962) represented this idea well through expressing that the "degree of empathic understanding is conceived as the extent to which one person is conscious of the immediate awareness of another" (p. 3).

There has been extensive research on the ability of people to develop empathic abilities and responses (for review, see Goldstein & Michaels, 1985). This body of research strengthens the argument that professionals can develop empathy for their clients. The leading models of empathy development are those of Martin Hoffman and Norma Feshback (see Goldstein & Michaels, 1985). Hoffman's model focuses on six modes of empathic arousal: (a) reactive newborn cry, (b) classical conditioning, (c) empathic distress as a result of observation, (d) motor mimicry, (e) symbolic association, and (f) more active role taking. The process goes from more automatic responses to the emotional experiences of others to deliberate efforts to take the perspective of the other and act on it (see Goldstein & Michaels, 1985, for a review of this theory). Hoffman (1982) argued that the final stage of empathic development requires high levels of cognitive maturity and motivation.

The other leading model of empathic development is by Feshback (1975, 1978). His model includes three factors, two that are affective and one that is cognitive. The first cognitive component is the ability that individuals develop as children to discriminate between emotional states of other people. This requires us to be able to identify emotional cues in other people that are often not only distinct from our own but also different from each other. The second cognitive component is our developing ability to assume the perspective and role of another, cognitively understanding a situation from a specific other viewpoint. The third is an affective component that includes developing an ability to experience the emotions that another person is experiencing. Both models emphasize a developmental pathway that people need to follow to gain the ability to experience empathy with others.

The predominating theories of empathy emphasize a developmental process wherein the majority of development occurs prior to the point at which individuals seek to become counselors, psychologists, or therapists (Clark, 2007). This raises a few issues to be considered. First, if between 65% and 85% of the process of developing into an empathic individual is supposed to have occurred prior to the beginning of training as a mental health professional, then how and when should said development be assessed? A common assumption is that empathy can be taught to a majority of developing practitioners in the mental health field as evidenced by numerous training programs that have been produced to encourage this development (see, e.g., Crabb, Moracco, & Bender, 1983; Egan, 1994; Erera, 1997; Goldstein & Michaels, 1985; Hepworth & Larsen, 1993; Ivey, 1994; Truax & Carkhuff, 1967).

Ivey and Ivey (2007) described empathic understanding in a therapeutic setting as responsive behaviors that fall into one of three categories: basic, additive, and subtractive. *Basic empathy* is the form of empathy in which therapist responses are basically interchangeable with those of the client. *Additive empathy* is described as the therapist accurately adding something beyond that which the client has said. *Subtractive empathy* is used when the therapist either diminishes or distorts that which the client has said. The Iveys offered a 5-point scale to examine empathy in the therapeutic setting. Similar to the work of Carl Rogers, the Iveys relate positive regard for the client to empathy, encouraging beginning therapists to assess their positive regard on the same 5-point scale.

Similarly, Egan (2002) described empathy as an interpersonal communication skill, in which helpers strive to understand their clients and communicate this understanding with a goal of helping the clients better understand themselves. Egan further clarified that empathy is a value orientation wherein the committed therapist works toward this understanding in three different ways. First, the therapist demonstrates a commitment to strive to understand each client from her or his perspective and surrounding emotions through consistent and appropriate communication of this understanding. Second, the therapist has a commitment to understand each client with a focus on the context of the client's life. Third, the therapist has a commitment to understand any dissonance between reality and the client's perspective.

Similar to the work of Ivey and Ivey (2007) and Egan (2002), most current models of empathy appear to emphasize the need to focus on culture, context, and issues relating to diversity. We have also found that most current models of empathy construe the development and use of empathy as an active process that can be learned and improved with effort and focus. Carl Rogers (1975) said it well when he explained that empathy "involves being sensitive, moment to moment, to the changing felt meanings which flow in the other person, to the fear or rage or tenderness or confusion or whatever, that he/she is experiencing" (p. 4).

CULTURAL ASSUMPTIONS OF EMPATHY: A CRITIQUE

The constructs of empathy described previously developed in a cultural context that favored individualism and described the connection of one individual with another individual. When the individual-to-individual paradigm is extended to helping relationships, the helper's role is defined in terms of helping a client resolve a problem. Regardless of the origins of the client's presenting problem, it is assumed that the client eventually will be able to use her or his individual agency to summon the resources needed to resolve the problem. Also underlying this helping model is the assumption that clients present themselves for therapy (or are persuaded by others, or even mandated by social service agencies, to receive therapy) to resolve a problem.

If you asked most Western-trained social service providers to describe what they do, many if not most would say they make individuals feel more pleasure and less pain, more happiness and less sadness, more success and less failure. This is a one-directional approach to social services, which is rooted in self-interest. A two-directional approach values both pleasure and pain inclusively. D. T. Miller (1999) examined the self-interest motive and the self-confirming role of assuming self-interest in textbook psychology and stated,

> It is proposed that a norm exists in Western cultures that specifies self-interest both is and ought to be a powerful determinant of behavior. This norm influences people's actions and opinions as well as the accounts they give for their actions and opinions. In particular, it leads people to act and speak as though they care more about their material self-interest than they do. (p. 1053)

The theory of self-interest has led to a psychological norm of self-interest fostering a powerful descriptive and prescriptive expectation in Western society. The evidence supporting a bias toward self-interest may speak more to the power of social norms than of innate proclivities in a self-fulfilling prophecy. D. T. Miller further noted, "The more powerful the norm of self-interest, the more evidence there is for the theory of self-interest, which, in turn, increases the power of the self-interest norm" (p. 1060). However, there are other participants informing this cultural bias as well.

Textbook psychology has also typically assumed that there is a fixed state of mind, whose observation is obscured by cultural distortions and that relates behaviors across cultures to some universal definition of normative behavior. A contrasting anthropological perspective assumes that cultural differences are clues to divergent attitudes, values, or perspectives in each context that differentiate one culture from another on the basis of a culture-specific viewpoint. Anthropologists have tended to take a relativist position when classifying and interpreting behavior across cultures. Psychologists, by contrast, have linked social characteristics and psychological phenomena with minimum attention to cultural differences. When counselors have applied the same interpretation of similar behaviors, regardless of the cultural context, cultural bias has been the consequence.

Although there has been much attention to internal validity in psychological research, there has been less emphasis on external validity. External validity is the extent to which one can generalize the results of research. According to S. Sue (1999), "The lack of internal validity does not allow causal inferences to be made without some degree of convincingness or credibility. The lack of external validity may render findings meaningless with the actual population of interest" (p. 1072). The greater the emphasis on internal validity, the more psychological research will be dominated by majority or dominant culture values. The presence of cultural bias in psychology requires that all research studies address external validity issues for the populations being researched, that different research approaches be used as appropriate to each population, and that the psychological implications of a population's ethnocultural belief system be considered in making comparisons across cultures (S. Sue, 1999).

A report by the Basic Behavioral Science Task Force (1996) of the National Advisory Mental Health Council (NAMHC) documents the extent of cultural encapsulation of mental health services. First, anthropological and cross-cultural research has demonstrated that cultural beliefs influence the diagnosis and treatment of mental illness. Second, the diagnosis of mental illness differs across cultures. Third, research has revealed differences in how individuals express symptoms in different cultural contexts. Fourth, culturally biased variations in diagnosis vary according to the diagnostic categories relevant to the majority population. Fifth, most providers come from a majority culture, whereas most clients are members of minority cultures. If the standard practices of mental health services are themselves encapsulated, as suggested by the NAMHC report, then these cultural biases will certainly influence the practice of psychology through counseling and therapy.

This report provides one more demonstration that the rhetoric about cultural diversity that has permeated the fields of human services has not had a significant impact on diminishing cultural encapsulation. The pool of service providers and leaders in the field is not much more diverse than 20 years ago

(D. W. Sue & Sue, 2003). However, the pool of clients receiving mental health care service is indeed becoming more diverse across the fields of human services so that clients who previously did not have access to professional help now have that opportunity (Pedersen, Draguns, Lonner, & Trimble, 2008) Consequently, the need for a culturally inclusive perspective is rapidly increasing while the resources to meet that need have not increased proportionately.

GLOBALIZATION OF COUNSELING AND PSYCHOTHERAPY

Economic globalization has resulted in mass migrations from rural to urban areas around the world. Consequently, indigenous social support systems, which were made possible largely by village living environments, have become less effective and no comparable urban support system has proved an adequate substitute. The consequence of this globalization process, in many societies, has been social revolution by the many against the few.

For example, the Chinese revolution grew out of a potential for unrestrained violence in the Chinese people. The Confucian order had stressed emotional restraint and "eating bitterness" as the appropriate response of subordinates, but the revolution rejected this dependency orientation. The workers renounced their previous passivity and took action. Where Confucianism had alluded to the virtues of tranquility and interpersonal harmony, Mao Tse-Tung made activism the key to the behavior of the ideal Party cadre. Where fear and avoidance of conflict characterized the "cultivated" response to social tension in the traditional society, Mao stressed the importance of criticism and controlled struggle in resolving those issues that blocked China's social advance (Solomon, 1971, p. 513). The revolution combined emotional manipulation and political education as complementary dimensions of mass mobilization. By 1949 China's revolution on the mainland provided an idealized, nonhierarchical brotherhood of friendship as a solution to problems of anger. However, the possibility of peer conflict, even in this idealized system, gave renewed meaning to the need for strong political authority, and the sense of ambivalence and tension remains unalleviated (Kim, Yang, & Hwang, 2006; Solomon, 1971; Wong & Wong, 2006).

Concurrent with economic globalization, individualistic patterns of thought have spread through the cultural diffusion of Western languages, educational and legal systems, and the media in the last several decades. These patterns have characterized efforts to "modernize" in the schools, language, research, and interpretations of the social sciences around the world. The popularity of Western models of counseling even among non-Western cultures creates an identity crisis in which neither the Western nor the indigenous model quite fits. Turtle (1987) described the rapid movement of psychology from the West toward the East. Given the theoretical dependence on principles of materialism, empiricism, and determinism in Western psychology, this transition is difficult at best. Turtle (1987) stated,

> To offer practical solutions to problems of social planning, to advise on maximal utilization of capacities of individuals, to claim the ability to counsel, to comfort and to cure those in trouble and distress, in the face of firmly established beliefs about the proper forms of social organization and the relation of the individual thereto, and of highly valued practices of guidance, consolation and spiritual healing, gives evidence either of remarkable self-confidence and/or powers of salesmanship in modern psychologists, or of extraordinary social disruption in the East, or of both. (p. 1)

Western influences have inhibited the development of indigenous psychologies in many developing countries (Moghaddam & Taylor, 1986), especially when counseling interventions were adapted superficially to the indigenous ideological backgrounds of different cultures. According to Berry, Poortinga, Segall, and Dasen (1992),

> On the one hand psychology is only a small part of Western thought and may not have direct and widespread impact on a functioning culture. On the other hand psychology may be part of a broader package of acculturative influences that affect many of the core institutions (educational, work, religious) through which all or most people pass in the course of their development. (p. 380)

The cultural assumptions underlying psychotherapy not only inhibit development of indigenous psychologies outside Western geographical spheres but also make for grave misinterpretations in majority–minority culture relationships within Western countries. We expand on the idea of developing indigenous psychologies in chapter 11 of this volume. Counseling and therapy have a history of protecting the status quo against change, as perceived by minority cultures in countries such as the United States. These attitudes are documented in "scientific racism" and "Euro-American ethnocentrism" (D. W. Sue & Sue, 1999). Cultural differences were explained by a *genetic deficiency* model that promoted the superiority of dominant cultures. This was matched to a *cultural deficit* model that described minorities as deprived or disadvantaged by their culture. According to D. W. Sue and Sue (2003), minorities were underrepresented among professional counselors and therapists, the topic of culture was trivialized at professional meetings, minority views were underrepresented in the research literature, and consequently the counseling profession was discredited among minority populations.

The dangers of applying Western-based methods inappropriately are particularly important in clinical applications. Segall, Dasen, Berry, and Poortinga (1990) contrasted Western individualism with non-Western collectivism to demonstrate the significant differences. These differences need not be antithetical, however. These two perspectives can be seen as complementary and can demonstrate how collectivist and individualist methods are being influenced as well as doing the influencing in modern counseling interventions. Psychologists and counselors working outside the European American envelope are developing indigenous approaches of helping, diagnoses, and treatment more appropriate to the local context (Kim et al., 2006). Refugees, for example, are an at-risk population suffering from pressures of acculturative stress in Westernized cultures whereby an appropriate intervention through primary prevention is called for. Bemak, Chung, and Pedersen (2003) provided extensive annotated bibliographies on special problems in counseling refugees.

THE INCLUSION OF FORMAL AND INFORMAL SUPPORT SYSTEMS

ICE acknowledges that many forms of counseling take place in informal contexts and through informal methods. In each person's identity, different social support systems are woven together in a fabric in which formal and informal elements, like texture or color in a weaving, provide a pattern or design that is unique. In each person's identity, a balance of formal and informal support systems is essential to good mental health. A multiculturally skilled counselor can balance formal and informal approaches in the treatment of culturally different populations (Pedersen, 2000a).

The pattern or design of social systems in Western cultures is significantly different from that in non-Western cultures. In a world perspective, the formal context of counseling and therapy is an exotic approach. In Western societies there is a tendency to locate the problem inside the isolated individual rather than relating a person's difficulty to other persons, the cosmology, or informal support systems from an inclusive perspective. From a systems perspective, counseling can occur in an informal as well as a formal mode. The place where counseling occurs and the method by which counseling is provided are defined by a balance of formal and informal support systems. The combination of formal and informal methods and contexts creates a dynamic combination of indigenous support systems that define one's personal culture.

An examination of Figure 1.1, which shows the full range of methods and contexts through which support systems function, from the most formal (wherein rules, structures, and definite expectations apply) to the more informal (wherein spontaneity and the lack of defined structures apply), reveals a paradigm for describing the range of formal and informal support systems.

Method

		Formal	Nonformal	Informal
Context	**Formal**	1 Office-scheduled therapy	4 Mental health training	7 Mental health presentation
	Nonformal	2 Community mental health	5 Support groups and friends	8 Family and service
	Informal	3 Professional advice	6 Self-help groups	9 Daily encounter

Figure 1.1. An inclusive model of counseling services by method and context.

The incorporation of formal and informal support systems has been included in previously published literature (Pedersen, 1997). Figure 1.1 incorporates the full range of previously identified possibilities for analyzing how the formal and informal systems complement one another. These combinations include a range of alternatives appropriate in various culturally diverse settings from Pedersen's practice of counseling university students in Asia.

Each cell of Figure 1.1 depicts a different combination of formal and nonformal features of counseling methods in various counseling contexts. Each cell in the figure illustrates a different context.

1. A formal method and formal context are involved when the counselor–specialist works with a fee-paying client in a scheduled office interview. Counseling as a professional activity occurs mostly in this cell.
2. A formal method and nonformal context are involved when the counselor–specialist works by invitation or appointment with a client in the client's home, office, or community. Semiformal meetings with individuals, families, or groups of foreign students are often best scheduled for locations outside the counseling

office. A location that is more familiar to the client can make it easier to establish rapport when discussing personal problems.

3. A formal method and informal context are involved when the counselor–specialist is consulted about a personal problem by a friend or relative at a party or on the street. In some cultures it is important for the person requesting help to accept the helper as a friend before it is appropriate for that person to disclose intimate problems. For example, when Pedersen counseled foreign students at the University of Minnesota, he first would have to be "checked out" at nationality-group parties or approached about personal problems informally on street corners and only later—if Pedersen passed the test—in an office or formal setting.

4. A nonformal method and formal context are involved when a person not functioning in the role of counselor is asked for psychological help or to provide a professional service, training, or presentation. When Pedersen counseled for 6 years in Asian universities, it became clear that the functions of a counselor were not well understood. The concept of a medical doctor was clear, but the counselor was more a special kind of "teacher." To accept help from a teacher was honorable and increased one's status in the community. Consequently, it was frequently useful to describe counseling as a special kind of teaching and learning interaction. An Asian student would be quite comfortable asking her or his teacher for advice and help on a personal problem.

5. A nonformal method and nonformal context are involved in the various support groups organized by persons to help one another through regular contact and an exchange of ideas, even though none of the participants are trained as a therapist. When Pedersen had Asian or other international students as clients who were unfamiliar with counseling, he frequently would ask them to bring a friend to the interview. The friend, although not trained as a counselor, would function almost as a cotherapist by providing constant support, clarifying the content of formal counseling interviews, and helping Pedersen to understand the client by acting as mediator and interpreter. This can be especially useful if there is a language problem between the client and counselor.

6. A nonformal method and informal context are involved when self-help groups and popular psychology are used as resources. A frequent indicator of culture shock is withdrawal from support groups and increased isolation from groups of others. There

are various self-help groups, such as Alcoholics Anonymous and other organizations for addicts, single persons, veterans, or those who share the common bond of a traumatic experience. Similarly, there is much literature on positive thinking or advice giving that is a frequent source of help. Pedersen's Chinese clients frequently first consulted the Confucian proverbs for advice and sought counseling only when the proverbs seemed inadequate.

7. An informal method and formal context are involved when a listener receives considerable assistance in solving a psychological problem from a formal, scheduled presentation or activity even if that was not the explicit intention of the program. In non-Western cultures, much of what people call counseling in Western settings occurs through religious institutions. Family meetings and activities also provide valuable vehicle for the functions of counseling and leave a great vacuum by their absence. These institutions are neither primarily psychological, nor is their primary purpose to promote mental health. The ritualistic context, however, is often formal and contributes significantly to healthy mental attitudes.

8. An informal method and nonformal context are involved when family and friends provide help to an individual. In many Asian cultures it would be unacceptable to go outside the family or a very close circle of friends to disclose personal problems. In some situations a foreign student under stress while in the United States may be helped by making contact with relatives or close friends who can serve as a resource and context for casual and indirect conversations that can promote healthy mental attitudes.

9. An informal method and informal context are involved in daily encounters in which individuals receive help spontaneously and unexpectedly from their contacts with other people, whether that help is intended or unintended. Spontaneous recovery from crises or stress takes many forms. Imagine, for example, that it is a nice day and you are walking down the street. Someone smiles. You smile back. You feel better. Each culture teaches its own repertoire of self-help mechanisms for healing.

A comprehensive picture of formal and informal support systems helps to classify the different sources of psychological help. Without an adequate framework to identify the resources, counselors are likely to rely too heavily on more formal, obvious support systems and ignore the less obvious, informal alternatives. If counselors seek to translate counseling and therapy to culturally different populations, they will need to complement the diverse informal influences in clients' support systems. The formal and informal framework highlights the complexity of a client's indigenous support systems and also indicates the importance of matching the right method and context so that culturally skilled counseling can occur.

CONCLUSION: POSSIBILITIES FOR EMPATHY

Recognizing the validity of one perspective on empathy does not require us to invalidate all other perspectives. Walsh (1989) described the relationship between Asian and Western psychologies as complementary. First, Asian and Western psychologies both focus on development, with the Asian systems focused on well-being and advanced stages of development in a more "transpersonal" focus, whereas Western systems focus on psychopathology and physical and mental development. Difficulty arises when a majority culture seeks to impose its perspective on a minority group. Pathologizing mystical experiences would be an example of Western models going beyond their boundaries in some cultures.

Alternative models of empathy are needed because, as it is currently conceived, empathy does not accommodate the fact that cultural patterns shape the way people view the self and relationships with others. The individuated self is being overtaken by a more relational or familial self, typical of the global majority. The recognition of family as an important resource, the emphasis on corporate cultures, and the political appeals to special interest groups are some examples of the relational trend. This trend, as it borrows from non-Western sources, is best described by Geertz (1975) as follows:

> The Western conception of the person as a bounded, unique, more or less integrated motivational and cognitive universe, a dynamic center of awareness, emotion, judgment and action organized into a distinctive whole and set contrastively both against other such wholes and against a social and natural background is, however incorrigible it may seem to us, a rather peculiar idea within the context of the world's cultures. (p. 48)

In the more collectivist non-Western cultures, relationships include not only the individual but the many "culture teachers" of that individual in a network of significant others. Being empathic in that cultural context requires a more inclusive perspective than in the typically more individualistic Western cultures. However, the relational self is a well-established concept in Western psychology also, with advocates that include Freud, Jung, Allport, Vygotsky, Adler, Meichenbaum, Ellis, and others (Pedersen, 2000a, 2000b).

Western and more individualistic cultures are described as more "idiocentric," emphasizing competition, self-confidence, and freedom, whereas the contrasting cultures are more "allocentric," emphasizing communal responsibility, social usefulness, and acceptance of authority. Alternative and complementary therapies have tended to be developed in the more allocentric cultural contexts. The frequent themes of inclusion, relationships, balance, subjectivity, and harmony in non-Western therapies are in sharp contrast to the frequent themes of dissonance reduction, individuality, exclusion, empiricism, linear thinking, and objective evidence in Western therapies. The labels *counseling, therapy,* and *human services* are relatively new, but the functions described by those labels have a long history. A comprehensive history of counseling interventions would need to go back to the beginning of recorded social relationships as a formal and sometimes informal process.

2

TOWARD MORE INCLUSIVE EMPATHY: A SURVEY OF RELATIONAL WORLDVIEWS AND ALTERNATIVE MODES OF HELPING

The emphasis on relationships in inclusive cultural empathy (ICE) is becoming ever more important as an alternative to conventional individualistic emphasis especially in more developed societies. This second chapter presents a variety of societies in which relationships are especially important, emphasizing non-Western and Asian cultures in particular. The idea of ICE has grown out of concepts familiar to these non-Western cultural contexts.

As the science and practice of psychology migrates to different parts of the world, our discipline is becoming more international in scope (Stevens & Wedding, 2004). The rapid development of societies through modernization and globalization makes it difficult to accurately describe the basic assumptions of both Western and non-Western psychologies, which are constantly changing, it is hoped toward a relationship-centered future through increased empathy. As West (1999) explained, "Empathy is not simply a matter of trying to imagine what others are going through, but having the will to muster enough courage to do something about it. In a way, empathy is predicated upon hope" (p. 12). Western and non-Western cultural contexts are in contrast with one another at least with regard to their starting points if not also in their future direction. Less individualistic non-Western cultures are more likely to conceptualize the person as a collectivity of identities and not as an isolated individual. To that extent, empathy presumes intergroup contact beyond mere interpersonal connections.

Nagda (2006) wrote about building bridges across differences as an interactional process for intergroup encounters:

> Intergroup dialogue represents one approach that incorporates inter-personal and intergroup elements, reflected in friendship and alliance building process, respectively. These joint friendship-alliances are marked by critical-dialogic empathy and are purposeful in that they carry a responsibility to engender justice. In situations of intergroup contact among groups located in stratified social structures, critical-dialogic empathy not only connects one through imagining the experience of the other but also engages one deeply in self-reflection, dialogue, and action to better the lived experience of both the other and the self. (pp. 573–574)

The term *critical-dialogic empathy* refers to the dialogue between people on which empathy is based and that is critical to a meaningful empathic relationship.

THE IMPORTANCE OF COLLECTIVISTIC AND INDIVIDUALISTIC THEORIES

In contrasting collectivistic with individualistic cultures, the nature of self becomes an important issue. The self in most collectivistic cultures is maintained and defined through active negotiation of facework, or the ways we present ourselves to others and respond to others' presentations of themselves. By contrast, in Western societies the self is grounded intrapsychically in self-love, self-definition, and self-direction. In the solidarity of a collectivistic setting, the self is not free. It is bound by mutual role obligations and duties as it is structured and nurtured in an ongoing process of give-and-take in facework negotiations. In the West, there must be high consistency between public face and private self-image. In Asian cultures, the self is not an individual but a relational construct. As Stevens and Wedding (2004) noted,

> Dissatisfaction with Western psychology has contributed to the increased prominence of international psychology. Two sources for this dissatisfaction are the emergence of economic and political systems in the developing world that are more person-centered and the limited utility of psychological paradigms imported from the West. (pp. 2–3)

D. T. Miller (1999) supported the importance of individualism in proposing that a norm exists in Western cultures declaring that self-interest both is and ought to be a powerful determinant of behavior. This norm influences people's actions and opinions as well as the accounts they give for their actions and opinions. The theory of self-interest has led to a psychological norm of self-interest fostering an individualistic prescriptive expectation in Western society. The more powerful the norm of self-interest, the more supporting evidence, the more powerful the self-interest norm becomes, in a circular self-fulfilling prophecy.

Non-Western cultures have typically been associated with *collectivistic* perspectives, whereas Western cultures have typically been associated with *individualistic* value systems (Kim, Triandis, Kagitçibasi, Choi, & Yoon, 1994). Individualism describes societies in which the connections between individuals are loose and each individual is expected to look after her- or himself, whereas collectivism describes societies in which people are part of strong cohesive ingroups that protect them in exchange for unquestioned lifetime loyalty (Hofstede, 1991). These cultural orientations are useful in predicting behavior. Individualistic cultures prefer direct, explicit communication strategies in managing relationships, whereas collectivistic cultures generally prefer indirect, more contextual communication strategies. "However, it is proposed that, in a multicultural workplace, cultural orientation alone may not predict choice of strategy, in that situational constraints may also contribute" (Brew & Cairns, 2004, p. 331).

Wei-Ming (2000) described "multiple modernities" as Asian models are adapted to the Western context and the dilemma this presents.

> The paradox, then, is our willingness and courage to understand radical otherness as a necessary step toward self-understanding. If the West takes East Asian modernity as a reference, it will begin to sharpen its vision of the strengths and weaknesses of its model for the rest of the world. The heightened self-reflexivity of the modern West will enable it to appreciate how primordial ties rooted in concrete living communities have helped to shape different configurations of the modern experience. (p. 266)

Western and non-Western cultures have become interdependent in their relationships. In Eastern traditions of scholarship, what is most important is not an abstract truth. The discovery of objective knowledge is less important than the discovery of spiritual interconnectedness (J. H. Liu & Liu, 1999).

Next, we provide some examples of international psychologies that exemplify alternative ways of thinking about health and the ideal outcomes of help-seeking. Some unique implications for counseling emerge as we examine viewpoints that challenge the basic assumptions of counseling theory as we know it. International psychologies we review in this chapter do not always fit easily into Western categories, sometimes providing answers to questions not being asked by Western psychologists.

THE IMPORTANCE OF HIGH- AND LOW-CONTEXT THEORIES

There is a similarity between counseling and conflict management even though different cultures may have their own preference between high- and low-context perspectives. High-context systems tend to be more inclusive in their outlook than systems in which the context is less important to the counseling process. Gudykunst and Ting-Toomey (1988) associated high and low context as a corollary of individualism and collectivism. Jandt and Pedersen (1996) found these dimensions helpful for managing conflict across cultures. Recognizing these patterns helps one construct favorable conditions for establishing empathy in counseling relationships in both high- and low-context conditions.

1. Low-context persons view indirect conflict management as weak, cowardly, or evasive, whereas high-context persons view direct conflict management as impolite and clumsy.
2. Low-context persons separate the conflict issue from the person, whereas high-context persons see the issue and person as interrelated.
3. Low-context persons seek to manage conflict to reach an objective and fair solution, whereas high-context persons focus on the affective, relational, personal, and subjective aspects that preclude open conflict.
4. Low-context persons have a linear and logical worldview that is problem oriented and sensitive to individuals, whereas high-context persons see the conflict, event, and all actors in a unified context.
5. Low-context persons value independence and are focused on autonomy, freedom, and personal rights, whereas high-context persons value inclusion, approval, and association.
6. Low-context cultures separate the conflict issue from the person, whereas high-context cultures see the issue and person as connected.
7. Low-context cultures seek to manage conflict toward an objective and fair solution, whereas high-context cultures focus on the affective, relational, personal, and subjective aspects that preclude open conflict.
8. Low-context cultures have a linear and logical worldview that is problem oriented and sensitive to individuals, whereas high-context cultures see the conflict, event, and all actors in a unified context.
9. Low-context cultures value independence and are focused on autonomy, freedom, and personal rights, whereas high-context cultures value inclusion, approval, and association.

Hall (1976) contrasted the American (low context) with the Japanese (high context) perspective regarding justice, for example. Trials in the Japanese legal system put the accused, the court, the public, and the injured parties together to work toward settling the dispute, compared with the protagonist–antagonist conflict model in an American court. The function of the trial in Japan is to locate the crime in context so that the criminal and society can see the consequence. In high-context systems people in authority are responsible for subordinates, whereas in low-context systems responsibility is diffused, making it difficult to fix blame. According to Hall (1976),

> Low context cultures generally refer to groups characterized by individualism, overt communication and heterogeneity. The United States, Canada and Central and Northern Europe are described as areas where low context cultural practices are most in evidence. High context cultures feature collective identity-focus, covert communication and homogeneity. This approach prevails in Asian countries including Japan, China and Korea as well as Latin American countries. (p. 39)

Some cultures emphasize the importance of context more than others in their communications and particularly in their conflict management strategies. Exhibit 2.1 presents a brief rating form that will help students assess the extent to which their own personal preference is high context or low context in its emphasis. There are no right or wrong answers, although cultures vary as to the emphasis that each places on various aspects of conflict and mediation. Thus, the assessment can be used to determine one's cultural assumptions and consequently compare them with other possible assumptions.

Low-context cultures tend to be more individualistic and more Western in their outlook than high-context cultures. The words *Western* and *non-Western* have less to do with geographical hemispheres and more to do with psychological perspectives or context of each culture. The scale shown in Exhibit 2.2 provides some examples of dimensions whereby one extreme is more typical of a Western perspective and the other extreme is more typical of a non-Western perspective. Students can assess their own perspective to see which of the two extremes is more relevant to themselves.

WHAT IS THE ESSENCE OF SELF?

It is appropriate to establish the nature of individuality itself as it differs across cultures. The very construct of *personality* assumes a particular view of the individual as a basic unit in the structure of psychology. Social inclusion implies a movement from individual-centered perspectives to group-oriented viewpoints as evidenced in educational diversity programs to reduce prejudice and promote intergroup harmony. The standard models of intergroup

EXHIBIT 2.1
Score Sheet for Self-Assessment of High- Versus Low-Context Thinking

Directions: Answer as honestly as possible and indicate your agreement or disagreement with each statement by circling one of the responses. Once you have responded to all 15 items, add up the numbers you circled and score your answer sheet. Neither high- nor low-context thinking is preferred. The emphasis should be on the consequences of high- or low-context thinking in relationship management. Some discussion questions include the following: (a) Which cultures do you think are higher context in their thinking? (b) Which cultures do you think are lower context in their thinking? (c) Can you see the advantages and disadvantages of both high- and low-context thinking as a strategy for managing conflict? (d) Were you surprised by your score on this rating sheet? (e) Would others be surprised by your score?

1. In resolving conflicts, personalities are more important than facts.

Strongly Disagree	Disagree	Disagree Somewhat	Don't Agree or Disagree	Agree Somewhat	Agree	Strongly Agree
1	2	3	4	5	6	7

2. A fair outcome requires a neutral mediator.

Strongly Disagree	Disagree	Disagree Somewhat	Don't Agree or Disagree	Agree Somewhat	Agree	Strongly Agree
1	2	3	4	5	6	7

3. In resolving conflicts, the status of the parties is an important consideration.

Strongly Disagree	Disagree	Disagree Somewhat	Don't Agree or Disagree	Agree Somewhat	Agree	Strongly Agree
1	2	3	4	5	6	7

4. It is normally possible to resolve conflicts if the people involved are honest and direct.

Strongly Disagree	Disagree	Disagree Somewhat	Don't Agree or Disagree	Agree Somewhat	Agree	Strongly Agree
1	2	3	4	5	6	7

5. The best mediator is one who knows the parties well.

Strongly Disagree	Disagree	Disagree Somewhat	Don't Agree or Disagree	Agree Somewhat	Agree	Strongly Agree
1	2	3	4	5	6	7

6. The first step to resolving a conflict is to get the parties to admit the conflict face-to-face.

Strongly Disagree	Disagree	Disagree Somewhat	Don't Agree or Disagree	Agree Somewhat	Agree	Strongly Agree
1	2	3	4	5	6	7

7. If I were asked to help resolve a conflict, the first thing I would want to know is some history of the people involved.

Strongly Disagree	Disagree	Disagree Somewhat	Don't Agree or Disagree	Agree Somewhat	Agree	Strongly Agree
1	2	3	4	5	6	7

8. It is not right to apologize if you are not at fault in a conflict.

Strongly Disagree	Disagree	Disagree Somewhat	Don't Agree or Disagree	Agree Somewhat	Agree	Strongly Agree
1	2	3	4	5	6	7

9. It is often wise to depend on someone else to work out your conflict for you.

Strongly Disagree 1	Disagree 2	Disagree Somewhat 3	Don't Agree or Disagree 4	Agree Somewhat 5	Agree 6	Strongly Agree 7

10. Formal rituals are necessary to successfully resolve declared conflicts.

Strongly Disagree 1	Disagree 2	Disagree Somewhat 3	Don't Agree or Disagree 4	Agree Somewhat 5	Agree 6	Strongly Agree 7

11. A mediator unknown to both parties is best because this assures neutrality and anonymity.

Strongly Disagree 1	Disagree 2	Disagree Somewhat 3	Don't Agree or Disagree 4	Agree Somewhat 5	Agree 6	Strongly Agree 7

12. Sometimes the best way to deal with a conflict is to keep silent.

Strongly Disagree 1	Disagree 2	Disagree Somewhat 3	Don't Agree or Disagree 4	Agree Somewhat 5	Agree 6	Strongly Agree 7

14. To ensure fairness in mediation, communication rules must be applied in the same way in all settings.

Strongly Disagree 1	Disagree 2	Disagree Somewhat 3	Don't Agree or Disagree 4	Agree Somewhat 5	Agree 6	Strongly Agree 7

15. One should look to the future and not the past when finding solutions to conflicts.

Strongly Disagree 1	Disagree 2	Disagree Somewhat 3	Don't Agree or Disagree 4	Agree Somewhat 5	Agree 6	Strongly Agree 7

Note. High context: Higher scores indicate a tendency to view conflict and mediation from this perspective; high-context items are 1, 3, 5, 7, 9, 10, and 12. Low context: Higher scores indicate a tendency to view conflict and mediation from this perspective; low-context items are 2, 4, 6, 8, 11, 14, and 15. From *110 Experiences for Multicultural Learning* (pp. 105–106), by P. B. Pedersen, 2004, Washington, DC: American Psychological Association. Copyright 2004 by Paul B. Pedersen. Adapted with permission.

relations training in universities focus on creating intergroup harmony in which members of identity groups are expected to know members of other groups *as individuals*, not as group members. This approach represents either a "decategorization" or a "recategorization" process. As Gurin (2006) noted,

> The decategorization model involves getting rid of group boundaries altogether primarily through activities and interactions in which everyone is merely an individual. . . . The recategorization approach also stresses reducing the salience of groups but by creating new in-group identity that brings in-groups and out-groups together. (pp. 626–627)

Accepting the individual without at the same time rejecting that individual's group is not always easy.

EXHIBIT 2.2
A Measure of Western Versus Non-Western Influence

Directions: Circle the number between 1 and 7 for each of the items below to indicate your own perspective, with a higher number indicating a non-Western preference and a lower number a Western perspective. Add up the numbers you circled and report their score. Although there are no right or wrong answers to this test of perspectives, you may be surprised. Some of the questions for you to think about may include the following: (a) How do you define the Western perspective? (b) How do you define the non-Western perspective? (c) Can you name countries likely to be more Western or non-Western? (d) What problems occur when the Western perspectives dominate a society? (e) What problems occur when the non-Western perspectives dominate a society?

Western	Rate yourself							Non-Western
Life before death	1	2	3	4	5	6	7	Life after death
Individualized self	1	2	3	4	5	6	7	Spiritualized self
Self-centered	1	2	3	4	5	6	7	Social centered
Independence as healthy	1	2	3	4	5	6	7	Dependence as healthy
Child is free	1	2	3	4	5	6	7	Child is interdependent
No obligation toward parents	1	2	3	4	5	6	7	Big obligation to parents
Child–parent interdependency	1	2	3	4	5	6	7	Child–parent dependency
Individualism	1	2	3	4	5	6	7	Collectivism
Truth is clear authority	1	2	3	4	5	6	7	Truth is paradoxical
Authority inhibits growth	1	2	3	4	5	6	7	Growth requires authority
Logic oriented	1	2	3	4	5	6	7	Experience oriented
One-directional norms	1	2	3	4	5	6	7	Two-directional balance
Personality is not contextual	1	2	3	4	5	6	7	Personality is contextual

Note. From *110 Experiences for Multicultural Learning* (pp. 38–39), by P. B. Pedersen, 2004, Washington, DC: American Psychological Association. Copyright 2004 by Paul B. Pedersen. Adapted with permission.

We normally think of an individual starting her or his personality at birth and ending it at death. According to the Hindu concept, however, the personality extends before the birth and after the death of a particular individual, a process of identity that extends over many generations. The Sanskrit equivalent of "individual" is *vyakti*. The concept is defined as a transitional state. To the extent that the individual is a self, it has independent reality. The ultimate end of spiritual freedom guides that individual's behavior in a particular way. To the extent that the self is embodied in the particular body as a product of nature, with a capacity to produce offspring, there is an indissoluble bond between the embodied individual and all other individuals. An individual caught in an otherwise hopeless web of misery can always hope for a better world after rebirth.

The implications of that doctrine are the rejection of the reality "mine," or one's own possessions up to and including one's own body. All these possessions are regarded as changeable, passed on to others after death, and therefore impermanent or temporary. What, then, is left to transmigrate from one existence to the next? Murphy and Murphy (1968) noted,

Life is like fire: its very nature is to burn its fuel. When one body dies it is as if one piece of fuel were burned: the vital process passes on and recommences in another, and, so long as there is desire of life, the provision of fuel fails not. (p. 22)

Throughout Indian philosophy, the self or *atman* is regarded as identical with the Absolute or Ultimate Self. Whereas there is disagreement among the various Indian religions about the essence of the *atman* as a metaphysical principle, there is no disagreement regarding the *atman*'s significance as the moral agent for individual action. Mastery of self is only a means to reach one's inner nature and is not heaven itself. The ultimate goal of the process of emancipation is the recovery or discovery of one's true self. "Hell" is continued bondage to others and to the desire of the senses; "heaven" is mastery of one's self and the blissful realization of one's divine nature. Thus, the true *atman* is the ultimate or pure wisdom without internality or externality, indestructible and imperishable.

The self therefore participates in this condition of unity with all things, with the changing manifestations of the phenomenal world being illusory and temporary. Humanistic conceptions of self-realization are far more individualistic than Buddhists or Hindus could accept. When these Asian conceptions are imported through Westernized humanistic theories, they are typically distorted and given an ego-oriented flavor. In Buddhist thought, however, the ego is the enemy. In Buddhism, the term *individual* is misleading or an illusion.

In the contemporary emphasis of humanistic psychology on rediscovering the nature of "real self," some religiophilosophical teachings of Indian thought have demonstrated their attractiveness. The emphasis is less on individual or particular surface qualities of the self and more on the relational meaning of personality to all other realities. This provides an unchanging stability at the core of personality that is genuinely eternal, participating in ultimate reality and demonstrating the unity of all things. Consequently, the more an object is individualized, the less it participates in the essence of reality.

The Indian view of self takes an ontological rather than an epistemological view of truth, leaning in the direction of monastic idealism and contending that all reality is ultimately one and ultimately spiritual. The emphasis is on the underlying features or essence of the individual rather than on surface qualities of the self. The individual or particular self is dependent on the universal, which supports and defines reality, emphasizing the *relational* meaning of a person or thing rather than its fundamental uniqueness. By fixing limits between self and nonself, the person limits and defines a place in the universe that gives her or him an identity. There is thus a balance due to the harmonious tension between self-affirmation and self-negation. The goals of maturity in India are satisfying and continuous dependency. Independency longings are considered to lead to neurosis, contrary to Western concepts of mental health and adjustment. The notion of dependency is viewed positively in the Indian notions of *bandha, sambandha,* or *bandhavya* (bond, bondship, kinship) and does not have the negative connotations of immaturity.

In terms of modern psychology, the tendency of self-affirmation is extraversive, directed toward the external world, whereas the tendency of self-negation is introversive, directed toward the inner world with which the ego-illusion is dissolved (because an ego can only be experienced in contrast to an external world). The extraversive and introversive movements are as necessary in the life of humanity as inhalation and exhalation in the life of an individual (Yang, Hwang, Pedersen, & Daibo, 2003).

A therapist working with a person from such a culture would seek to reconcile independency strivings or to submerge the individual's complex interdependence. The concept of "mine/not mine" applied to material objects, time, thoughts, and emotions is branded as selfishness inside the extended family. A Western therapist working with a Western person would probably move in a nearly opposite direction.

In Japan, *amae* means to expect and depend on another's benevolence and nurturance. The term is generally used to describe a child's relationship emphasizing her or his emotional qualities toward parents, particularly the mother, but it can also describe a special relationship between two adults, such as husband and wife or master and subordinate. There is no such concept in English, which reflects a difference in psychological viewpoint between the two identities.

The unique aspect of Japanese dependency is the fluidity of relationships without fixed roles of inferiority and superiority. There is rather a mutuality in the bond of *amaeru,* implying the tendency and necessity to presume upon another person. This dependency need is both accessible and acceptable to the consciousness of a Japanese adult, and in fact social sanctions encourage it. The positive value of dependency sharply contrasts with Western views that characterize dependency negatively (Doi, 1969, p. 339). This positive attitude toward dependency is greatly influenced by an emphasis on immediate personal relations as a basic principle of Japanese culture.

Doi (1969) reviewed the importance of *amae* relationships for understanding Japanese culture. With the decline of loyalty to the emperor, and deemphasis on repaying one's "*on,*" or spiritual debts to emperor, parents, and ancestors that had regulated the psychology of *amae,* the delicate balance of powers maintaining Japanese personality is being disrupted. *On* strengthens ingroup bonds but ultimately defines outgroup members as beings for whom one does not need to show any moral consideration whatsoever.

Relationships in Japanese culture stress collectivism rather than individualism. Whereas the basic social unit in the West is the individual, and groups of individuals compose the state, the Japanese society is more accurately understood as an aggregation of family units. Considerable importance is attached to esteem of the hierarchical order, with each person well defined in her or his role. Special attention is given to the family, clan, and nation as instrumental in defining loyalty through mutual exchange of obligation.

Chinese child-rearing practices, when contrasted with typical American practices, also offer insights into networks of dependency relations (Chiu, 1972). Chinese elders use more severe discipline than American parents; Chinese parents emphasize mutual dependence in the family rather than self-reliance and independence; Chinese children see the world in terms of relationships rather than with an individualistic self-orientation; Chinese are more strongly tradition oriented and more situation centered, as well as more sensitive to environmental factors. Consequently, Chinese children develop a cognitive style attuned to interdependence of relationships, whereas American children prefer to differentiate, analyze, and classify a stimulus complex in a more independent manner (Chiu, 1972). A key aspect to understanding these cultural differences lies in the parental role and family context.

Traditionally, Chinese babies are normally breast-fed whenever they cry, even in public, and are carried on their mother's back and sleep in their parents' bed. Breast-feeding is prolonged, and the mother is typically extremely protective of the baby's bodily health, giving the baby herbs or medicines even when the baby is not sick. Continuous and immediate gratification is the ideal form of child rearing. Toilet training is very permissive. The mother trains herself and sensitizes herself to the baby's rhythm. She does not train the infant to control herself or himself. The mother assumes responsibility for her baby's function (Tseng & Hsu, 1972).

The Chinese child is taught to handle hostility without expressing anger. Aggressive behavior is severely punished. Sharing and collaterality are encouraged, thereby developing at first a "shame-oriented" conscience in the child that later must lead to "internalized shame." There is little or at least more subtle and controlled sibling rivalry for parental favoritism, because both children would be punished for aggressive, competitive behavior toward one another. The handling of the child changes abruptly by about school age (6 years old), at which time the teacher is expected to assume control over the child's discipline. The contrast between indulgence for young children and subsequent harshness to instill discipline in maturing youngsters indicates a way of handling aggressive impulses through the basic social rhythm of ho-p'ing (harmony) and hun-luan (the confusion of vented aggression). The earlier permissiveness instills a strong sense of self-esteem and feelings of self-worth in children, just as subsequent discipline teaches commitment to a family above self. As noted by Solomon (1971),

> Thus, the subsequent harsh disciplines of youth represent the parents' effort to arrest the development of that self-esteem which is the legacy of an indulged infancy. The child matures with a "selfish" longing to recapture the oral pleasures and the sense of power known early in life. (p. 80)

The system of filial piety resembles a mutual exchange. Parents devote themselves to children, who in turn are expected to support the parents in old age. Relationships among family members provide a model for a moral virtue in all areas of society, with the ideals of family government becoming the basis of national statesmanship, sanctioned not merely by the family's emotional needs or political necessity but also by intellectual rationales with inherently religious meaning. Western parents send their maturing child into the world to gratify hostile or pleasure-seeking impulses outside the family. Solomon (1971) observed,

> The Confucian solution, however, rejects "abandonment" as a solution to generational conflict in favor of the greater ends of parental security and the integrity of the family group. The son is to realize his social identity in a lifelong prolongation of his original state of dependency. (p. 36)

In this interdependent relationship, the child depends on parents and, later, the aging parent depends on her or his children, in a full cycle of reciprocity.

At the present time there are coexisting traditional and modern family styles in Asia, as a consequence of rapid social change. Traditional values are less rigidly adhered to in nontraditional families, and self-direction displaces passive compliance to parental commands; differential role expectations are allowed for men and women; and role differences of age-graded siblings place less responsibility on the eldest son. At the same time, the traditional values are maintained to some extent as ideals and thereby continue to influence the development of personality (Yang et al., 2003).

SYNTHETIC CULTURE EXAMPLES OF CULTURAL DIVERSITY

In addition to non-Western examples, it is useful to look at the synthetic cultures described in Appendixes A and B to this book. Synthetic cultures do not occur naturally but are constructed for use in simulations or role plays that temporarily combine patterns of culturally learned behavior. They are useful in constructing a safe context in which real world consequences of the simulation are minimal. On the basis of Hofstede's (2001) 70,000-subject and 55-country database, research on values came up with four and later a fifth dimension of values. These 10 synthetic cultures are artificially constructed extremes of each end of the five dimensions. Exhibit 2.3 matches selected behaviors with expectations for each of the 10 synthetic cultures. This brief outline showing how the 10 cultures are similar and dissimilar is described in a framework of the cultural grid whereby expectations are separated from behaviors. It is useful to point out (a) how the same behavior may have different meanings and different behaviors may have the same meaning,

EXHIBIT 2.3
Behaviors and Expectations in Synthetic Cultures

Behavior	Expectation
High-power distance (primary directive: respect for status)	
Soft-spoken, polite, listening	Friendly
Quiet, polite, but not listening	Unfriendly
Asks for help and direction	Trust
Does not ask for help and direction	Distrust
Positive and animated, but no eye contact	Interest
Expressionless and unanimated, but with eye contact	Boredom
Low-power distance (primary directive: all people are equal)	
Loud, direct, and very verbal	Friendly
Loud, direct, but not saying much	Unfriendly
Offers help and direction	Trust
Does not offer help and direction	Distrust
Challenging with direct eye contact	Interest
Passive and no direct eye contact	Boredom
High-uncertainty avoidance (primary directive: respect for the truth)	
Detailed response, formal, specific, and unambiguous	Friendly
Generalized, ambiguous response, anxious to end interview	Unfriendly
Separates right from wrong unambiguously	Trust
Openly critical, challenging the credentials of others	Distrust
Verbal, task-oriented, questioning with direct eye contact	Interest
Passive and quiet with no direct eye contact	Boredom
Low-uncertainty avoidance (primary directive: tolerance for ambiguity)	
Ambiguous, informal, and general	Friendly
Specific, rude, and antagonistic	Unfriendly
Rightness and wrongness are relative to the situation	Trust
Secretive and nondisclosing	Distrust
Quiet, relationship oriented, and empathic	Interest
Aggressive and direct	Boredom
High individualism (primary directive: respect for individual freedom)	
Verbal and self-disclosing	Friendly
Critical and likely to subvert or sabotage	Unfriendly
Aggressively debates issues and controls the interview	Trust
Noncommittal, passive, ambiguous, and defensive	Distrust
Loudly verbal, questioning, touching, physical contact	Interest
Physical distance, no questions, and no eye contact	Boredom
High collectivism (primary directive: respect for friendship)	
Nonverbal and modestly polite	Friendly
Disengaged and likely to withdraw from contact	Unfriendly
Listens carefully and show respect to the guest	Trust
Nondisclosing, nonresponsive, but polite	Distrust
Listening carefully, seeking to learn, and respectful	Interest
Nonresponsive, disengaging, and distant	Boredom
High masculine (primary directive: to win at all costs)	
Physical contact, seductive, and loud	Friendly
Physical distance, sarcastic, and punishing	Unfriendly
Competitive, challenging, and dominating	Trust

(continued)

EXHIBIT 2.3
Behaviors and Expectations in Synthetic Cultures (*Continued*)

Openly critical, disparaging, and eager to end the interview	Distrust
Sports oriented, eager to debate, engaging	Interest
No eye contact, discourteous, and drowsy	Boredom
High feminine (primary directive: respect for the weak)	
Modest, quiet, and receptive to the other person's ideas	Friendly
Polite but disengaging, nonresponsive, and distant	Unfriendly
Cooperative, trusting, and seeking to please	Trust
Noncommittal, cold, and nondisclosing	Distrust
Relationship oriented, warm, and receptive to others	Interest
Distant, preoccupied, and nonreceptive	Boredom
Long-term perspective (primary directive: delay of gratification)	
Direct, questioning, and cooperative	Friendly
Disengaging, distant, and exclusionary	Unfriendly
Sharing, invested, and purposeful	Trust
Separate, uptight, stressed, and restrained	Distrust
Hardworking, future oriented, idealistic	Interest
Nondisclosing, quiet, distant, and judgmental	Boredom
Short-term perspective (primary directive: immediate gratification)	
Extravagant, generous, happy, and smiling	Friendly
Blaming, angry, distressed, rude	Unfriendly
Warm, formal, and eager to work together	Trust
Disappointed, betrayed, and disengaged	Distrust
Eager to please, generous, respectful of traditions	Interest
Blaming, disrespectful, and eager to end the interview	Boredom

Note. From *110 Experiences for Multicultural Learning* (pp. 135–138), by P. B. Pedersen, 2004, Washington, DC: American Psychological Association. Copyright 2004 by Paul B. Pedersen. Adapted with permission.

(b) the primary directive of each culture can be achieved without contradicting the primary directive of any other synthetic culture, and (c) the common ground shared by all participants, such as finding a constructive solution to the local problem, is difficult to identify when participants behave in different and presumed hostile ways (Hofstede, Pedersen, & Hofstede, 2002). Given that the same expectation may prescribe different behaviors and different expectations may prescribe similar behaviors, it is easy to see how misunderstandings can disrupt empathy across cultures.

Each synthetic culture might be open to an empathic relationship but only on its own terms, whether those terms are defined inclusively or exclusively. As you review the 10 synthetic culture identities, some questions for discussion might include the following: (a) Were you able to understand each synthetic culture role accurately? (b) Did you find aspects of all 10 synthetic cultures in yourself? (c) Can you find common ground across these synthetic cultures? (d) Did you find aspects of some synthetic cultures in stereotypes of different cultures? (e) Is it possible to find common ground without sacrificing cultural integrity or giving up the synthetic culture's primary directive in the process?

A SURVEY OF NON-WESTERN THERAPIES

In addition to national differences, it is also useful to examine the inclusive variety of belief systems that provide a contrast with Western perspectives. The following examples are not complete but provide an assortment of belief systems from non-Western cultures in which an inclusive perspective is more likely to be preferred than in Western belief systems.

Ayurvedic therapies from India combine the word for life, vitality, health, and longevity (*dyus*) with the word for science or knowledge (*veda*), focusing on promoting a comprehensive and spiritual notion of health and life rather than healing or curing any specific illness. Ayurvedic treatments are combined with conventional therapies more frequently in Europe than in the United States (Kim et al., 2006). Health is treated as more than the absence of disease and involves a spiritual reciprocity between mind and body. Western-based research has documented the efficacy of Ayurvedic therapies (Kim et al., 2006)

Yoga has a history of thousands of years as a viable therapy. The word *yoga* is based on the Sanskrit root *yuj*, meaning to yoke or bind the body–mind–soul to God. Yoga has its main source in the *Bhagavad Gita*, Hindu's most sacred text, in understanding the connection of the individual to the cosmos. Research on yoga has demonstrated benefits in lowering blood pressure and stress levels through meditation, personality change, and therapeutic self-discovery (Kim et al., 2006).

Chinese therapies include an elegant array of approaches based on the concepts of the *Tao* or the way, *ch'i* or the energy force, and *yin/yang* or the balance of opposites. The various systems of Chinese therapies are grounded in religion and philosophy by the mystical union with God or the Cosmos and nature. The Tao describes those patterns that lead toward harmony. The ch'i describes a system of pathways called meridians in the body through which energy flows. The yin/yang describes the balance of paradoxes, each essential to the other.

Buddhist therapy is based on the absence of a separate self, impermanence of all things, and the fact of suffering. People endure striving to possess and desire things, which are impermanent. The cure is to reach a higher state of being to eliminate delusion, attachment, and desire in the interrelationship of mind and body. Elements of cognitive restructuring, behavioral techniques, and insight-oriented methods are involved in the healing process (Kim et al., 2006).

Sufism is the mystical aspect of Islam inside the person. The outward dimension *sharia* is like the circumference of a circle with the inner truth *haqiqa* being the circle's center and the path *tariqa* to that center going beyond rituals to ultimate peace and health. The Sufi's goal is to enable people to live simple, harmonious, and happy lives. Jung's analytical psychology and Freud's interpretation of the fragmented person are similar but more objective in their emphasis than the Sufi who seeks to go beyond the limited understanding of objective knowledge.

Japanese therapies of *Zen Buddhism*, *Naikan*, and *Morita therapy* focus on "constructive living," and their aim is for people to become more "natural." Morita Masatake (1874–1938), a professor of psychiatry at Jikei University School of Medicine in Tokyo, developed principles of Zen Buddhist psychology. Yoshimoto Ishin (1916–1988) was a successful businessman who became a lay priest at Nara and developed Naikan therapies in the Jodo Shinshu Buddhist psychology. Morita therapy is a way to accept and embrace our feelings rather than ignore them or attempt to escape from them. Naikan therapy emphasizes how many good things we have received from others and the inadequacy of our repayment.

Shamanism is a family of therapies involving altered states of consciousness in which people experience their spiritual being to heal themselves or others. Shamanism is found from Siberia and the Native American Indian cultures to Africa and Australia going back perhaps 25,000 years. Shamans heal through spirit travel, soul flights, or soul journeys, which distinguishes them from priests, mediums, or medicine men. These altered states include psychological, social, and physiological approaches to modify consciousness (Kottler, Carlson, & Keeney, 2005).

Native American healers recognize four main causes of illness: offending the spirits or breaking taboos, intrusion of a spirit into the body, soul loss, or witchcraft. Illness can be a divine retribution for breaking a taboo or offending divine powers requiring that the patient be purified with song, prayers, and rituals. In the same way a healer restores health by removing objects or spirits from the body. When the soul is separated from the body or possessed by harmful powers, it must be brought back to energize the patient, and sometimes the shaman must travel to the land of the dead to bring the soul back. Finally, witchcraft causes illness by projecting toxic substances into the patient.

The Kabbalah of Jewish mysticism was developed by the Zohar schools of Spain and Provence in the 13th and 14th centuries and the Cordoverian and Lurianic schools in Safed in the 16th century and was a major influence in the development of classical Hasidism of the late 18th century. The Kabbalah describes a four-world cosmology with the body. The four worlds are defined as *Atziluth* (world of emanation), *Beri'ah* (world of creation), *Yetzirah* (world of formation), and *Asiyah* (world of action). The Kabbalah brings individuals to inner states through levels of reality and by maintaining careful balance in a personal encounter.

African healing as described by Airhihenbuwa (1995) is based in cultural values and is available, acceptable, and affordable. Even today African divinities, diviners, and healers continue to be popular in a religious or psychosocial dimension of health that goes beyond medical care. Health depends on a balance both within the individual and between the individual and the environment or cosmos. According to traditional beliefs and symbolic representations of tribal realities, illness can result from hot–cold imbalance, dislocation of internal organs, impure blood, unclean air, moral transgression, interpersonal struggle, or conflict with the spirit world. Similarities with allopathic medicine are evident.

A great variety of other systems exist, among them Christian mysticism, homeopathy, osteopathy, chiropractic, herbalism, healing touch, naturopathic medicine, Qigong, Curanderismo, and Tibetan medicine. Each system is, in turn, divided into a great variety of different traditions. However, the same patterns of spiritual reality, mind–body relationships, balance, and subjective reality run through many non-Western therapies. For more extensive reviews of non-Western therapies, see Sheikh and Sheikh (1989).

CONCLUSION

Our intent in presenting these examples of relational worldviews and alternative or complementary therapies is to prepare the reader to receive our argument for ICE in the next chapter. It will be clear to the reader by now that the functions of counseling exist in many different cultural contexts, but the ways in which help-giving is manifested may be strikingly different from a Western cultural context. This idea will be expanded in the following chapters to show that counseling can and does occur in different gender cultures, age cultures, economic status cultures, and so on. The task of empathic helping professionals, then, is to question their own and their client's assumptions to articulate the problem or imbalance and to understand what kind of help the client is seeking.

3

DEFINING INCLUSIVE CULTURAL EMPATHY

Informed by a concept of empathy that evolved within an individualistic worldview, today's helping professionals generally learn that empathy occurs when one person vicariously experiences the feelings, perceptions, and thoughts of another (Clark, 2007). Our purpose in this book, as stated before, is to expand concepts of empathy to accommodate different cultural worldviews, different reasons for seeking help, and different expectations of helping professionals. In this chapter we present *inclusive cultural empathy* (ICE) and show how it incorporates—and adds to—multicultural competencies. We justify its relevance in the context of postmodernism and explain how it is inclusive of many definitions of culture, healthy outcomes, and helping relationships. Next we sketch out the three stages of ICE development: awareness, knowledge, and skill. Finally, we explicate the assumptions behind ICE.

A CONCEPTUAL MODEL OF INCLUSIVE CULTURAL EMPATHY

The conceptual model of ICE is a revision of the conventional empathy concept applied to a culture-centered perspective of counseling. Conventional empathy typically develops out of similarities between two people.

ICE describes a dynamic perspective that balances both similarities and differences, at the same time integrating skills developed to nurture a deep comprehensive understanding of the counseling relationship in its cultural context. ICE has two defining features: (a) Culture is defined broadly to include culture teachers from the client's ethnographic (ethnicity and nationality), demographic (age, gender, lifestyle, residence), status (social, educational, economic), and affiliation (formal or informal) backgrounds and (b) the empathic counseling relationship values the full range of differences and similarities or positive and negative features as contributing to the quality of that relationship in a dynamic balance. ICE goes beyond the exclusive interaction of a counselor with a client to include the comprehensive network of interrelationships with culture teachers in the client's cultural context.

The revision of research on the conventional concept of empathy can be illustrated in two figures contrasting conventional and convergent empathy (Figure 3.1) with inclusive and divergent cultural empathy (Figure 3.2).

The contextual and cultural background

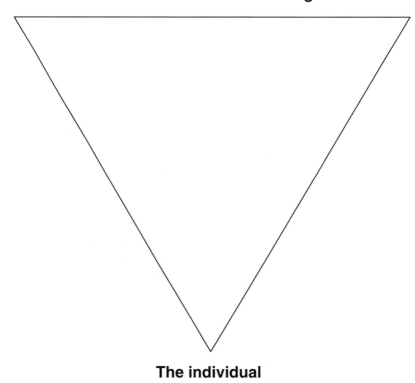

The individual

Figure 3.1. Conventional and Western-based convergent empathy.

The individual

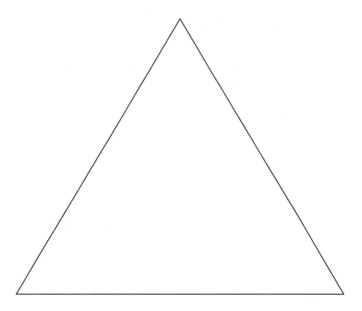

The contextual and cultural background relationships

Figure 3.2. Inclusive and Asian-based divergent or inclusive cultural empathy.

Empathy is constructed over a period of time during counseling as the foundation of a strong and positive working relationship. The conventional description of empathy moves from a broadly defined context to the individual person convergently, like a pyramid upside down (see Figure 3.1). The revised version of empathy moves from the individual person toward inclusion of the broadly defined cultural contexts in which that individual lives, like a pyramid (see Figure 3.2).

ICE is a reframing and enlargement of the relationship focus to encompass both similarities and differences in an increasingly comprehensive and culturally inclusive perspective. The conventional definition of empathy has emphasized similarities as the basis of comembership in a one-directional focus that does not include differences (Ridley & Lingle, 1996; Ridley & Udipi, 2002). According to Ridley and Lingle (1996), "The new construct of cultural empathy presented in much of the literature appears to be indistinguishable from generic empathy except that it is used in multicultural contexts to achieve an understanding of the client's cultural experience" (p. 30). ICE is therefore the learned ability of counselors to accurately understand and respond appropriately to the client's comprehensive cultural context, both in its similarities and differences, which may include confrontation and conflict (Ridley, Ethington, & Heppner, 2008).

HOW ICE INCORPORATES AND ADDS TO MULTICULTURAL COMPETENCE

Clemmont Vontress, who has been active in debate over multicultural counseling competencies, mainly emphasized shared experience in his definition of empathy:

> Empathy derives from the German word *Einfühlung,* which means "one feeling." It suggests a person's subjective reaction to one or more proximate individuals. It therefore must be understood in cultural context. Humans necessarily share commonalities. Shared experiences and conditions produce common cultures. They also enable participants to empathize with their fellows, because they have "been there and done that." They easily identify with them. (C. Vontress, personal communication, January 30, 2006)

Vontress identified at least five shared conditions or sets of experiences that contribute to empathy. First, as members of the same species, we humans are housed in a fragile biological system that is universally invariable. Therefore, to exist, we behave in predictable ways, to maintain and perpetuate life. We understand what it is like to love, to become parents, to be hungry, to be without shelter, to be threatened physically or psychologically, or to grieve when loved ones die. Second, people who live in similar geographical zones understand what it is like to inhabit such areas of the world. For example, natives of Mali can empathize with others who endure the extreme heat and humidity of sub-Saharan Africa. Third, inhabitants of a nation adapt to the rules, regulations, values, and attitudes pervasive in that country. They also understand and empathize with joys and hardships of their fellow countrymen. Fourth, in large countries, people adjust to specific regions of the country in which they live. They often instinctively understand and sense what others feel from the same region. Finally, members of racial and ethnic communities usually share a bond that people external to their community may not understand. Empathizing easily with their racial or ethnic fellows, they immediately know "where they are coming from." Cultural empathy is therefore the learned ability of counselors to accurately understand and respond appropriately to each culturally different client.

ICE goes beyond accommodating cultural differences toward a dynamic balance of similarities and differences between the client and counselor. As we stated earlier, culture is broadly defined to include ethnographic (ethnicity and nationality), demographic (age, gender, lifestyle, residence), status (social, educational, economic), and affiliation (formal and informal) categories. Each category can be conceptualized through a multiplicity of culture teachers. Both client and counselor have many different culture teachers who are similar in some ways and different in others. ICE is a generic counseling perspective that requires the counselor to manage both similarities and differences at the same time.

This inclusive approach is in sharp contrast to the exclusive perspective of dissonance reduction in conventional empathy. By reframing the whole counseling relationship into multicultural categories, it becomes possible for the counselor and the client to accept the counseling relationship as it is—ambiguous and complex—without first having to change it toward the counselor's cultural perspective. ICE does not require the compromising exclusion of categories to find common ground but rather enriches the counseling relationship through inclusion of both the counselor's and the client's diverse perspectives as they contribute to the growing and ever-changing relationship. This complex and somewhat chaotic perspective is what distinguishes ICE from other descriptions of empathy and even of cultural empathy.

Just as it is important to say what ICE is, it is also important to say what ICE is not. Stewart (1981) suggested that the exclusive emphasis on similarities is likely to result in sympathy rather than empathy. "The current definition of empathy is often confused with a second potential interface between persons—sympathy, a concept with a much longer and troubled history" (p. 69). The conventional definition of empathy has emphasized similarities as the basis of comembership in a relationship that minimizes differences and has a one-directional focus toward solving a problem. ICE introduces a type of relationship in which similarities and differences are acknowledged and honored, and in which a two-directional focus toward life balance is possible.

It is also important to distinguish between ICE and countertransference from a psychodynamic perspective. Countertransference has the potential to do considerable damage. Although counselors in a multicultural society are challenged to expand one's capacity for empathy beyond the barriers of visible and invisible differences, cultural countertransference limits one's capacity for cross-cultural empathy. Avoiding the dangers of cultural countertransference requires one to develop cognitive and affective awareness of oneself and others at an articulate level of consciousness. Corey (2004) illustrated that problem: "To the degree that countertransference is present, group therapists react to members as if they were significant figures of their own original family" (p. 145). The familial analogy suggests the powerful potential of countertransference for either good or bad outcomes. Corey described countertransference as frequently occurring in group counseling. The good or bad consequences depend on how well it is managed by the counselor.

With ICE, it becomes possible for a counselor to identify common ground between two people whose positive expectations and ultimate goals are the same even though their behaviors may be very different, without the counselor having to disregard or minimize those differences. Even the same individual may change his or her cultural referent group during the course of the interview, from emphasizing gender, to age, to socioeconomic status, to nationality or ethnicity, to one or another affiliation. Unless the counselor is skilled enough to understand that each changing and potentially salient identity will require a different understanding and interpretation of that person's behavior, the counselor is not likely to be accurate in assessing the person's changing identity. The same culturally learned behavior may have very different meanings across people and even for the same person across times and situations (Pedersen, 2000a).

It is important to interpret behaviors accurately in terms of the intended expectation. If two people share the same positive expectation—for success, accuracy, fairness, or safety—they do not have to display the same behaviors to find common ground. Smiling is an ambiguous behavior, for example. It may imply trust and friendliness or it may not. The smile may be interpreted accurately or it may not. Outside of its culturally learned context, the smile has no fixed meaning. Two people may both expect trust and friendliness even though one is smiling and the other is not. If these similar positive expectations such as trust or respect are undiscovered or disregarded, then differences of behavior will be presumed to indicate negative expectation, resulting in conflict. If, however, the two culturally different persons understand how they perhaps really have the same positive expectations even though their behaviors may be very different, they may agree to disagree or recognize that they are both approaching the same goal from different directions in complementary ways. The obvious differences in behavior across cultures are typically overemphasized, whereas the more difficult-to-discover similarities of positive expectations are typically underemphasized. A visual tool called the *intrapersonal cultural grid* is introduced in chapter 5 as a way to help conceptualize the skill of separating behaviors from expectations.

Wrightsman (1992) explained how the perspectives of behaviorism, psychoanalysis, and humanism are supplemented by a more inclusive perspective based on George Kelly's (1955) personal construct theory. Wrightsman (1992) described this new movement as more collectivistic, resembling non-Western indigenous psychologies:

> We are living in a time when the conventional wisdom about human nature and the nature of society is under attack. Technology has run amok; many now question our ability to bring technology under manageable control. Bureaucracy—a social structure originally established to provide for personal growth—now stifles human development and generates a philosophy that human nature is lazy, irresponsible and extrinsically motivated. The communal movement has challenged a pessimistic drift

in our society. Through study of the movement's assumptions, aims, procedures and outcomes, we may gain an understanding of the future of philosophies of human nature. (p. 293)

Complex and dynamic psychosocial theories that incorporate culture have been available for a long time. The postmodern survivors are "shapeshifters" (Lifton, 1993) with multiple identities as a source of strength, and they provide a new psychological ideal for the postmodern world. Lifton contrasted the shapeshifting self with an alternative "fundamentalist self" who avoids fragmentation by being consistent. In the postmodern world, discontinuous change seems to be a permanent feature. This need not result in chaos. The value of ICE is to incorporate the cultural context in a comprehensive way, recognizing its own self-regulating dynamic as the counseling relationship develops. Imposing the counselor's perspective can also remove the chaotic features but at the expense of devaluing the client.

AN INCLUSIVE DEFINITION OF CULTURE

By defining culture broadly to include ethnographic, demographic, status, and affiliation categories, the multicultural construct becomes relevant to all counseling relationships. Narrower definitions of culture have limited multiculturalism to what might more appropriately be called "multiethnic" or "multinational" relationships between groups with a shared sociocultural heritage that includes similarities of religion, history, and common ancestry. Ethnicity and nationality are important to individual and familial identity as one aspect of culture, but a more broadly defined construct of culture goes beyond national or ethnic boundaries. People from the same ethnic or nationality group may still experience cultural differences. Not all Blacks have the same experience, nor do all Asians, all American Indians, all Hispanics, all women, all old people, or all people with disabilities, and so on. No particular group is rigidly unified in its perspective. Therefore the broad definition of culture is particularly important in preparing counselors to deal with the complex differences among clients from every cultural group.

Poortinga (1992) defined culture as "shared constraints that limit the behavior repertoire available to members of a certain sociocultural group in a way different from individuals belonging to some other group" (p. 10). Segall, Dasen, Berry, and Poortinga (1990) affirmed that ecological forces are the prime movers and shapers of cultural forms, which in turn shape behaviors: "Given these characteristics of culture, it becomes possible to define it simply as the totality of whatever all persons learn from all other persons" (p. 26). Culture is part of the environment and all behavior is shaped by culture, so that it is rare (perhaps even impossible) for any human being ever to behave without responding to culturally learned patterns.

Another implication of the broad definition of culture is cultural psychology, which presumes every sociocultural environment depends on the way human beings give each cultural context meaning and are in turn changed in response to that environment. Cultural psychology studies the ways cultural traditions and social practices regulate, express, and transform people in patterned ways. Shweder (1990) stated, "Cultural psychology is the study of the ways subject and object, self and other, psyche and culture, person and context, figure and ground, practitioner and practice live together, require each other, and dynamically, dialectically and jointly make each other up" (p. 1).

Counselors have sometimes been misled by dichotomous thinking habits in their search for objectivity. There is a tendency to oversimplify a context and even a client by measuring everything on a 7-point scale of either–or categorizations from good to bad or normal to abnormal in ways that ignore the possibility of both–and thinking from quantum theory (Butz, 1992). As a consequence of our search for dissonance reduction, we may distort our perspective of the client and the client's cultural context. Just as differentiation and integration are complementary processes, so are the emic (culture specific) and etic (culture general) perspectives necessarily interrelated. The terms *emic* and *etic* were borrowed from "phonemic" and "phonetic" analysis in linguistics describing the rules of language to imply a separation of general from specific aspects (Pike, 1966). Even Pike in his original conceptualization of this dichotomy suggested that the two elements not be treated as a rigid dichotomy, but as a way of presenting the same data from two complementary viewpoints. Although research on the usefulness of emic and etic categories has been extensive, the notion of a "culture-free" (universal) etic has been just as elusive as the notion of a "culture-pure" (totally isolated) emic.

The basic problem facing counselors is how to describe behavior in terms that are true to a particular individual in a specific culture while also generalizing from those behaviors to one or more other cultures (Pedersen, 2000b). Combining the specific and general viewpoints provides a multicultural perspective. This larger, inclusive perspective is an essential starting point for mental health professionals seeking to be more accurate and to avoid cultural encapsulation by their own culture-specific assumptions.

The multicultural perspective, broadly defined, complements rather than competes with traditional theories of behavioral, psychodynamic, or humanist counseling. Counseling from whatever theoretical perspective is interpreted from the counselor's own cultural self-awareness and is applied to the client's cultural context. D. W. Sue et al. (1998) specified the importance of counselor self-awareness and an awareness of the client's cultural context to the delivery of effective counseling services.

The broad and inclusive definition of culture has been mistakenly criticized for reducing culture to individual differences. The distinction between individual differences and cultural differences is real and important. Your skin color at birth was an individual difference, but what that skin color has come to mean over time and socialization has turned skin color into a cultural factor. We learn our individual identity in a cultural context. The cultural identities to which we belong are no more or less important than our individual identity. Although culture has traditionally been defined as a multigenerational geographic phenomenon, the broad definition of culture suggests that cultural identities and culturally significant shared beliefs may develop in a contemporary time frame independent of geography and still be distinguished from individual differences.

Frequently, we hear about how multiculturalism or cultural differences present problems to counselors and counseling, usually in the form of quotas or measures of imposed equity. Culture has frequently been seen as a barrier to counseling rather than as a tool for helping counselors be more accurate and as a means of facilitating ICE. As long as our understanding of culture is limited to labels for narrowly defined perspectives, the generic relevance of cultural contexts to multicultural counseling is not likely to be appreciated.

The rhetoric in support of recognizing cultural complexity as part of multicultural counseling has been in professional documents of accreditation, certification, and licensure for many years now. From the narrow definition of culture, these statements have been perceived as political, favoring the special interests of one group or another. From the perspective of a broad definition of culture, however, multiculturalism goes beyond the self-interests of any particular group to redefine the very basis of identity for both the counselor and the client, regardless of their skin color, age, gender, socioeconomic status, or affiliations. The argument on which much of multicultural counseling rhetoric has been based has been largely humanitarian in its basis. The argument from a broad definition of culture is based on functional accuracy or utilitarian goals of ICE in the counseling relationship, without diminishing the humanitarian imperative.

The cultural context provides a force field of contrasting influences, which can be kept in balance through ICE. There are several implications of considering ICE to be necessary for good counseling to occur. Each implication contributes toward a capability for understanding and facilitating a balanced perspective in multicultural counseling. Can a counselor hope to know about all possible cultures to which the client belongs? Probably not, but the counselor can still aspire to know about as many cultural identities as possible, just as in aspirational ethics, whereby the counselor tries always to do good but never expects to achieve absolute goodness.

Individualism by itself is proving to be dysfunctional and needs to be combined with other perspectives for different cultures to exist together. Helgesen (2005) described society as a living system that rejuvenates itself when confronting inefficiencies through a "web of inclusion" that combines the group and the individual approach in a dynamic unity. The web of inclusion follows an open and flowing architecture of organizations in ways that are similar to the percepts of the Tao in Chinese philosophy in the search for a kind of balance.

> In the physical sciences, a state of equilibrium does not imply a healthy balance, but refers rather to random dispersal of energy—a kind of death. The more coherent or rigid the structure, the tighter and more organized, the more immune it is to the living energies of transformation. (Helgesen, 2005, p. 287)

This dynamic and inclusive form of "syntropy" is appropriate to our interconnected world and may define the next stage of our evolution as a species.

AN INCLUSIVE DEFINITION OF POSITIVE THERAPY OUTCOMES

Healthy functioning in a multicultural context may require a person to maintain multiple conflicting and culturally learned roles without the opportunity to resolve the resulting dissonance. Balance, as a construct for ICE, involves the identification of different or even conflicting culturally learned perspectives without necessarily resolving that difference or dissonance in favor of either viewpoint.

The construct of balance was defined by Heider (1958) and Newcomb (1953) in consistency theory as the search for an enduring consistency in an otherwise volatile situation. Cognitive balance is achieved by changing, ignoring, differentiating, or transcending inconsistencies to avoid dissonance (Triandis, 1977). From another more complicated perspective, however, asymmetrical balance can be described as requiring a tolerance for ambiguity, inconsistency, and dissonance (Pedersen, 2000b) rather than rushing to resolve differences too quickly.

Change in this context is perceived as a continuous and not an episodic process. Balance as a construct seeks to reflect the metaphors of organismic systems in holistic health. Problems, pain, and otherwise negative aspects of one's experience may also provide necessary resources for understanding the dark side of healthy functioning, as in ecological analysis of psychological process (Berry, 1980).

Health is more than the absence of illness; it is a positive force with its own separate definition. The construct of balance is useful for understanding this unique characteristic of health as a goal orientation of counseling. By attending to the client's cultural context, a skilled counselor will find it necessary to respond differently even to the same presenting symptoms. The counselor acts much as a social engineer compensating for a lack of harmony in the cultural context by increasing the influence of a counterbalancing perspective for the client.

The function of counseling is to restore balance in the client's cultural context. There are several examples of empathic balance in the counseling literature. Tseng and Hsu (1980) discussed how therapy compensates for culturally different features. Highly controlled and overregulated cultures might encourage therapies that provide a safety-valve release for feelings and emotions, whereas underregulated or cultural contexts with less rigid norms might encourage therapies with externalized social control at the expense of self-expression. Lin and Lin (1978) attributed mental illness to five harmful emanations affecting the yin and yang when they are disturbed or out of balance.

In some cases the balance has been restored through therapy by bringing in a mediator as a third person in addition to the counselor and client. Bolman (1968) advocated the approach of using two professionals, one from each culture, collaborating in cross-cultural counseling with traditional healers as cocounselors. Weidman (1975) introduced the notion of a culture broker as an intermediary for working with culturally different clients. Slack and Slack (1976) suggested bringing in a coclient who has already effectively solved similar problems in working with chemically dependent clients. Satir (1964) introduced mediators in family therapy for problems of pathogenic coalitions with the therapist mediating to change pathogenic-relating styles. Counseling itself is a "go-between" process whereby the therapist or mediator is the catalyst for resolving conflict.

Trimble (1981) suggested that, in some cultures such as American Indian cultures, a third person as mediator might work better than in other cultures. However, if the mediator is poorly chosen, bringing in a third person as mediator or interpreter may seriously distress clients through embarrassment, misinterpretations, inaccuracies, invasions of privacy, and for a variety of other reasons (LeVine & Padilla, 1980). If counselors are themselves trained to be bicultural and bilingual, the mediating function is internalized within the counselor's range of skills. This internalized mediation goes back to the earliest Greek role of the counselor as a mediator between the client and a superordinate world of powers and values.

Pope-Davis, Coleman, Liu, and Toporek (2003) provided a comprehensive survey of multicultural competencies that demonstrate the importance of balance. Professionals who practice ICE help clients achieve balance when they use skills such as the following:

- *The ability to see positive implications in an otherwise negative experience from the client's cultural viewpoint.* Ivey and Ivey (2007) emphasized the importance of a "positive asset search" in counseling. It would be simplistic of a provider to assume that the negative experiences of culturally different clients are not also related to positive outcomes and consequences.

- *The ability to anticipate potential negative implications from an otherwise positive experience.* Each solution a counselor brings to a culturally different client will almost certainly also have potential negative effects that must also be considered from the client's viewpoint.
- *The ability to articulate statements of meaning.* This helps to interpret or integrate positive and negative events in a constructive way without requiring the client to resolve the dissonance in favor of one or another culture. The role of the counselor is to help clients articulate the meaning of an otherwise difficult situation for their lives and for their future. The meaning of each event will include both positive and negative elements, which must be understood in a cultural context. Ivey and Ivey's (2007) microskill "reflection of meaning" requires counselors to explore basic and often conflicting concepts in their multiple cultural identities.
- *The ability to avoid simple solutions to complex problems and acknowledge the complicated constraints of a client's cultural context.* Ivey and Ivey (2007) described the "premature solution" as the most frequent mistake of beginning counselors. This is even truer in a multicultural setting. Pedersen (2000b) suggested that it is useful to anthropomorphize the problem as a third-person metaphor to help counselors better understand the complexity of problems in culturally different settings.
- *Sensitivity to how collective forces influence an individual's behaviors.* Ivey and Ivey (2007) frequently pointed out how traditional counseling is biased toward an individualistic perspective. In a more collectivist culture, the welfare of the unit or collective forces may be more important than the individual. Good multicultural counseling may require balancing the welfare of the individual client against the welfare of those collective forces in a way that satisfies the individual and the collective.
- *Sensitivity to the changing power of the client over time.* Strong (1978) described social influence theory's contribution to understanding the importance of power in counseling. Power is culturally defined, and good multicultural counseling will be sensitive to whether counseling is enhancing or diminishing a client's power.
- *Sensitivity to the changing power of the client across different topical areas.* This reduces stereotyping. Differentiation by counselors requires them to note changes in social influence and power across topics as well as across time. A good multicultural counselor should be able to identify clients' areas of

expertise as well as areas of deficiency. The importance of self-esteem and the destructive effects of perceived helplessness apply especially to a client attempting to cope in a culturally unfamiliar context.

- *Sensitivity to the changing power of the client in culturally different social roles.* Clients who function at a very adequate level in some roles may not function adequately in other roles. Culturally biased counselors frequently disregard differences in role-functioning ability.

- *The ability to adjust the amount of culturally defined influence by the interviewer.* This can facilitate the independent growth of the other person. To facilitate a balanced perspective, the counselor will need to provide enough but not too much control, influence, or power as defined by the cultural context. If the counselor exerts too much control to a strong client, the client may rebel and reject the counselor as more troublesome than the problem. If the counselor exerts too little control toward a weak client, the client may abandon the counselor as inadequate and unable to provide the necessary protection (Pedersen, 2000a).

- *The ability to maintain harmony within the interview.* Ivey and Ivey (2007) commented on the importance of competence in counseling techniques being measured by the counselor's contribution to a harmonious rapport between client and counselor, even though they may be from different cultural backgrounds. Although the construct of dynamic balance through ICE is elusive, the preceding examples of observable counselor behaviors describe some of the essential aspects. These examples are rooted in the traditional counseling research literature and are not, by themselves, controversial. Because these examples are familiar, they may provide a bridge for counselors to understanding how ICE can expand the possibilities for human services. Further discussion of these and other specific skills can be found in chapters 8 and 9 of this volume.

DEVELOPING INCLUSIVE CULTURAL EMPATHY

In the next chapters, the development of ICE is presented following a three-stage sequence of multicultural competence, moving from awareness (of culturally learned assumptions, context, and experiences) to knowledge (information gaps and essential facts about the cultural context) to skill (making decisions and taking action on the basis of accurate awareness and a meaningful understanding of the cultural context). The following equation describes the dynamic process of developing ICE:

Affective acceptance + Intellectual understanding +

Appropriate interaction = Inclusive cultural empathy

Affective acceptance is defined as the development and emotional acknowledgment or awareness of culturally learned assumptions and a network of comemberships across cultural boundaries that include both cultural patterns of similarity and difference. Intellectual understanding is the increase in knowledge and comprehension of specific similarities and differences within a counseling relationship. Appropriate interaction–intervention requires developing the skills and abilities to incorporate both similarities and differences in a plan for working together by reframing the culturally learned assumptions and information to bring about constructive change.

Now that readers have been introduced to the basic concepts of ICE, we can reveal assumptions behind the ICE model. Underlying all the assumptions listed next is this main assumption: that cultural patterns of thinking and acting were being prepared for us even before we were born, to guide our lives, shape our decisions, and put our lives in order. We inherited these culturally learned assumptions from our parents and teachers, who taught us the rules of life. As we learned more about ourselves and others, we learned that our own way of thinking was one of many different ways. By that time, however, we had come to believe that our way was the best of all possible ways, and even when we found new or better ways, it was not always possible to change. We are more likely to see the world through our own eyes and to assume that others see the same world in the same way using a self-reference criterion. Multiculturalism, infused with inclusion, offers a contrasting perspective.

D. W. Sue, Ivey, and Pedersen (1996) identified the underlying assumptions for multicultural counseling and therapy. Building on that foundation, they identified the following eight assumptions behind ICE so that readers can more easily find points of agreement and disagreement.

1. We are both similar and different at the same time. No matter how different another person is from you, there is always some degree of similarity. No matter how similar the other person is to you, there is always some degree of difference. If either similarities or differences are overemphasized, you will get into trouble. If you overemphasize diversity and differences between people, you end up with stereotyped, disconnected categories that tend to be hostile toward one another. If you overemphasize similarities, you rob persons and groups of their individual identities.

2. Culture is complex and not simple. Complexity is your friend, not your enemy, because it protects you against accepting easy answers to difficult questions. It is tempting to create simple models that can be explained and understood but that do not reflect the complexity of a real-world cultural context. It is dangerous to confuse these simple explanations and labels with the more complex reality.

3. Behaviors by themselves are not meaningful. Behaviors are not meaningful data until and unless they are understood in the context of a person's culturally learned expectations. Behaviors can only be accurately interpreted in their cultural context. Similar behaviors might have different meanings and different behaviors might have the same meaning. If two persons share the same expectation for trust and respect, they do not have to display the same behaviors to get along with one another.

4. Not all racism is intentional. Counselors who presume they are free of racism underestimate the power of social pressure, modern advertising, and privilege. In many cases this racism emerges as an unintentional action by well-meaning, right-thinking, good-hearted, caring professionals who are probably no more or less free from cultural bias than the general public. Racism is defined as a pattern of systematic behaviors resulting in the denial of opportunities or privileges to one social group by another. Racism can refer therefore to aversive behavior by individuals or institutionalized social groups. Overt racism is intentional, whereby a particular group is judged inferior and/or undeserving. Covert racism is unintentional, whereby misinformation or wrong assumptions lead to inaccurate assessments or inappropriate treatments. Covert, unintentional racism is less likely to be challenged or changed.

5. We are all vulnerable to cultural encapsulation. Wrenn (1962, 1985) first introduced the concept of cultural encapsulation. A person who has fallen victim to cultural encapsulation defines reality according to her or his own set of cultural assumptions. The person is insensitive to cultural variations among individuals and assumes her or his own view is the only right one. The person's assumptions are not dependent on reasonable proof or rational consistency but are believed true regardless of evidence to the contrary. Everyone is judged from the viewpoint of the person's self-reference criterion without regard for the other person's separate cultural context. In particular, a culturally encapsulated helping professional tends to seek technique-oriented short-term solutions with little attempt to accommodate the client's needs.

6. Inclusion is more likely to define a cultural context than exclusion. A broad and inclusive definition of counseling interventions includes both the educational and the medical model to accommodate the diversity of culturally different consumer populations. "Even our definitions of health and pathology can be culture-bound, especially in the area of mental health. Thus what constitutes healthy human development may also vary according to the socio-cultural context" (Kagitcibasi, 1988, p. 25). The task is to match aspects of each cultural context with significant and salient antecedents to achieve appropriate outcomes in a purposive way. It is essential to recognize the importance of an inclusive perspective for accurately understanding each cultural context.

7. Internal spiritual resources are important. In many cultures the client may seek help from "intrapsychic resources" within the person, using self-righting mechanisms such as the client's natural support system. These endogenous resources are frequently overlooked as one of the treatment modes available. In many cultures conditions of stress lead to a mobilization of these self-healing modes that might result in altered states of consciousness as in dreams, dissociated states, religious experiences, or even psychotic reactions.

8. Ambiguity, although inconvenient, has potentially positive value. Levine (1985) suggested that the social sciences have failed to deal with ambiguity as an empirical phenomenon and have ignored the constructive possibilities of ambiguity for theory and analysis. "The toleration of ambiguity can be productive if it is taken not as a warrant for sloppy thinking but as an invitation to deal responsibly with ideas of great complexity" (p. 17). Complexity theory in the social sciences (Waldrop, 1992) grew out of chaos theory in the physical sciences, seeking to redefine conventional categories. "They believe that they are forging the first rigorous alternative to the kind of linear, reductionistic thinking that has dominated science since the time of Newton—and that has now gone about as far as it can go in addressing the problems of our modern world" (p. 13).

Knowledge has many forms. Concepts of knowledge must be enlarged to go beyond the boundaries of rational process. Knowledge in other cultures has many forms. There are many ways to gain knowledge, for example, intuition and other forms of knowledge accumulated through experience. Although reasoning is a valuable skill, in some cultures it is presumed to get in the way of knowledge because it excludes potentially valuable sources of information. For that reason, logical inconsistency and paradox become valuable approximations of truth in many societies. Logic is only one form of validation, dependent on a linear, empirical, and exclusionary principle to describe human behavior. The criteria of balance suggest other sources of qualitative validation as well.

THE CONTRASTING PROCESS OF MORAL EXCLUSION

Cultural encapsulation becomes most visible in the actions of exclusion. Insiders are separated from outsiders. Certain individuals or groups are judged to be outside the boundaries, and the normal rules of fairness no longer apply. Those who are excluded are nonentities, expendable, and undeserving, so doing harm to them is acceptable if not perhaps appropriate and justified. Ranging from discrimination to genocide and ethnic cleansing, victims are blamed for allowing themselves to become victims!

By better understanding the process of moral exclusion, we can better build a system of ethical guidelines for the future of counseling. This phenomenon is most evident in two nations at war, but subtle forms of moral exclusion are evident elsewhere as well. When intergroup contact fails, it often results in exclusionary behavior. Moral exclusion—meaning exclusion of a group or person for moral reasons—results from severe conflict or from feelings of unconnectedness and antipathy. Opotow (1990) listed the rationalizations and justifications that support moral exclusion of minorities, which help to identify otherwise hidden examples of moral exclusion through psychological distancing, displacing responsibility, defining group loyalty, and normalizing or glorifying violence.

According to Opotow (1990), some examples of moral exclusion and consequent behaviors include the following: (a) biased evaluation: making unflattering comparisons; (b) derogation: disparaging and denigrating others; (c) dehumanization: repudiating others' dignity and humanity; (d) fear of contamination: perceiving contact as threatening; (e) expanding the target: redefining legitimate victims; (f) accelerating harm doing: engaging in destructive acts; (g) approving destructive behavior: condoning harm doing; (h) reducing moral standards: defining harmful as proper; (i) blaming the victim: displacing the blame for actions; (j) self-righteous comparisons: justifying retaliation; and (k) desecration: harming others to demonstrate contempt.

Other more subtle, hidden, and covert processes of moral exclusion and their consequences include the following: (a) groupthink: striving for group unanimity; (b) transcendent ideologies: exalting the group experience; (c) deindividuation: feeling anonymous in the group; (d) moral engulfment: replacing ethical standards; (e) psychological distancing: not feeling others' presence; (f) technical orientation: focusing on efficient means; (g) double standards: having different sets of moral rules; (h) unflattering comparisons: emphasizing one's superiority; (i) euphemisms: conferring respectability on hurtful behavior; (j) displacing responsibility: appealing to higher authority; (k) diffusing responsibility: doing harm collectively; (l) concealing the effects: minimizing injurious outcomes; (m) glorifying violence: making violence legitimate; (n) normalizing violence: accepting violent behavior; and (o) temporal containment: allowing a necessary exception (Opotow, 1990).

Moral exclusion is the obvious consequence of cultural encapsulation and can occur in degrees from overt and malicious evil to passive unconcern when intergroup contact fails. It is possible to be exclusionary by what you do not do as well as by what you do. Moral exclusion is pervasive and not isolated. Psychological and social supports may condone otherwise unacceptable attitudes, intentionally or unintentionally. Opotow (1990) noted, "As severity of conflict and threat escalates, harm and sanctioned aggression become more likely. As harm doing escalates, societal structures change, the scope of justice shrinks, and the boundaries of harm doing expand" (p. 13). This model can also be applied to counseling and other areas of psychology. Opotow and Weiss (2000) demonstrated how moral orientations of inclusion and exclusion underlie and fuel environmental conflicts. A typology of denial in environmental conflict demonstrates "a form of selective inattention toward threat-provoking aspects of a situation to protect a person from anxiety, guilt, or other ego threats" (p. 479). As Opotow and Weiss pointed out, (a) we are all victims of exclusion, (b) we are all violators of inclusion, and (c) we all need to work on increasing our inclusionary perspective in problem solving through dialogue.

Palombi and Mundt (2005, p. 175) developed a model for inclusion with regard to gender and disabilities by combining the themes of wellness and liberation at the personal, relational, and collective levels. Personal needs involve mastery and control. Relational needs include support and affective bonds. The collective perspective combines the need for economic security, shelter, and safety nets. The community model of embeddedness, interdependence, intradependence, and evolution combines consideration of the target, purpose, and method of intervention as the basis of social justice.

Usually, moral exclusion results from severe conflict or from feelings of unconnectedness as relationships are perceived. Opotow (1990) listed the rationalizations and justifications that support moral exclusion and help to identify otherwise hidden examples of moral exclusion. Other examples of moral exclusion might include psychological distancing, displacing responsibility, group loyalty, and normalizing or glorifying violence. The list of examples is provided to demonstrate that moral exclusion can be so ordinary an occurrence that it fails to attract attention.

CONCLUSION

In this chapter we have described—by way of definitions, comparisons, contrasts, examples, and assumptions—our inclusive cultural empathy or ICE model. The first stage in developing ICE is awareness of assumptions. Whether we know it or not, we are all taught to assume certain things about who we are and how to behave. Most of these assumptions are unspoken but can be brought to a level of consciousness whereby we can articulate them. We have also examined the processes and manifestation of moral exclusion to describe why the alternatives to inclusion are unacceptable. In the next two chapters we explore how to develop awareness, both of our own cultural assumptions and of the possibly different assumptions of others.

4

AFFECTIVE ACCEPTANCE: RELATING TO AND UNDERSTANDING OURSELVES AND OTHERS

Affective acceptance is the development, emotional acknowledgment, or awareness of both culturally learned assumptions and a network of comemberships across cultural boundaries (i.e., the way that people share some things culturally with each other yet do not share other things) that include both cultural patterns of similarity and difference. As helping professionals strive to develop affective acceptance, it is important to keep in mind the fact that culture is not static but rather permeable and constantly changing because of internal and external forces (Harper, 2003). Cultures and contexts are in constant flux, as are the similarities and differences between them. Therefore, competent counselors are mindful that affective acceptance is not an endpoint that can ultimately be attained, but instead an ongoing process throughout our careers, developed and maintained by effort and vigilance across numerous factors.

D. W. Sue and Sue (2003) clarified five necessary factors that the culturally competent mental health professional must develop in relation to affective acceptance. The culturally aware mental health professional

1. has moved from being culturally unaware to being aware and sensitive to her or his own cultural heritage and to valuing and respecting differences.

2. is aware of her or his own values and biases and how they may affect minority clients.
3. is comfortable with differences that exist between [her- or himself and the] client in terms of race, gender, sexual orientation, and other sociodemographic variables.
4. is sensitive to circumstances (personal biases; stand of racial, gender, and sexual orientation identity; sociopolitical influences; etc.) that may dictate referral of the client to a member of her or his own sociodemographic group or to another therapist in general.
5. acknowledges and is aware of her or his own racist, sexist, heterosexist, or other detrimental attitudes, beliefs, and feelings. (p. 19)

In this section, we clarify how affective acceptance is a key variable in the development of inclusive cultural empathy. We accomplish this through the integration of D. W. Sue and Sue's (2003) five factors of a culturally competent mental health provider under the structure of the eight assumptions about culture-centered counseling discussed in chapter 3 of this volume. These eight assumptions are as follows:

1. We are both similar and different at the same time.
2. Culture is complex and not simple.
3. Behaviors by themselves are not meaningful.
4. Not all racism is intentional.
5. We are all vulnerable to cultural encapsulation.
6. Inclusion is more likely to define a cultural context than exclusion.
7. Internal spiritual resources are important.
8. Ambiguity, although inconvenient, has potentially positive value.

These eight assumptions will be integrated with the factors of a culturally competent mental health provider delineated by D. W. Sue and Sue. This chapter explores the first four assumptions, and the next four assumptions will be covered in chapter 5. Suggested activities and discussions will accompany much of this and the remaining chapters, offering readers the ability to learn through action and application.

ASSUMPTION 1: WE ARE BOTH SIMILAR AND DIFFERENT AT THE SAME TIME

A significant key to developing inclusive cultural empathy in a helping relationship is an awareness that each therapeutic relationship is between people who are distinct in many ways yet also have numerous commonalities.

The zones of difference and similarity within and between cultures can be referred to as *cultural borderlands* (Falicov, 1996). These cultural borderlands function to either assist or hinder the efficacy of a therapeutic relationship. These zones give rise to commonalities and resonance among groups and individuals (similarities) as well as internal inconsistencies, conflicts, and contradictions (differences). As the therapist develops an understanding of the commonalities and differences in each therapeutic relationship, he or she acquires the type of awareness necessary to become inclusively empathic.

Traditional approaches to developing a therapeutic relationship have emphasized that similarities should be the focus and emphasis and differences should be avoided. The logic behind this approach is that a focus on differences will create a rift between the client and the counselor. Thus many traditional approaches to counseling and therapy call for a focus on what exists in common between the therapist and the client and to build from this shared ground. The dilemma with this approach is that it reinforces ignorance about the very different experiences and opportunities that others have in life.

Let us imagine, for example, Larry, a middle-aged male therapist who was raised in a comfortable home in the suburbs of a Midwestern city. Larry has begun working with a young woman recently emigrated from Mexico named Concha. Concha is 26 years old and has recently had her third child. She and her family live in a small home shared with another family because of financial burdens. Concha arrived at counseling because of pressure from her social worker, who feels that her depressive affect may be affecting her ability to cope well with challenges before her. She and her husband are experiencing great difficulty in making ends meet as they are unable to get good-paying work owing to their recently emigrated status. Although both Concha and her husband were well educated in Mexico and had developed skills in their respective fields, good-paying work opportunities do not seem to be surfacing for either of them in the United States. Thus, they are forced to live in a very small apartment in a relatively poor neighborhood. Concha also appears to not be very forthright about her troubles and concerns up front in session.

If Larry approaches Concha solely paying heed to similarities she has to his life and context without also focusing on differences, he will likely make assumptions that overlook significant issues. He might, for example, assume that what Concha needs most is help feeling good about herself and to become more focused and goal directed. In this way, Larry might assume Concha can then move forth and make better choices that turn her life around and bring her the kinds of rewards available to all in society. Although this example of assumptions might seem a bit extreme, this set of goals and accompanying assumptions is not terribly uncommon among therapists who have not acquired multicultural awareness.

Falicov (1996) introduced four distinct ways in which therapists can approach the exploration of similarities and differences with clients: the universalist approach, the particularist approach, the ethnic-focused approach, and the both/and approach. In the *universalist* approach, the therapist emphasizes similarities instead of differences in intrapersonal and interpersonal processes. Therapists using this approach might respond to Concha in a manner quite similar to that of Larry in the previously discussed story. These behaviors are built on assumptions of stable processes across all peoples, including family interaction, individual needs, and patterns of behavior and thought. Therapists who assume a strictly universalist outlook consider culture and context as peripheral to effective therapy.

The opposite extreme to the universalist approach is the *particularist* approach, which purports that people are more dissimilar than they are alike. This approach presumes that all interactions within the family as well as the broader context are ultimately idiosyncratic responses to each family's customs, conventions, themes, and traditions, passed along generationally in a given family. The concept of culture, from a particularist perspective, refers to the beliefs and actions of a given person or family more than a reflection of broader social context. Each individual is seen as independently idiosyncratic and unrelated to larger cultural issues. This approach dismisses culture as a valuable variable in helping clients overcome their individual and interior conflicts. Particularist issues override all context-based challenges.

The *ethnic-focused* approach stresses that ethnicity is the key variable responsible for diversity of attitudes, feelings, thoughts, and behavior among different groups of people. Although the growth of this approach has been critical in the development of the understanding of and sensitivity to ethnic and cultural differences, it also has some shortfalls. In its tendency to systematize shared concepts due to ethnicity, it may lead some professionals to assume that ethnic and cultural groups are more homogeneous than they really are (Falicov, 1996). Approaching similarities and differences from an ethnic focus alone requires a tremendous amount of knowledge on the part of the therapist prior to meeting most any client. Such knowledge is challenging to accumulate and maintain because of a large amount of ethnicities and subgroups that exist as well as the complexity involved in the overlapping of multiple cultural identities.

The *both/and* approach is proposed as a way to respond with respect for all variables that come into play as well as the complexity that their overlapping creates. This approach requires the therapist to release the either/or ways of thinking, ranging from the topical universalist approach to the culture-refuting particularist approach to the oversimplifying ethnic-focused approach (D. W. Sue, Ivey, & Pedersen, 1996). The both/and approach combines information about specific cultures relevant to the therapeutic relationship with the "not-knowing" stance of Anderson and Goolishian (1998). Therapists using the not-knowing stance will approach clients with curiosity, encouraging dialog that takes into account cultural, personal, and universal issues. The not-knowing therapist emphasizes the client's ability to teach and inform the therapist about the interplay of the previously discussed issue areas. The both/and approach combines the gentle, nonassumptive style of not-knowing with the informed, culturally sensitive style of the ethnic-focused approach. This approach also takes into account issues emanating from both the universalist and the particularist perspective. Thus respect is given to the fact that universal issues exist and often apply to all people. In a similar fashion, individual differences are seen as important in how they shape response to all issues, from individual through cultural.

As we clarified in chapter 1, regardless of how different another person is from the therapist, there is always some measure of similarity. Likewise, regardless of how similar another person is, there are always differences that apply. As helping professionals, if we overemphasize either differences or similarities, we will likely err and overlook significant issues that could allow us to be of the most use to our clients. If we overemphasize diversity and differences between people, we result with stereotyped, disconnected categories that tend to collide unnecessarily with one another. If we overemphasize similarities, we do not allow our clients and their associated groups to maintain independent or interdependent identities. The both/and approach to similarities and differences creates and mediates a balance between these issues.

When exploring similarities and differences, the type of approach used is key to coming to a rich understanding while developing a warm and accepting therapeutic relationship. We advocate that therapists consider using something along the lines of the both/and approach, as explained previously. The skills necessary to accomplish this will be part of the focus of chapter 6. The key issue to know at this point is to approach your clients with a blend of inquisitiveness, humility, and awareness of where to focus to develop an understanding of key similarities and differences. D. W. Sue et al. (1996) also stressed the importance of not overemphasizing either cultural differences or cultural similarities. An overemphasis on cultural differences "produces a stereotyped, exclusionary, politicized, and combative perspective based on zero-sum assumptions," whereas an overemphasis on cultural similarities "results in exploitation of less powerful by more powerful groups and the pretense of a melting pot that disregards essential features of cultural identity" (p. 15).

Key Arenas of Similarity and Difference

Competent counselors can identify shared or overlapping features of cultural, contextual, and experiential comembership with each client, regardless of how different they may appear. This common ground can serve as a useful point of reference in developing a good therapeutic relationship. Awareness of this converging comembership is critical in the development of meaningful therapeutic alliance. The cultural borderlands of similarities and differences between the counselor and the client can be appraised by a focus on the following key areas: (a) cultural norms, expectations, and values; (b) contextual issues; and (c) experiential issues.

Each person is raised with a specific set of cultural norms, expectations, and values that has been prepared prior to her or his existence. This is also true of every person a therapist sees as a client. The issue is that each person has a different set of voices speaking to her or him at the same time about what is correct, appropriate, normal, and important in any given situation. Clients also have their own set of cultural voices speaking to them about these same issues, but from a different perspective. Perspective on significant issues can differ and overlap from culture to culture in a striking manner. Table 4.1 clarifies just a few issue areas that can serve as dividers and as bridges between a therapist with a mainstream perspective and a client from a nonmainstream perspective.

To emphasize how any one of the previously discussed variables can become significant in the therapeutic relationship as well as in an ability to develop inclusive cultural empathy, we briefly look at the issue area of perspective of time. Different perspectives of time and timeliness have often been a challenging component for counselors working with clients of various cultural backgrounds. Argyle (1996) argued that rules of punctuality are among the most difficult to navigate when people move across cultures. One of the authors of this book previously worked in Brownsville, Texas, where he discovered that several of his clients responded much better to counseling appointments when he scheduled them in to see him in broad swaths of time. For example, he had a number of clients whom he would schedule to meet him on "Tuesday afternoon." Although that afternoon was commonly somewhat booked, there were invariably clients scheduled on the hour who were not able

TABLE 4.1
Mainstream U.S. Perspective Versus Eastern or Other Perspectives

Issue area	Mainstream U.S. perspective	Eastern or other perspective
Definition of family	Nuclear and biological	Extended
Connectivity and independence	Independent	Interdependent
Social obligation	To self (looking out for number one)	To family and broader society
Social perspective	Individualistic	Collectivistic
Relationship to authority	Challenge authority	Accept authority
Religious	Salvation	Reincarnation
Relationship to parents	Independence at adulthood	Ongoing reverence, respect, and obedience into adulthood
Perspective of time	Importance of being on time	Things will happen in due time
Negative motivating force	Guilt	Shame

to come, for whatever reason. The clients scheduled for the "afternoon," in a broader sense, came in when they did and were very patient about waiting to be seen when they arrived. If a time slot opened up and they were there, they filled it. If it did not, they scheduled for another broad swath of time. The therapist's lack of rigidity in scheduling them was met with flexibility in waiting to see him. Most days, this sort of arrangement worked very well, and most hours were filled with sessions. This is an example of the type of response that can come from cultural awareness.

Although contextual experience can vary greatly from person to person, there are a number of key contextual variables to be aware of when working with clients. First, there is the variable of *family migration history context* and accompanying cultural change. Important issues to attend to include why, when, and how a client and her or his family came to migrate to the United States. Stories of migration vary nearly as much as we do as a people in the United States. Several other nations are also woven out of various people who have emigrated from all over the world. Examples include Australia, Argentina, Brazil, and Canada. The world is becoming increasingly global, and immigration is growing along with the global influx. As you prepare to discuss migration history with your clients, it is important that you also become aware of your own family migration history. The relatively small numbers of people in the United States whose families do not have a migration history to the states often have a family migration history, commonly forced, within the country. Native Americans have a history of being affected by the migration of others. This story is actually quite common throughout the Americas as well for most Native Americans. African Americans generally have a common familial migration history that is attached to the U.S. history with slavery. Many of the vestiges of slavery arguably affect the context of African Americans to this day. Just because the client did not migrate her- or himself does not mean that her or his family's migration history is not relevant to the client's context and experience in the world. Exhibit 4.1 is designed to heighten awareness of the importance of differences and similarities in family migration history as a contextual variable.

Another important variant of context has been referred to as *ecological context* (Falicov, 1996). This variant of context refers to how, where, and with whom the client lives and fits into the broader environment. Key components of ecological context include class and socioeconomic status, religious community, ethnicity, quality of available education, quality of living environment, quality and availability of transportation to work and other various opportunities, and proximal availability of resources (food, banking, day care, etc.). The larger the number of ecological variables working against the individual and her or his family, the more significant ecological context becomes as an important variable in therapeutic relationships. A common error in counseling is for the counselor to assume something akin to the following: "All she has to do is want

EXHIBIT 4.1
Family Migration History

Directions: Have the participants break up into groups of 3 or do this activity with someone you have met in the past few years. Each individual in every triad will be interviewed by the other two individuals in the triad on her or his family migration history. The following are examples of some useful questions to ask:

- How did you come to live in the town/city/region in which you live today?
- Where do your parents claim as their hometown(s)? How did their families come to be there?
- What knowledge do you have of how your family came to live in the United States?
- If your family originally came from another country or countries, are you connected emotionally or in any other manner to these locations and their respective cultures?
- If they came from other points of origin, under what circumstances did they immigrate here?
- Did your family come from a different region of the country prior to being here?
- If so, are you still connected emotionally or in any other sense to that region or state?
- How does your family's migration history affect your personal identity?
- Do people treat you and/or your family in any particular manner because of your migration history?
- If you are unaware of your family's emigrational history, or it is unclear, how does this feel to you?

After the triads have completed the family migration interviews, discuss the experience as a large group.

- Did you learn anything about those with whom you were speaking that you did not expect?
- Did you learn anything about yourself during the interview process?
- How does your identity as related to family migration history vary from the identities of the others with whom you spoke?
- How do you feel about the emotional impact of discussing family migration history?
- What can you take from this activity that will help you in coming to understand your clients' cultural perspectives better?

change bad enough to work for it to happen and things will begin to improve." Although, at face value, such a statement may be at least partially true for all clients, it is less true for clients who live in very challenging ecological contexts. The activity in Exhibit 4.2 is designed to help increase awareness of differences and similarities in ecological contexts. Each individual's personal as well as family history of ecological context is also important in defining how he or she interacts with the world.

Differences and Context

The dominant culture of any society generally creates assumptions about how people should be, act, and believe. This dominant cultural push comes in direct conflict with people who come from cultural backgrounds that differ from the dominant culture. Many clients experience this dominant

EXHIBIT 4.2
Ecological Context

Directions:

1. Have the participants break up into groups of 3. This activity may also be done outside of the class setting in dyads and then discussed later in class, or a reader may do this with another person whom he or she has met in the past few years.
2. Each individual in every triad or dyad will be interviewed by the other individuals in the triad on her or his ecological context. The following are examples of some useful questions to ask.

Ecological Context of Rearing

When you grew up, what was your neighborhood like? How safe did your family feel it was to go outside at night? How far away was the nearest grocery store? How did your family get to that store? When your parents wanted babysitting help, how did they get it? Who helped care for you and your siblings? What were your schools like? Were you allowed to take textbooks home to study during high school? Were your class texts purchased by the school, your family, or some other source? How were you provided lunch while at school? How many cars did your family have when you were growing up? If your family did not have cars, how did you get around? How often did your family take vacations when you were a kid? If your family did take vacations, what types of vacations were they? How old were you when you first got a job? What was the reason you got your first job? Did your family attend church or synagogue or other place of worship when you were a child? How important was religion in your family?

Current Ecological Context

What is your current living situation? How many people do you live with and in what setting? What do you and your significant others use as transportation? How near is the nearest grocery store and how do you get to it? Do you consider yourself religious? If so, what role does religion play in your family life? Do you have any children? If so, how do you procure child care when you need it? How safe do you consider your neighborhood at night?

After the triads have completed the family ecological interviews, discuss the experience as a large group.

- Did you learn anything about those with whom you were speaking that you did not expect?
- Did you learn anything about yourself during the interview process?
- How does your identity as related to ecological context vary from the identities of the others with whom you spoke?
- How do you feel about the emotional impact of discussing ecological context?
- What topic areas were most uncomfortable for you and why?
- What can you take from this activity that will help you in coming to understand your clients' cultural perspectives better?

cultural push as a form of oppression, wherein they are marginalized or ostracized for not fitting into the norms of the "mainstream." Many problems that clients bring to the therapeutic relationship are not caused solely within the client but instead are based on environmental challenges of the interface discussed earlier. Inclusive empathy requires the counselor to develop an awareness and understanding of the challenges faced by clients that are different from her or his own experience. Making assumptions about client feelings without such an understanding is culturally encapsulated instead of culturally competent. Examples of experiences and perspectives include race and ethnicity, gender, sex, socioeconomic status, differential physical and mental abilities, and sexual orientation. Exhibit 4.3 provides guidelines to help counselors understand and predict how people from various cultures make decisions.

ASSUMPTION 2: CULTURE IS COMPLEX AND NOT SIMPLE

As we clarified in chapter 1, counselors should see complexity as our companion and not our enemy as it protects us against accepting easy answers to difficult questions. Oetting and Beauvais (1991) developed an orthogonal model of coexisting identities that clarifies the manner in which humans are culturally complex beings. This model explains that greater identification with any one sociocultural identity variable does not require decreased identification with other sociocultural identity variables. An individual's true identity is a distinct combination of multiple sociocultural identities each independent and overlapping in any of numerous complex combinations. Sometimes

EXHIBIT 4.3
Predicting the Decision of a Resource Person

Objective
- To learn how people from other cultural backgrounds make decisions.

Procedure
- Bring a resource person into the class from a culture or population with which the group members are not likely to have had previous contact. It is important to find a resource person who is both articulate and authentic. It is easy to find people who are authentic to a population but not articulate or who are articulate but not authentic.
- Ask the resource person to describe difficult decisions he or she has had to make. Have that person describe the situation up to but not including the actual decision that was made. Stop the resource person at that point and have each group member predict what decision the resource person will have made and why. When everyone has made their prediction, then have the resource person explain what decision was made and why it was made that way.
- In debriefing this exercise, it is a good idea to have worked with the resource person ahead of time and coached that person to help you teach the concepts of logical consequences or reflection of meaning as it is different in each cultural context.
- Allow the group members to ask their questions directly of the resource person and back off as a leader as much as you can. Be open to the possibility that the resource person's style might be quite different from your own.

Insight
The "self-reference criterion" that reflects our own view may not apply to others.

Note. From *110 Experiences for Multicultural Learning* (pp. 68–69), by P. B. Pedersen, 2004, Washington, DC: American Psychological Association. Copyright 2004 by Paul B. Pedersen. Adapted with permission.

within-group cultural differences seem to exceed between-groups differences as people identify the complex and dynamic salience of cultural self-identity moving from one situation to another. This theory of cultural identification does not polarize cultures but instead acknowledges the simultaneous multiplicity of coexisting identities in each individual. This orthogonal model recognizes that increased identification with one culture does not require decreased identification with other cultures. An individual can belong to many different cultures at the same time.

The five most frequently used alternative models of cultural identity are less complex but also less adequate. The *dominant majority* model simply imposes a dominant culture on all minority groups, regardless of the consequences. The *transitional* model presumes a movement toward the dominant culture as an appropriate adjustment. The *alienation* model seeks to avoid stress from anomie by assisting people in transition to make successful adjustments and treats different cultures as pathology. The *multidimensional* model presumes transition on several dimensions at the same time, with different degrees of change on each dimension toward a reconciled identity. The *bicultural* model presumes that one can adapt to a new culture without losing contact with an earlier culture. Oetting and Beauvais's (1991) orthogonal model, however, suggests that adapting any one culture is independent from simultaneously adapting too many other cultures, providing an unlimited combination of patterns. The orthogonal model presumes a higher level of complexity and a more comprehensive inclusion of cultural identities. The orthogonal model offers several advantages. Pedersen (1999) clarified the following nine advantages to the use of the orthogonal approach to individual identity.

1. Cultural groups may exist in association with one another without isolating themselves or competing with one another.
2. Minority cultures need not be eliminated or absorbed to coexist.
3. A permanent multicultural society may be possible that is multifaceted and multidimensional without becoming a melting pot.
4. Conflicts of value and belief do not present insurmountable barriers but may be combined in a realistic pluralism. Although some primary values and beliefs of each cultural group cannot be compromised, other secondary values and beliefs can be adapted and modified to fit a changing society.
5. Cultural conflict may become a positive rather than a negative force from the perspective of shared common-ground expectations.
6. Members of minority groups may be less inclined toward militancy when their survival is not threatened.
7. Interaction between minority and majority cultures may be less destructive for all parties. The orthogonal model describes a

win-win outcome for conflict among culturally different clients and counselors.

8. There are economic advantages of releasing resources previously consumed by cultural conflict. Imposed and enforced harmony is expensive and frequently ineffective in the long range. Voluntary harmony promotes the best interests of all clients if it can be achieved through willing cooperation.

9. There are already models of orthogonal relationships in healthy bicultural and multicultural social units. These models have appeared briefly but have then usually been overcome by the need for power by a dominant majority or the need to protect special interests by a hostile minority. Pluralism is neither easy to achieve nor simple to maintain. However, the alternatives are likely to be more expensive in the long term.

Ridley, Mendoza, Kanitz, Angermeier, and Zenk (1994) argued that the therapist's cultural sensitivity depends on the presence of five cognitive and behavioral variables. First, a culturally sensitive therapist understands that clients are representatives of multiple cultural groups, with each cultural identity variable overlapping with the others to create a unique individual identity. As we mentioned in chapter 1, in this way, each individual has at least 1,000 cultures to which he or she belongs at any given time, each playing a role in the person's perspective and identity. Second, a culturally sensitive therapist proceeds as if he or she is unsure of which hypotheses and beliefs concerning culturally different clients will hold true with each case encountered. Because of the complexity involved in the overlapping of multiple identities, it is not possible to have a clear understanding of a client's cultural identity and experiences prior to a vigorous check of the goodness of fit of cultural norms to the individual. Third, a therapist cannot become effective in selection of therapeutic interventions without first developing cultural sensitivity. Deficits in the ability to be culturally sensitive leave therapists in the position to make errors in judgment based on cultural misunderstandings. Fourth, therapist efficacy and cultural sensitivity can be negatively affected by cultural differences that are not clearly examined and acknowledged. If therapists do not take the time to develop a clear awareness of cultural differences, their responses to their clients can be based on assumptions of shared perception and values that are inaccurate. Finally, to be culturally sensitive, counselors must acquire, develop, and actively use an accurate cultural perceptual schema in the therapeutic relationship. This is to say that counselors need to develop the ability to maintain flexible and consistently evolving ways of perceiving their clients and all the variables that make up their sense of identity and perspective. To become and remain culturally sensitive to our clients, we must continually analyze ourselves, unearthing any private agendas we have, enthusiastically striving to eradicate any prejudicial or stereo-typic perceptions of our clients.

Every person we encounter exists in a dynamic interaction of multiple layers of complexity. As discussed earlier, individuals have many cultural identities that overlap and interact on an ongoing basis. We also undergo varying levels of development in our various cultural identities. Embracing complexity is useful in that it helps us avoid oversimplifying our responses to our clients. As we embrace complexity, we come to realize that the old saying of "the more I know, the less I know" becomes increasingly evident as a truism. We each have numerous cultural identities that shape who we are, how we think, and how we act. These identity categories include race, language, ethnicity, religion and spirituality, gender, familial migration history, affectional orientation (also known as sexual orientation), age and cohort, physical and mental capacities, socioeconomic situation and history, education, and history of traumatic experience. Chapter 5 focuses more directly on these cultural identity constructs.

The complexities we face in working with our clients should ultimately shape the decisions we make about how we theoretically approach our work. Leaders in multicultural counseling have long argued that there is no single theory or approach that can be applied equally to all clients in all situations with all problems (Ivey, 1986; D. W. Sue, 1991; D. W. Sue et al., 1996). Culturally aware counselors understand the importance of shifting their counseling approaches and theories applied to adjust to cultural, contextual, and sociopolitical aspects of their clientele. This flexibility includes the development of abilities to integrate alternative helping modalities, such as indigenous healing and spirituality and religion.

Within our diverse cultural identities, we also vary in cultural identity development. Models of cultural identity development include the minority identity development model (Atkinson, Morten, & Sue, 1998), identity development for White counselors (Ponterotto, 1988), White racial identity development (Helms, 1984), White racial consciousness (Rowe, Bennett, & Atkinson, 1994), biracial identity development (Poston, 1990), feminist identity development, and lesbian and gay identity (Cass, 1979; McCarn & Fassinger, 1996; Troiden, 1989), among many others. D. W. Sue et al. (1996) combined the general findings of the various cultural identity development models into a set of cognitive, emotional, and behavioral stages. The sequence of the stages is as follows:

> (1) naïveté and embedded awareness of self as a cultural being, (2) encountering the reality of cultural issues, (3) naming of these cultural issues, (4) reflection on the meaning of self as a cultural being, and (5) some form of internalization and multiperspective thought about self-in-system. (D. W. Sue et al., 1996, p. 17)

As the individual passes through each stage, he or she experiences different attitudes and emotions toward others as well as different attitudes and emotions about him- or herself. To become more aware of our cultural identity, we need to evaluate ourselves on the appropriate cultural identity development models. Awareness of our current status in cultural identity development is the first and one of the most important steps we need to take to develop toward internalization of cultural identity and a realistic and broad perspective of ourselves as interacting with others and society in a systemic manner.

Another significant layer of complexity is that of each individual's context and experience. The various things we experience throughout our lives can dramatically affect our beliefs, perspectives, and behaviors. For example, surviving a traumatic experience, such as the terrorist attack on the federal building in Oklahoma City, a fatal car wreck, a hostage experience, or a close call in a fire can all change the way a person interfaces with the world around her or him. Experience that is repeated on a daily or regular basis becomes a person's context. Context can be at least as powerful a shaper of perspective as any single significant and solitary experience. For example, the ongoing experience of being an African American in U.S. society can serve as a context of ongoing experience that creates great challenges for many people. Cornel West (1999) summed up much of this experience in the following description:

> The sheer absurdity of being a black human being whose black body is viewed as an abomination, whose black thoughts and ideas are perceived as debased and whose black pain and grief are rendered invisible on the human and moral scale is the New World context in which black culture emerged. (p. 101)

West further argued that "to be a black human being under circumstances in which one's humanity is questioned is not only to face a difficult challenge, but also to exercise a demanding discipline" (p. 101).

Finally, the complexity of culture is heightened by the fact that various cultural identities, cultural identity development, experience, and context do not exist in any person's life independently. Instead, at any given point in time, people are consistently responding to voices from any number of different variables that make up who they are. As these different voices speak simultaneously, they often create an interaction effect that results in a product much different than would come from any one voice alone. Ultimately, the whole of who we are as cultural beings is much more than a simple sum of our various parts. This whole identity and reality is also undergoing constant and unpredictable change. According to the metatheory of multicultural counseling and therapy, our cultural identity is constantly evolving as is the relative importance of our various cultural affiliations (D. W. Sue et al., 1996). The interaction of who we are, who we have been, what we experience, and current and past contexts constantly causes the salience of any given cultural referent. The definition of any human as a cultural being is ultimately very complex. A culturally aware counselor will strive to master the ability to work with her or his client's in co-construction of the client's cultural and social realities en route to helping her or him work toward a culturally based definition of wellness. Exhibit 4.4 is

EXHIBIT 4.4
Clarifying Cultural Identity Variables

Objective
To identify the complex culturally learned roles and perspectives that contribute to an individual's identity.

Procedure
In the blanks below, please write answers to the simple question, "Who are you?" Give as many answers as you can think of. Write the answers in the order that they occur to you. Go along fairly quickly. You will have 8 minutes.

I am_____

I am_____

I am_____

I am_____

I am_____

I am_____

I am_____

I am_____

I am_____

I am_____

and so forth.

- Now, select the top 10 variables of who you are and put them in order from most important in self-definition to least.
- Each person next is invited to write her or his top five self-identifiers on the board in front of the class. After all participants have written their top five on the board, discuss what you see.

Some useful discussion questions include the following:

- What are some trends you see as you look across the group?
- What types of variables seem to be most important in self-description for people in this group?
- What types of variables appear to be least important in self-description for people in this group?
- Would your answers change if you were in a different setting? If so, what kind of setting and why?
- What do you learn from this activity that will help you better understand your clientele?

Note. From *Culture-Centered Counseling Interventions* (pp. 25–26), by P. B. Pedersen, 1997. Thousand Oaks, CA: Sage. Copyright 1997 by Sage Publications. Adapted with permission.

designed to help counselors identify the complex culturally learned roles and perspectives that contribute to a person's identity, and Exhibit 4.5 provides an example of how to work with a person's multidimensionality.

ASSUMPTION 3: BEHAVIORS BY THEMSELVES ARE NOT MEANINGFUL

A common error made by less culturally aware therapists is to presume to understand their clients' motives on the basis of meaning derived from observation and tracking of their behaviors without paying attention to the contexts of said behaviors. This error occurs because behavior does not have specific meaning until and unless it is understood as it relates to a given person's culturally learned expectations and other contextual variables.

The social constructivist approach can be very helpful in developing a more accurate understanding of a client's behavior. Watts (1992) clarified

---

EXHIBIT 4.5
Focusing on Clients' Cultural Multidimensionality

An African American, lesbian, physically disabled client has come to counseling because she is feeling "very depressed." In the first counseling session, this client indicated that much of her depression revolves around the fact that her disability has resulted in long-term unemployment. She has used up all of her savings long ago and has been completely financially dependent on governmental assistance programs for an extended period of time.

During her initial session with the White male counselor who was assigned to her case, the client indicated that her strong religious beliefs and family support were all "that I had left in my life." She also stated how much she hated being "poor, Black, and disabled."

- Given this scenario, which aspect(s) of this client's multidimensionality would you focus on in this initial counseling session?
- What issues would you keep in mind when addressing this client's expressed concerns about being "poor, Black, and disabled"?
- How would you tap into this client's religious beliefs and family support to foster positive counseling outcomes?
- How do you think the fact that this client was assigned to a White, physically abled, male counselor might impact the helping process in this particular situation?
- Does the fact that this client is a lesbian have any relevance for counseling? If so, what considerations should the counselor keep in mind about the counselor's own sexual identity/orientation as they continue to work together in the future?

These questions are presented to (a) underscore the importance of recognizing how a client's multidimensionality affects the counseling process, (b) highlight some of the specific challenges mental health practitioners face when they intentionally strive to respectfully address their clients' multidimensionality in the helping process, and (c) encourage you to consider how your own multidimensionality may affect the counseling process with this and other clients with whom you work.

Note. Exhibit contributed with permission from J. Daniels and M. D'Andrea, University of Hawaii.

three key principles of social constructivism that apply when evaluating behavior. First, people interact with the environment because of the ways that historical, cultural, and social conditioning have had an influence on their perspective and beliefs. Second, people exist within cultural contexts that are ultimately unique and best understood when evaluated in reference to themselves and not to any other culture, particularly the dominant culture. Finally, it is inappropriate and unjust for one group, sharing a culture, to impose its standards on another group, as this creates a dynamic of dominance and subordinance that ultimately can be oppressive. Therefore, "truths" and "realities" exist both within and beyond Western empirical traditions. Behaviors of others are best understood within the context of their occurrence. This context is often embedded within other contexts or at least with overlapping contexts (Szapocznik & Kurtines, 1993). The culturally aware counselor emotionally accepts the fact that what a particular behavior might mean to her or him does not necessarily take on the same meaning to her or his client in differing contexts.

Outside of cultural context, most behaviors have no set meaning. What a person is feeling can be displayed with a large variety of behaviors, many of which vary by cultural context. Even what one does with one's body parts is ultimately translated in cultural context. For example, in the United States, an up-and-down nod of the head is commonly understood as indicating agreement. In India, agreement is signified by rocking one's head from side to side. Another example is use of right versus left hand. In Indian culture, anything important must be done with the right hand; the left is traditionally reserved for personal hygiene. Even if a person is left-handed, in India, he or she should not touch food with the left hand. Also, if one is given a gift in India, he or she should never accept it with the left hand, as that will very likely be perceived as an insult. If these rules seem a bit arbitrary to the reader, imagine how arbitrary culturally and contextually oriented rules of behavior seem to people coming from distinct cultures to the United States.

In the same manner, how a person derives meaning from a particular event or occasion is shaped by that person's cultural context. For example, diverse cultures view rituals and superstitions differently. Rituals and superstition both play critical roles in people's perception and emotional response. One group's rituals can collide directly with another group's superstitions. Exploring both differences and similarities in the interaction of rituals and superstitions can be crucial in avoiding misunderstandings.

The culture currently dominant in the United States has many assumptions built into it regarding human thought and behavior. These assumptions generally skew the manner in which we perceive and respond to the behaviors of others. We clarify a few of these assumptions in an effort to illuminate the role they play in the culturally unaware counselor's tendency to mistranslate the actions and intentions of their clients. First, an overriding assumption is that what is "normal" is set, fixed, and unable to waiver. Cultural definitions of what is normal tend to serve as the measuring stick by which all other behaviors are observed and measured. Under this assumption, that which is normal does not take into account the effect that context has on people's behaviors. Such assumptions lead to cultural encapsulation, which is discussed later in this chapter.

Second, it is assumed that the concept of individualism is universally important. Any person or culture that perceives individualism differently is perceived to be wrong or even maladjusted. Any person who is thus dependent on others is perceived as pathological. Third, a common assumption is that both the source and the solution to all problems lie within the individual. Thus the individual is expected to adjust when pathology is evident. Systems and the broader society are presumed to be appropriate and thus beyond reproach. Fourth, related to the previous two assumptions, it is commonly assumed that all people are ultimately and equivalently self-aware. This assumption negates the reality that in many cultures, people only see themselves in relation to others. Fifth, also related to this assumption is the cultural construct that presumes that support systems are ultimately unimportant. Clients are commonly seen as existing independent of others.

Sixth, linear thought is assumed to be the preferred, most effective, and most healthy way of thinking. More global processes are assumed to be ultimately of less use and value. Seventh, the history of a person and those of her or his system is presumed to be irrelevant to their current behaviors. A person's experience, particularly in interaction with historical context, is not taken into account when evaluating behavior. Finally, less culturally aware counselors tend to see the boundaries of professional behavior and demeanor as fixed. Rules of propriety in interaction are set by Eurocentric and andocentric norms and not seen as in need of adjustment on the basis of the cultural contexts of clients (Highlen, 1994). The activity in Exhibit 4.6 is designed to show the importance of placing behavior within a cultural context by using the following three scenarios as examples.

Natasha

At age 18, Natasha fled Lithuania, her country of birth, at the end of the cold war. She was not allowed to attend college in her home country because her father, who left behind Natasha and her mother in the late 1960s to come to America, had been labeled a political dissident. When Natasha arrived in the United States, she hoped that her father would help her find work and a place to live. He did not, but instead left her to fend for herself. In desperation, Natasha married a man who offered her what she thought would be a stable home. Although her home was comfortable, Natasha was abused with such regularity that she felt forced to divorce her

EXHIBIT 4.6
Behavior in Context

Have the class break into groups of four to six students. It can be particularly useful to have two or more groups assigned to discuss each scenario.

Procedure
1. Assign each group one of the three following scenarios (see the text) to discuss.
2. Each group is to discuss the behavioral patterns of the people involved in each scenario. The groups' job is to come up with as many possible ways of understanding the relationship between contextual issues and the decisions that the individuals involved made and will need to make in the future.

Discussion
After the groups have had up to 10 minutes to discuss the scenarios, lead a group conversation about the results of their discussions. Independent readers may also read the scenarios and come up with their own responses. Questions to discuss include the following:

- How relevant did you find contextual issues to the behaviors of the people involved in your scenarios?
- How did context appear to affect the choices available to the people in your scenarios?
- If you were the counselor for the people in your scenarios, how might you approach them while demonstrating respect for contextual issues involved in their lives?
- What questions might you want answered in order to be most helpful to these clients?

husband. Natasha now is 40 years old, a single mother with a teenage daughter from her marriage. Although she tries to find a fulfilling relationship, Natasha seems to not have any luck finding men who treat her with consistent respect. Although Natasha desires a relationship with long-term commitment, she continues to be involved with men who are not interested in committing. She tends to cycle in and out of a few relationships that are each only partially fulfilling.

The Sandberg Family

The eight members of the Sandberg family in rural Nebraska live in impoverished conditions. Their extended family has lived in the area for three generations. None of them have attended college and only a few have finished high school. The Sandbergs are members of a fundamentalist Christian church in the nearby town. The mother stays at home and the father has only been able to find seasonal work. Their oldest daughter, Marsha, is now pregnant with no prospects for marriage or even support from her boyfriend. It is very likely that Marsha will drop out of school. About the same time, the mother found out she was also pregnant with her seventh child. To make matters more challenging, they expect complications with this pregnancy because she had medical problems with her last one. One of the fears the family has is that Mrs. Sandberg has a high risk of dying or at least losing the baby during childbirth.

Laura

Laura was raised in a home with two alcoholic parents. Her home life was turbulent throughout her youth, with her parents often fighting and eventually divorcing when she was 10. When she was 11 she was sexually abused by her uncle. Laura ran away from home when she was 16 and now supports herself as a stripper. She has a drug habit and struggles with depression. She lives in her car when she is not living with her current boyfriend. Laura has been having trouble building relationships with stable men who do not use drugs and who respect her. She desperately wants to be able to have her own home and family.

ASSUMPTION 4: NOT ALL RACISM IS INTENTIONAL

The premise we raised in chapter 1 was that racism commonly emerges as an unintentional action of well-meaning people. This has a lot to do with the fact that racism is built into the fabric of our society. Racism can be defined as a pattern of belief and accompanying behavior that, solely because of race or culture, denies access to opportunity or privilege to members of one of more racial groups while affording access to members of another racial or cultural group (Ridley, 1989). Racism may also include the belief that racial or ethnic groups other than one's own are intellectually, psychologically, or physically inferior, as well as the view that there are qualitative differences across racial lines. The inclusion of behavioral aspects in the definition of racism shifts the focus from intentions and outlooks to actual customs of the perpetrator. It has been argued that the most insidious forms of racism are unintentional or done despite good intentions (Ridley, 1995). D'Andrea and Daniels (2000) argued that

> most of the racism that exists in the United States is perpetuated by millions of well-meaning, liberal-thinking White persons who react with passive acceptance and apathy to the pervasive ways in which this problem continues to be embedded in our institutional structures. (p. 294)

Racism exists in at least three forms: individual, institutional, and cultural. Individual racism is the concept most people think of when the term *racism* is used. This form of racism includes both beliefs and actions. The beliefs come in the form of personal attitudes, prejudices, and assumptions designed to convince oneself of the superiority of one's race over another's.

The actions of individual racism include various forms of discrimination toward others on the basis of their race. Both actions and beliefs can be intentional or unintentional in nature. Unintentional forms include rationalizing racial differences with "color blindness"; attributing problems in others to "cultural deficits"; overcompensating when relating with people of color because of underlying feelings of guilt, discomfort, uneasiness, and fear when in the presence of people of color; and ongoing nonacceptance of the existence of "White privilege." White privilege is discussed later in this section. Unintentional individual racism appears to have a tendency to materialize as a form of discrimination that appears only when the unintentional racist can easily rationalize her or his behavior as nondiscriminatory (Gaertner & Dovidio, 1977).

Institutional racism includes sets of laws, regulations, public policy, priorities, and practices in decision making that function to maintain the social and economic advantage of the racial group in power through subjugation, oppression, and forced dependence on the larger society (Jones, 1997). This form of racism presents as differential access to power, commodities, services, and opportunities by race. Institutional racism is generally legal, or presumed to be legal, and thus is embedded within laws, customs, traditions, expectations, and all levels of institutional organizations. Historic examples of institutional racism are the Jim Crow laws of the South that legally separated people in eating establishments, how they could use public transportation, where they could sit in theaters, and what restrooms, schools, and water fountains they could use. The civil rights movement brought the legal use of overt institutional racism to an end. This does not mean that it still does not exist. It is often embedded in other forms of oppression to avoid the appearance of racism. Examples include differential funding of public schools and other public facilities on the basis of class and the use of language to divide and separate. Institutional racism, in its many forms, is commonly overlooked by many counselors, particularly those who are not directly victimized by its existence.

Cultural racism is the most deeply ingrained form of racism, and thus the most difficult to overcome. It includes societal beliefs and customs that promote the assumption that the commodities of the dominant race (e.g., language, traditions, appearance) are better than those of other races. Cultural racism leads to rigid definitions of beauty, competence, and intelligence. It can limit the range of a person's perceived choices, dreams, and rights to creative expression and self-determination. For example, cultural racism can become internalized to the point that it leads individuals to dislike themselves because they do not have "beautiful skin" (leading to skin bleaching) or not straight enough hair (leading to hair straighteners, hair extensions, and wigs), or the right body type (as a result of clothing designed for White body types that are portrayed as the definition of attractiveness). Cultural racism can also lead to the formation of institutional racism. An example of this is the passage of a law in California disallowing bilingual education for Spanish-speaking children despite overwhelming evidence that it is in their best interest to offer it.

Unintentional Racism as White Privilege

A significant nexus of the forms of racism plays out through the concept of White privilege. Privilege is not only a state of being preferred or favored but also a set of conditions that systematically empower select groups on the basis of variables such as race while systematically not empowering others. In general, those of us who have different forms of privilege commonly have a great deal of difficulty acknowledging the privilege we experience on a daily basis. We are taught to not recognize White privilege. White people who do not make the effort to understand and respond to White privilege are taking part in oppression, albeit unpremeditated in nature. Such oppression is a form of unintentional racism. This difference in rights and privileges is normative in society and commonly overlooked in discussions of racism. To become empathetic on issues of race, we need to come to a higher understanding of the role that privilege plays in our lives and those of our clients.

In Western society, the common experience of people who consider themselves White is to be taught that the experiences they have and the opportunities they have are average everyday experiences for most people. White people learn to practice unintentional racism through the perpetuation of a system of White privilege of which most of them are totally unaware. Jackson (1999) defined White privilege as a club that enlists select people at birth, does so without requesting consent, then indoctrinates them with expectations and rules that are portrayed as normative.

The following is a brief list of daily privileges of being a White person excerpted from a much longer list written by Peggy McIntosh (1992). As you read this list, contemplate how it might feel to those who do not have these same privileges to work with others who do, yet do not recognize that they are relatively overempowered. McIntosh explained the following list of privileges as an invisible container of unearned assets that a White person can count on cashing in each day but about which she or he was intended to remain unmindful. A much more thorough listing of daily White privileges can be found in McIntosh (1992).

- I can turn on the television or open to the front page of the paper and see people of my race widely represented.
- When I am told about our national heritage or about "civilization," I am shown that people of my color made it what it is.
- I can go into a music shop and count on finding the music of my race represented, into a supermarket and find the staple foods

which fit with my cultural traditions, into a hairdresser's shop and find someone who can cut my hair.

- I do not have to educate my children to be aware of systemic racism for their own daily physical protection.
- I can swear, or dress in second-hand clothes, or not answer letters, without having people attribute these choices to the bad morals, the poverty, or the illiteracy of my race.
- I can do well in a challenging situation without being called a credit to my race.
- I am never asked to speak for all the people of my racial group.
- I can remain oblivious of the language and customs of persons of color who constitute the world's majority without feeling in my culture any penalty for such oblivion.
- I can be pretty sure that if I ask to talk to the "person in charge," I will be facing a person of my race.
- If a traffic cop pulls me over or if the IRS audits my tax return, I can be sure I haven't been singled out because of my race.
- I can take a job with an affirmative action employer without having my coworkers on the job suspect that I got it because of my race.
- I can be late to a meeting without having the lateness reflect on my race.
- I can be sure that if I need legal or medical help, my race will not work against me.
- I can easily find academic courses and institutions which give attention only to people of my race.
- I can choose blemish cover or bandages in "flesh" color and have them more or less match my skin.

Exhibit 4.7 provides a list of questions designed to help you explore your own ideas and feelings of White privilege.

As we discuss the concept of racism, it is important to note a few distinctions in terminology. Locke (1998) clarified that prejudice is placing judgment prior to carefully and fully examining the object of evaluation. He explained that racial prejudice is the passing of judgment on the basis of ethnic, racial, and cultural group membership prior to this same careful and full examination. Finally, he clarified that racism is a combination of racial prejudice with power to act on this prejudice. Ivey and Ivey (2001) argued that oppression creates a sense of ongoing trauma through which people who are not of majority status must live on a daily basis. They explained racism and similar forms of prejudice as specific cases of trauma as well as ongoing trauma of living in a society that is racist and oppressive. The ongoing realization that things are as they are and will not likely improve tremendously combined

EXHIBIT 4.7
Discussion Questions on White Privilege

1. As you read the list of White privileges (see the text), what feelings do you experience?
2. If any of the feelings you experience are negative or angry, what do you think is at the root of such feelings?
3. If you were to describe the experience of being a Person of Color in a society based on White privilege, how would you describe it?
4. Now that you have familiarized yourself with the concept of White privilege, what other privileges do you think exist in the daily lives of White people in Western society?
5. How do you think such privileges came to exist?
6. What is it that has maintained White privilege as an "invisible knapsack" of assets for so many years?
7. If a person wanted to do something constructive in response to White privilege, what might he or she do?
8. Are there different things that White people can do in constructive response to White privilege than People of Color can do?

with the ongoing fear or expectation of experiencing oppression creates a sort of long-term, ongoing oppression.

Lack of awareness of differential preference and the accompanying intentional and unintentional oppression do not only exist for White people as members of the dominant culture in the United States but also for those who have majority status on many variables. The hierarchical order of society is actually more of a set of interlocking variables. As racism exists in intentional and unintentional formats, so do other forms of oppression in society. Other forms of unintentional oppression include sexism, classism, heterosexism, ableism, ageism, ethnocentrism, and religious bias. The following few pages focus on issues similar to those regarding unintentional racism, but in other areas of unintentional oppression. Owing to space limitations, we focus briefly on unintentional heterosexism, followed by a few words on other unintentional "isms." Chapter 5 will focus more thoroughly on issues surrounding the development of the knowledge necessary to acquire inclusive cultural empathy. This section ends with an activity created to heighten awareness of the unintentional roles we play in various forms of privilege, as described previously.

Unintentional Heterosexism as Straight Privilege

To become empathic toward the experience of people of affectional orientations aside from heterosexuality, it is important that heterosexuals become aware of how the daily life experiences of nonheterosexuals differ from their own experiences. In response to McIntosh's (1992) working paper on White privilege, a group of students at Earlham College in Indiana collaboratively drafted a list of daily privileges that straight people have in soci-

ety. The following are privileges excerpted from the complete list (some paraphrased; see Hunter, 2005).

On a daily basis as a straight person,

1. If I pick up a magazine, watch TV, or play music, I can be certain my sexual orientation will be represented.
2. When I talk about my heterosexuality (e.g., in a joke or talking about my relationships), I will not be accused of pushing my sexual orientation onto others.
3. I do not have to fear that if my family or friends find out about my sexual orientation there will be economic, emotional, physical, or psychological consequences.
4. I did not grow up with games that attack my sexual orientation (i.e., "fag tag" or "smear the queer").
5. I am not accused of being abused, warped, or psychologically confused because of my sexual orientation.
6. I can go home from most meetings, classes, and conversations without feeling excluded, fearful, attacked, isolated, outnumbered, unheard, held at a distance, stereotyped, or feared because of my sexual orientation.
7. I am never asked to speak for everyone who is heterosexual.
8. I can be sure that my classes will require curricular materials that testify to the existence of people with my sexual orientation.
9. People don't ask why I made my choice of sexual orientation.
10. People don't ask why I made my choice to be public about my sexual orientation.
11. I do not have to fear revealing my sexual orientation to friends or family. It's assumed.
12. People of my gender do not try to convince me to change my sexual orientation.
13. I can easily find a religious community that will not exclude me for being heterosexual.
14. I can count on finding a therapist or doctor willing and able to talk about my sexuality.
15. I am guaranteed to find sex education literature for couples with my sexual orientation.
16. My masculinity or femininity is not challenged because of my sexual orientation.
17. I am not identified by my sexual orientation.
18. I can be sure that if I need legal or medical help my sexual orientation will not work against me.
19. Whether I rent or I go to a theater, I can be sure I will not have trouble finding my sexual orientation represented.

20. I can walk in public with my significant other and not have people double-take or stare.
21. I can choose to not think politically about my sexual orientation.
22. I can remain oblivious of the language and culture of LGBTQ (lesbian, gay, bisexual, transgender, queer) folk without feeling in my culture any penalty for such oblivion.
23. I can go for months without being called straight and nobody calls me straight with maliciousness.
24. My individual behavior does not reflect on people who identity as heterosexual.
25. In everyday conversation, the language my friends and I use generally assumes my sexual orientation. For example, the term *sex* inappropriately is used to refer to only heterosexual sex or family meaning heterosexual relationships with kids.
26. People do not assume I am experienced in sex (or that I even have it!) merely because of my sexual orientation.
27. I can be open about my sexual orientation without worrying about my job.[1]

Exhibit 4.8 presents a list of questions counselors can ask themselves to evaluate their awareness of heterosexual privilege.

Other Forms of Unintentional Oppression

Unintentional oppression exists virtually anywhere in which there is a culture that is dominant. In oppression, there are two key forms of players, those doing the oppressing and the oppressed. For the purposes of this book, we use the terms *targets* and *agents* to refer to these two types of players in oppression. Targets are members of social identity groups that are disenfranchised, exploited, marginalized, victimized, and made powerless in a variety of ways by oppressors and the oppressors' systems and institutions (M. Adams, Bell, & Griffin, 1997). Targets are subject to exploitation and containment, maintained in situations that keep their choices and movement restricted and limited. They are seen as replaceable and expendable, and lumped into narrowly defined roles of their prescribed groups in which they exist virtually devoid of individual identities. Agents, however, are affiliates of dominant social groups privileged from birth or attainment, who deliberately or unwittingly exploit and gain unfair advantage over members of target groups (M. Adams et al., 1997).

Rich (1986) argued that a person's status as a heterosexual generally goes unquestioned because its alleged naturalness and normalcy place it beyond

---

[1]From *Unpacking the Invisible Knapsack II: Sexual Orientation*, by Daniel Hunter, 2005. Reprinted with permission from the author.

EXHIBIT 4.8
Discussion Questions on Heterosexual Privilege

---

1. As you read the list of heterosexual privileges (see the text), what emotions do you experience?
2. If any of the feelings you experience are negative or angry, what do you think is at the root of such feelings?
3. If you were to describe the experience of not being heterosexual in a heterosexual world, how would you describe it?
4. Now that you have familiarized yourself with the concept of heterosexual privilege, what other privileges do you think exist in the daily lives of heterosexual people in Western society?
5. How do you think such privileges came to exist?
6. What is it that has maintained heterosexual privilege as an "invisible knapsack" of assets?
7. If a person wanted to do something constructive in response to heterosexual privilege, what might he or she do?
8. Are there different things that heterosexual people can do in constructive response to heterosexual privilege than can homosexual or bisexual people?

---

the realm of political analysis. It is our view that the presumptions of "naturalness and normalcy" pertain to all agent statuses in society. People who have status within any target area presume to be above labels, as their status is presumed to be normal, whereas people of target status tend to be given the label. It is for this very reason that advocates and members of many of the target groups put effort into labeling those in the agent groups against whom they are constantly compared and contrasted.

Targets and agents take a number of forms in society. Each target status is generally matched with a specific agent status. Target and agent statuses are not exclusive in nature; as we mentioned, people have multiple identities wherein they can be more than one form of a target, more than one form of an agent, as well as a target and an agent at the same time in different areas. For example, in the United States, when examining race as a variable, target and agent status varies, with people who are White sharing agent status and Persons of Color filling the associated target status. When considering gender as a variable, boys and men have agent status, whereas girls and women have the associated target status. Status varies with regard to sexual/affectional orientation, with people who are heterosexual filling the agent status and people who are homosexual, lesbian, and bisexual filling the target status. When considering sex as a variable (defined as physiological differences between people), males and females exist in the agent status together, and individuals who are intersex reside in the target status. In terms of religious status, people who consider themselves Christian are in the agent status, whereas people who identify as Jewish, Muslim, Pagan, Wicca, atheist, Hindu, agnostic, Buddhist and so forth are in the target status. Other common target statuses include people in the middle and upper class, middle-aged adults, people of average weight, and people who have the relationship status of being part of a couple.

The associated agent statuses include the working poor and impoverished, children and the elderly, people perceived to be overweight, and those who have the relationship status of single (M. Adams et al., 1997). It is important to reiterate that a person can share a number of agent statuses at the same time that he or she also has other target statuses. Furthermore, a person's agent status does not necessarily mean that he or she does anything to intentionally oppress people of the associated target status. Oppression is often unintentional, in that it can result from an agent's lack of understanding of his or her own relative social privilege.

An important issue to point out regarding the various forms of privilege in society is that not all privilege is the same. Some forms of privilege can override other forms. For example, privileges regarding race, gender, and ability tend to override or at least have greater impact than other forms of privilege, as systemic and institutionalized bias against people on the basis of these variables is deeply ingrained in society. It is also clear that individuals without privilege in these areas do not necessarily have the ability to avoid prejudiced and otherwise biased responses to them. For example, a person of color cannot generally "pass" as White and thus must respond to individual, cultural, and institutional racism on a regular basis. An individual who is physically disabled has needs that supersede those who are "abled" and also encounters individual, cultural, and institutional bias. Women and girls are confronted with gender bias and gender role expectations that limit and control them in ways that men and boys do not experience. In all three of these forms of disempowerment, the targets are not in situations in which they can readily "pass" or hide their less privileged status. Belonging in target statuses such as having nonheterosexual orientation or non-Christian religion can be more readily disguised if the person who is a target desires to not make her or his status public.

Therapists and counselors who desire to be culturally empathic need to be aware of the various target and agent statuses and how they affect their clients and those within their systems. Unintentional oppression plays a key role in the experience and living situations of each person we serve on a daily basis. For example, a professor who is a friend of one of the authors serves in a Midwestern university where she refers to her experience of unintentional oppression as having to "pay taxes" that others around her do not have to pay. Although very respected in her field, she feels that she pays a "double tax" because of her status as a woman and an African American working in a Research 1 university. Because of these two statuses, administrators and other leaders expect her to serve on more committees and have more duties than others. It appears that her experience is such that the compounding of her target statuses compounds the difficulties she encounters throughout her career and life.

Unintentional Oppression in the Form of Religious and Other Privileges

Like the previous discussions on White and heterosexual privilege, the following list and Exhibit 4.9 are designed to help participants develop more awareness of the various ways that religious privilege plays a role in their lives. Religious privilege will vary in accordance with whatever religion is dominant in a given culture. For example, because Christian religions dominate in current U.S. cultures, those of this faith experience the greatest amount of privilege. Review the following list of examples of religious privilege and while reading try to think of more examples of regular privilege experienced by Christians in the United States. See Exhibit 4.9 for discussion questions and note that this activity can be used for privilege based on gender, ability, class, sex, age, or size as well.

Examples of religious privilege include the following:

- I can move anywhere in the country and be confident that I can find places of worship representative of my religion.
- I can go to events and if there is an invocation, my religious perspective will likely be included.
- I can wear symbols of my religion without being concerned that other people will make me feel uncomfortable or need to worry about my physical safety.
- I am assured that the majority of religious holidays will be reflective of my religion (Merry Christmas vs. Happy Holidays).
- I can be assured that my religious perspective will be represented in textbooks and discussions of culture and history in school.

EXHIBIT 4.9
Discussion Questions for Religious Privilege

1. As you read the list of religious privileges (see the text), what emotions do you experience?
2. If any of the feelings you experience are negative or angry, what do you think is at the root of such feelings?
3. If you were to describe the experience of being non-Christian in a predominantly Christian society, how would you describe it?
4. What is it that has maintained religious privilege as an "invisible knapsack" of assets?
5. If a person wanted to do something constructive in response to religious privilege, what might he or she do?
6. How might a therapist or counselor appropriately respond to the existence of religious privilege with her or his clients?

- I can easily buy greeting cards, music, and decorations for celebrations, food, clothing, toys, books, and magazines featuring my religion.
- I can watch movies and television in which my religion is presented in a positive light.

Exhibit 4.10 presents the Level Playing Field exercise, designed to highlight the emotional experience of privilege, and thus oppression, in a group setting.

EXHIBIT 4.10

Level Playing Field: An Exercise in Privilege and Systemic Oppression

The origins of the Level Playing Field activity were not available to us upon investigation. This activity has been passed among teaching professionals long enough that we are unsure who deserves credit for its original creation. This activity was designed to create the emotional experience of privilege, and thus oppression, in a group setting. The activity obviously works best when administered to a group of people who have less power than the facilitator and are unaware of what the activity will entail.

Have the class line up across a large room or field shoulder to shoulder. Announce to the class that the object of the activity is to cross a line you have set a determined number of feet in front of them. If they cross the line, they will receive a reward (such as the freedom to skip a quiz in the course).

Now announce the following, in order, allowing the students sufficient time to respond to the commands:

- Everyone who attended a private school, take one step forward.
- Everyone who went to an inner-city public school, take one step backward.
- Everyone who grew up in a two-parent household, take one step forward.
- Everyone who is male, take two steps forward.
- Everyone who is a member of a family that owns a car, take one step forward.
- Everyone who is a member of a family with at least two functioning cars, take one step forward.
- Everyone who considers her- or himself to be White or Caucasian, take two steps forward.
- Everyone who got at least a 3.0 GPA in high school, take one step forward.
- Everyone who worked during the weekdays in high school, take one step backward.
- Everyone who has parents whose primary language in their youth was not English, take one step backward.
- Everyone whose parents had white-collar jobs, take two steps forward.
- Everyone whose family owned their home, take one step forward.

Now announce that you are going to be Mother (or Father) Fate.

- Everyone wearing red (or some uncommon color in the group), you are now handicapped. Take three steps backward.
- Everyone wearing a gold necklace or chain, you were selected to go to an academic charter school. Take two steps forward.
- Everyone with white shoes (or something uncommon), you are now not heterosexual. Take one step backward.
- Everyone with white shoes and pants, you are not only not heterosexual but also you have been "outed." Take one more step backward.

- Everyone with a watch on, you are now a member of the majority religion. Take three steps forward.
- Everyone whose name does not end in "z," "o," "a," "es," or "as," you are not in the group of people whose names keep them from being considered at many corporate jobs. You may take two steps forward.
- Everyone wearing glasses, you were raised in a well-funded school district. Take two steps forward.
- Everyone wearing blue, you were born a citizen of this country. Take two steps forward. If you are wearing blue and white, both of your parents were also citizens. Take one more step forward.

Now, have the class remain where they are and ask the following discussion questions:

1. How do you feel about this game?
2. How do you feel about where you are?
3. Do you feel that it was fair?
4. Were any of you tempted to try to "pass" or fake a trait in order to move forward or avoid having to move back?
5. What do you think about the reward system?
6. How do you feel about the amount and direction of the steps "awarded" in this game?
7. How do you feel this activity relates to the experience of privilege in society?

The title of the activity (Level Playing Field) refers to the way that some people feel that all people are born with equal opportunity. This view seems to overlook the various privileges that people have and do not recognize as well as the unintentional oppression that accompanies ignorance of differential privilege. How do you feel about the belief that all people have equal opportunity?

CONCLUSION

In this chapter we discussed the importance of coming to affective acceptance about how people are all similar and different at the same time and how their differences and similarities define who they are in relation to each other. We then discussed how culture as a complex concept must be approached on the path to culturally inclusive empathy. Next, we addressed the importance of people focusing on more than observable behaviors when trying to understand others. Finally, we discussed unintentional oppression, first through the phenomenon of unintentional racism. Counselors seeking to develop the affective acceptance necessary to become empathic in a culturally inclusive manner will need to work to develop in these four areas as well as those covered in chapter 5.

5

AFFECTIVE ACCEPTANCE: EMBRACING INCLUSION AND DEVELOPING EMPATHY

In this chapter, we complete coverage of the eight assumptions involved in developing affective acceptance. First, we discuss the importance of realizing counselors' vulnerability to cultural encapsulation, followed by the importance of embracing inclusion in the developing of empathy. We then focus on the importance of internal spiritual resources and conclude with the importance of embracing ambiguity in the process of developing inclusive cultural empathy (ICE).

ASSUMPTION 5: COUNSELORS ARE ALL VULNERABLE TO CULTURAL ENCAPSULATION

As therapists, we are vulnerable to the experience of cultural encapsulation as well as its negative effects on our ability to become empathic with our clients. The concept of cultural encapsulation was introduced by Wrenn

---

Parts of chapter 5 are from *Culture-Centered Counseling and Interviewing Skills*, by P. Pedersen and A. E. Ivey, 1993, Westport, CT: Praeger/Greenwood Press. Copyright 1993 by Praeger/Greenwood Press. Adapted with permission.

(1962) in a discussion about the problematic manner in which many school counselors approach their students. Since this introduction, the concept has been broadened to use with all counselors, psychologists, social workers, and other mental health workers. A culturally encapsulated counselor sees the world through a cultural lens without recognizing that many of her or his perceptions may in fact be biased and thus damaging to clients. Cultural encapsulation is built on five basic identifying features.

First, a culturally encapsulated person defines reality and truth on one rigidly maintained set of cultural assumptions. This set of assumptions is presumed to be constant and unchanging. Although truth and reality are seen as constant for many people, the truths each person perceives tend to be very different. These differences are based on the cultural patterns of thinking and acting that were prepared for each individual before he or she was born. People who use their own value systems and experiences as the solitary reference point from which to interpret and judge behavior, thoughts, and emotions are commonly referred to as *ethnocentric*. Ethnocentrism is the tendency to use one's own group's standards as the standard when looking at other groups, to position these standards at the top of a hierarchy in which all others are ranked lower in comparison (Berry, Poortinga, Segall, & Dasen, 1992).

Second, the culturally encapsulated individual assumes that her or his perspective is correct and is thus not sensitive to cultural variations among individuals. In this way, the encapsulated individual is trapped into one particular way of thinking that resists adaptation and rejects alternatives. A key issue in the maintenance of cultural encapsulation is the fact that most people are somewhat ensnared in our ways of perceiving the world by the comfort of believing that we have resolved the significant issues in life (or that they have already been resolved for us). When we believe that we know what is true, regardless of the actual veracity of our convictions, we tend to become comfortable, as if in an emotional homeostasis. Within this emotional homeostasis, most people are unlikely to seek out or pay heed to any information that might contradict their beliefs. This emotional homeostasis is upset with a form of cognitive dissonance when we are confronted with new information contrary to our assumed "truths." The portion of the section on the value of ambiguity (see Assumption 8) in developing ICE will focus more on this issue.

Third, maintenance of perspective is based on unreasoned assumptions without proof and regard to empirical reality. When confronted with evidence contrary to the encapsulated assumptions, the culturally encapsulated individual ignores or otherwise invalidates the information presented. Encapsulated people have a tendency to be surprised or even unbelieving when confronted with evidence of changes in truth or new truths. An example given by Wrenn (1962) was the "truth" of the shape of the world. At one point in time the truth was that the world was flat. Obviously, now this "truth" has been refuted with new "truth" about the shape of the world. When faced with the viewpoints of others, the culturally encapsulated individual will put between little and no effort into evaluating them as presented. In this way, he or she will make very little attempt to accommodate the needs of others. The exhibit accompanying this section is designed to present a current "truth" with new information that presents a new "truth" (see Exhibit 5.1). It is intended to help readers come to understand how vulnerable people all are to cultural encapsulation and how constant vigilance is necessary to overcome it and remain outside of it.

Fourth, the culturally encapsulated individual will not put in the effort to carefully evaluate the viewpoints of others when those viewpoints are not similar to her or his own and instead will seek technique-oriented short-term solutions. This individual will also make little effort to accommodate the needs of others who are different. The encapsulated presumption made is that everyone was born with the same opportunities and realities and thus only minimal accommodations are needed. Such encapsulated individuals will often see that accommodations are needed for others when someone close enough to them newly requires them. For example, it is common for people not to be very aware of the way much of the world does not cater to differential needs of people with physical disabilities until a family member becomes

EXHIBIT 5.1
Testing the Underlying Truth

Objective
To see how people from different cultures experience a different "truth" from the perspective of their cultural values.

Procedure
1. Ask each member of the class to write down a statement they believe to be true. (As an alternative, the whole group might identify a statement that all members believe to be true.)
2. Ask each member to write a sentence explaining why the statement is true.
3. Next ask each member to write a second statement explaining why her or his first explanation is true.
4. Next ask each member to write a third statement explaining why her or his second explanation is true.
5. You may go on to asking members to write a fourth, fifth, and more statements, but usually by this time the class has become hostile and refuses to continue the exercise saying "I don't know or care *why* it's true! It's *just true!*"
6. Ask the members to present their chain of linked explanations leading back to the statement of truth and look for similarities and differences among the chain of explanations among class members.
7. When we are pushed back to the "reasons behind the reasons" of how we define truth (as in arguments on religion or politics or emotional topics), we typically become quickly upset and anxious.

Note. From *110 Experiences for Multicultural Learning* (pp. 74–75), by P. B. Pedersen, 2004, Washington, DC: American Psychological Association. Copyright 2004 by Paul B. Pedersen. Adapted with permission.

disabled. This form of selective accommodation also occurs with different viewpoints. For example, it is often the case that individuals adamantly opposed to the rights of nonheterosexual people will only soften their views when they discover that a close relative or friend is not and has long not been heterosexual. Even when a new viewpoint is integrated into the perspective of a culturally encapsulated individual, it is not uncommon for this person to choose not to see that such accommodations are likely due to many other people in many other contexts. In a therapeutic setting, the culturally encapsulated counselor will be less likely to recognize when her or his client is having distress because of oppression or lack of societal privilege.

As with the identifying features we mentioned previously, the fifth feature behaviorally overlaps with the others. The culturally encapsulated individual judges everyone from the viewpoint of her or his own self-reference criterion without regard for the cultural context of the other person. A challenge we all have in confronting our vulnerability to cultural encapsulation is the fact that many of the things we do on a daily basis inherently reinforce its ongoing existence. Pedersen (2003a) clarified that the criteria we use in referring to ourselves can serve as a danger in fostering ongoing cultural encapsulation. This is to say that the terms and culturally prescribed definitions thereof serve as a tool to maintain our stance within a given cultural perspective. Most terms we use in self-description are culturally laden and not value free. Even if we do not say anything directly negative about another person or culture, our self-descriptions automatically place priorities on certain values, actions, thoughts, and attitudes.

For example, a man who consistently refers to himself as "self-made" and "independent" is choosing to define himself in terms that highlight specific culturally encapsulated values. The value-given preference in such a self-reference is a preference for individualism over collectivism. Using such self-labels highlights a cultural perspective while simultaneously deemphasizing or even denigrating other cultural perspectives. This man may consider his self-description as stating he is competent, hardworking, and accomplished. His perceived ability to do what he has done in his life "on his own" is what he sees as a personal strength, and thus a positive self-reference. To another person, coming from another cultural perspective, this self-description may have a very different meaning. The man may instead be seen as self-centered, selfish, not family oriented, not community oriented, and thus without honor. This man's example conveys that it is ultimately best if a person learns how to care for her- or himself over caring for the community or system within which she or he exists.

In this particular example, even if the listener comes from a cultural perspective that values independence and self-promotion, such a self-description can still be problematic. The man describing himself as independent and self-made may be overlooking societal advantages he has had from birth. The fact that he is a man already means that he has had advantages over women in "making himself." He may also be overlooking overempowerment coming from having been born White, heterosexual, in a family with both parents intact, without any physical or mental impairments, in a safe and comfortable home, raised as a member of the dominant religion of his area, having been able to go to better funded schools than others, and so forth. Others not born with such relative advantages may experience frustration, envy, or lower self-esteem when talking with this self-made and independent man who has had a good deal of the advantages given by society as a sort of birthright.

As we discuss these issues with counselors and therapists in training, we commonly have students posit that cultural encapsulation is really more a thing of the past and nowhere near as present today as it was when Wrenn (1962) first discussed it. To the contrary, we feel that cultural encapsulation may be more common today than it has ever been in the past.

Ten Ways That Cultural Encapsulation Is Common Today

The following is a list of ways that cultural encapsulation manifests itself on a regular basis today:

1. The portraying of diversity with hostile stereotypes.
2. The dominant culture's overemphasis of universal issues while ignoring cultural issues.
3. A preference for exclusion and exclusivity rather than inclusion and inclusivity.
4. The common portrayal of diversity and universalist alternatives as polar opposites.
5. A preference for competition over cooperation.
6. A propensity to define reality according to monocultural assumptions.
7. An insensitivity to, if not complete ignorance of, the existence and validity of cultural variations.
8. A tendency for those in power to protect unreasoned assumptions against perceived challenge.
9. A general preference for technique-oriented, simple solutions.
10. A reluctance to evaluate alternative viewpoints fairly and openly.

Many, if not all, of the previously discussed tendencies are built on fear of the unknown. This fear is fed by lack of experience with varying cultures and peoples as well as the worldviews, traditions, beliefs, and values that accompany them. As we come to realize the ongoing challenge of combating our vulnerability to cultural encapsulation, a game plan to confront this challenge becomes useful.

Eight Ways to Combat Vulnerability to Cultural Encapsulation

The following are eight actions counselors can take to avoid maintaining and developing encapsulated perspectives and responses to the experiences and behaviors of others:

1. Develop an awareness of our own culture and worldview. To avoid approaching others with cultural encapsulation, individuals need a clear awareness of stereotypes and assumptions we make or have traditionally made of others. People are often guilty of oversimplifying the cultures and experiences of others with biases based on values we have developed as part of our worldviews. It is not uncommon for people who have majority status to perceive themselves as devoid of culture, when in fact it is their culture that determines the way that they respond and interact to others around them.

2. Develop an understanding of how our life experiences, attitudes, values, biases, and culture influence the way we respond to others. As our awareness of these issues becomes clarified, we need to take time to evaluate how they shape our feelings, thoughts, and reactions to others around us. Such evaluation will begin to clarify why we might respond negatively to situations that might have a neutral effect on others. Talking with others from different cultures and who have different values about similar situations might help to highlight attitudes, values, and biases that shape our emotional and behavioral responses to others.

3. Get to know people who come from different cultural and contextual backgrounds than you. For example, if the majority of the people you know well grew up in a similar environment to yours (say, suburban or inner city), then you will be well served to get to know people from quite disparate experiences than yourself.

4. Get to know more about the content of hearts and minds of people who grew up in very different environments. On top of meeting and getting to know people from different cultures and contexts individually, we have found that reading the writings of people from different backgrounds can dispel a great deal of myths, biases, and stereotypes. When made to read and respond to writings by people with different life experiences and perspectives, our students have commonly reported that the exercise was powerful and even life altering. Of course, after reading such a strong statement, some readers will presume that this is overstated. Keep in mind that that majority of fiction and essay

that the average person reads is written by others coming from very similar cultures and contexts. Examples of books that have had a powerful effect on people from disparate backgrounds include *The Bluest Eye*, by Toni Morrison; *Bone: A Novel*, by Fae M. Ng; *There Are No Children Here: The Story of Two Boys Growing Up in the Other America*, by Alex Kotlowitz; and *The Circuit: Stories From the Life of a Migrant Child*, by Francisco Jiménez.

5. Seek for understanding on ways that diverse cultures share common ground. As we have mentioned before, a focus only on differences will not foster a productive relationship or the needed collaborative set that makes therapeutic relationships therapeutic. As we learn of the different experiences, values, and cultures of others, a key to the development of empathy is the development of an ability to connect with others in the cultural borderlands we share.

6. Persevere in a routine of unlearning something every day. This suggestion was made by Wrenn (1962) when he first introduced the concept of the culturally encapsulated counselor. This is based on the fact that truth is not static but instead evolves as new information is introduced. We can combat our vulnerability to cultural encapsulation with an ongoing regime focused on replacing outdated things we have learned with new things we learn. As we discard that which is no longer true, we make way for new truths. We need to remember that the very things we hold most important in our beliefs may be the very things that others have every reason to not believe.

7. Learn to trust others to have solutions to problems to which we see no solutions. Our inability to generate effective solutions is often based on the limited viewpoints from which we study our challenges. As we learn to trust others who come from different perspectives and contexts, we learn the true meaning of celebrating the power of diversity. We learn that differences are not best when tolerated, but instead best when seen as something akin to a broad platform on which we can stand with confidence.

8. Develop new standards for assessing "appropriate" behavior aside from our own reference groups. The fatal flaw of cultural encapsulation is our tendency to compare all others with what we are most familiar. The integrations of diverse definitions of propriety allow us to alter ourselves mentally and emotionally on the basis of the various contexts and cultures of people with whom we come in contact. We should take time to ask others what they see as appropriate and follow up with garnering information on why they see things the way they do. This process is not so much

about augmenting our own values as it is about developing comfort with values that are not the same as our own.

Further Discussion on Cultural Encapsulation

A common culturally based perspective on human sexuality is that sexual intimacy occurs in one of three categories. Sexual intimacy occurs between opposite sexes (male and female), which is defined as heterosexual; between same sexes (male and male or female and female), which is defined as homosexual; or with people of either the same or the opposite sex, which is defined as bisexual.

This culturally based perspective is founded on the assumption that all people are born either male or female. This is actually not accurate. A large number of individuals throughout the world are born with ambiguous sexual reproduction systems. These people, once known as hermaphrodites, among other labels, now prefer to call themselves intersex. Although the term *intersex* is most commonly used to refer to developmental anomalies that result in ambiguous differentiation of external genitalia, it may be used to describe the lack of concordance in the chromosomal, gonadal, hormonal, or genital characteristics of an individual. Thus a person with an intersex condition is born with sex chromosomes, external genitalia, or an internal reproductive system that is not considered "standard" for either male or female.

The instance of intersex anomalies has been estimated to be between 1 in every 100 to 1 in every 4,500 (1 in 2,000 is cited most often). This means that it is likely that more babies are born intersexed than those born with cystic fibrosis, the incidence of which is 1 in 2,500 (Blackless et al., 2000; Dreger, 1998).

In the United States, the current response of choice (or correct treatment) for intersex individuals is to "normalize" the abnormal genitals using cosmetic surgical technologies, cosmetic hormone technologies, and so on. Doing so is thought to eliminate the potential for psychological distress. In the past several years, numbers of people born intersexed have joined together to advocate for the "normalization" processes to be stopped with intersex children until they are old enough to consent to the treatment.

A brother of one of the authors was born intersex. After the doctors and his parents chose his gender to be male, he was medically treated to appear more masculine. On top of other medical treatments, he was treated with a powerful regime of male hormones. He has been happily married for over 16 years to a heterosexual woman. In the past several years, Hale has become an advocate for the rights of unborn intersex people, appearing on a documentary with the Discovery Channel and in interviews with the online magazine, *Salon.*

Given the previous information, consider the following questions to help explore your level of encapsulation:

1. What does the information about intersex say to you about the construct of gender?
2. If gender can be assigned to people at birth, despite the reality of their biology, is gender an appropriate factor to use in deciding who may marry whom in society?
3. In the case of Hale and his wife, what type of relationship do they have? (heterosexual, homosexual?)
4. If you consider it a heterosexual relationship, what criterion are you using to make that distinction?
5. What if, at birth, the doctors had decided to make Hale into a female? How would that affect your views about his relationship with his wife?
6. In several cultures throughout the world, children who are born intersex are not treated like they were born with birth defects but instead are revered as special. How do you see cultural encapsulation playing a role in the Western approach to the response to intersex newborns?

ASSUMPTION 6: INCLUSION IS MORE LIKELY TO DEFINE A CULTURAL CONTEXT THAN EXCLUSION

Historically, most of the research on therapeutic process and outcomes has focused almost uniformly on either individuals or families (Ivey, Ivey, & Simek-Morgan, 1993). This approach to thinking about psychotherapeutic relationships has overlooked broader social units such as organizations and social systems and thus falls short of comprehending the entirety of the human experience (D. W. Sue, 1995). This research is reflective of a cultural bias historically inherent in the approaches of counselors and psychologists. Many counselors continue to focus therapeutic work on the individual and her or his perceived needs while overlooking how that person is an interactive component of a cluster of many other systems. As the family systems approach introduced the concept of the self-in-system over 4 decades ago, a systemic perspective is beginning to take hold in the work of many therapists. Although this movement is in the right direction to allow for a much more inclusive approach to the perspectives and approaches used in counseling relationships, the field still needs to become even more inclusive. Many therapists using a systemic approach have a tendency to define the client's system as her or his immediate family and little more. This approach still falls short of the reality of the experience of a great deal of our clientele. A more culturally aware approach to counseling will include self-in-relation and family-system-in-relation to broader systems within varied contexts. D. W. Sue, Ivey, and Pedersen (1996) summed up the issue well when they emphasized that "a part of every counseling session needs to attend to significant others and contextual issues" (p. 37).

The key to inclusivity within cultural context is an awareness of the fact that a therapeutic focus on individual or narrowly defined systemic problems is very likely overlooking many key factors related to the client's needs. Arguably, a portion of every single counseling session should focus on issues of context and the client's existence as a person-in-relation to others as well as context. Therefore, homosexual people experiencing symptoms of anxiety, women with depressive symptomatology, and differently abled people experiencing issues of self-esteem should be helped from a perspective that includes not only their individual challenges but also issues of homophobia, sexism, and ableism, respectively. Ultimately, the culturally aware counselor will use a culture- and context-centered approach to counseling instead of the more simplistic client-centered approach.

Inclusion Activity: The Intrapersonal Cultural Grid

The intrapersonal cultural grid (ICG) provides a means to describe and understand specific behaviors in the context of the expectations and values behind that behavior (see Figure 5.1). The ICG defines cultural context broadly to include all salient social system variables. The interaction of the personal variables and cultural teachers in the ICG assumes that culture is so dynamic and complex that the cultural context changes across individuals and across situations. Rather than describe a person's "culture" as a static or unchanging label, this grid describes how each behavior is controlled by salient expectations and culturally learned values. This broad definition of culture makes the following three assumptions.

1. Each person's multicultural identity is complex, incorporating a combination of salient social system variables.
2. Each person's multicultural identity is orthogonal, including a multiplicity of salient social system roles simultaneously.
3. Each person's multicultural identity is dynamic, changing from time to time and place to place as different social system roles become salient.

Rather than describe a person's culture in the abstract, the ICG seeks to identify a specific individual's personal cultural orientation in a particular situation through understanding each specified behavior in the appropriate cultural context. The grid combines personal (behavior, expectation, and value) with social system variables (cultural teachers).

The ICG is based on the notion that culture is "within the person," providing a framework for linking intrapersonal with interpersonal variables. Each person's behavior by itself does not communicate a clear message or intention.

PERSONAL VARIABLES

	Where you learned to do it	Why you did it	What you did

CULTURAL TEACHERS

	Where you learned to do it	Why you did it	What you did
1. **Family relations** Relatives Fellow countrypersons Ancestors Shared beliefs			
2. **Power relationships** Social friends Sponsors and mentors Subordinates Supervisors and superiors			
3. **Memberships** Coworkers Organizations Gender and age groups Workplace colleagues			
4. **Nonfamily relationships** Friendships Classmates Neighbors People like me			

Figure 5.1. The intrapersonal cultural grid. From *A Handbook for Developing Multicultural Awareness, Third Edition* (p. 96), by P. B. Pedersen, 2000, Alexandria, VA: American Counseling Association. Copyright 2000 by the American Counseling Association. Reprinted with permission.

Only when that behavior is analyzed within the context of the person's salient social system variables does the person's intended message become clear. The context is best described by what is called *expectations*. Expectations are cognitive variables that include behavior–outcome and stimulus–outcome expectancies that guide individual choices. "If I do this . . . (insert behavior), then that . . . (insert expectation) is likely to occur." The social system variables are essential to both persons in a relationship for understanding one another's anticipated outcomes. The skill of extrapolating expectations from social system variables and linking specific behaviors with expectations improves with practice. The ICG is designed to help you analyze your behavior by first matching it with relevant expectations, then identifying the values behind each expectation, and finally identifying the social system variables that taught those values.

Use the following steps to analyze your behavior with the ICG:

Step 1: Identify a particular behavior in yourself or someone else. Let's look at your behavior in deciding to read this chapter.

Step 2: Evaluate the expectation behind the behavior. What do you expect to happen as a result of your reading this chapter? Let's assume you expect to learn something you do not already know, although there are actually many different and sometimes conflicting expectations attached to a single behavior.

Step 3: Identify the values on which each expectation is based. If we assume you are reading this chapter to learn something, then perhaps learning is an important value for you. Again, there are many different values behind each expectation, some more conscious than others.

Step 4: Find out from where those values came. Who taught you the values that shape your expectations and direct your behavior? We may well search for the source of your values by looking at social system variables. Each value, such as learning, may well come from many sources, such as family, religion, educational group, socioeconomic group, ethnic or nationality group, affectional orientation, and gender group, to name but a few of the likely candidates. In any case, you know for certain that those values were taught to you by someone and did not "simply happen."

By identifying each social system variable for a person's specific behaviors, the ICG helps to deconstruct the context of the expectations and values behind each behavior and highlights the importance of defining cultural context broadly.

ASSUMPTION 7: INTERNAL SPIRITUAL RESOURCES ARE IMPORTANT

It is helpful to be aware of the clients' spirituality and religiosity and of the roles that religion and spirituality play in their lives. Religion and spirituality play large roles in the lives of most U.S. citizens. According to a poll, 88% of Americans describe themselves as religious or spiritual, although a larger percentage of Americans see themselves as spiritual rather than as religious (L. Miller, 2005). This same poll reported that 81% of Americans practice Christian religions, whereas 4% practice non-Christian religions and 15%

practice no religion. A very high percentage of Americans believe in a God (96%), and three quarters of the U.S. population see religion as a very important part of their lives (Corey, Corey, & Callanan, 2003). The predominant religions in the United States are Roman Catholic, Baptist, Methodist, and Lutheran, with Roman Catholic and Baptist coming in as the two most commonly identified religions by state. From the data, it becomes clear that the overwhelming majority of Americans see themselves as Christian, whereas those who practice any non-Christian religion are in a very small minority.

Although people throughout the world have known it for centuries, social scientists are increasingly finding empirical evidence that religious and spiritual values and associated behaviors can promote wellness (Richards & Bergin, 1997; Richards, Rector, & Tjeltveit, 1999). Numerous studies have found evidence of a relationship between spirituality and perceived ability to cope with chronic illness, disabilities, and other stressful life events (e.g., Brooks & Matson, 1982; Carson & Green, 1992; Crigger, 1996; Kilpatrick & McCullough, 1999; Tix & Frasier, 1998). A common thread across these studies was the fact that when faced with crises, people have a tendency to turn to their religious and spiritual beliefs and customs for comfort. Ironically, merely one third of psychologists appear to view religious faith as important in their own lives (Plante, 1999). Thus, there appears to be a lack of connection between the perspectives of clients and the perspectives of psychologists when it comes to religion and spirituality.

If religion and spirituality are important to our clients' worldviews, then they should also be important to us as culturally inclusive counselors. Stanard, Sandhu, and Painter (2000) argued that because of the growing body of empirical evidence of the importance of spirituality and religion in clients' perceptions and wellness, spirituality should be considered the "fifth force" in counseling and psychology. Although up to 95% of professionals see a connection between spirituality and mental health, coursework on spirituality in therapy is relatively rare in training programs (Carlson, Kirkpatrick, Hecker, & Kilmer, 2002). Religion and spirituality may have been historically excluded from the field of psychology because of its origins as an empirical discipline (Wolf & Stevens, 2001). The field of psychology seems to have long avoided the area of study despite Jung's (1933) teaching that healing is not possible without a spiritual awakening or at minimum a focus on the issues relevant to spiritual distress. It is our view that competent mental health professionals will take extra effort to study religion and spirituality as they pertain to wellness and apply this learning in their therapeutic relationships. If we continue to relate to our clients ignoring spiritual and religious issues, we may miss crucial variables that would be of the utmost help to them. For example, Rodriguez (2004) argued that in Latino cultures, spirituality and religion are so integrated that a focus on the client's culture separated from spirituality creates a false dichotomy and thus does a disservice to Latino clients.

An important component to effective awareness of religion and spirituality as key factors in the therapeutic relationship is the therapist's recognition of her or his own religiosity and spirituality. Various authors have argued that personal religious and value clarity is key to effectively relating to clients on spiritual grounds (e.g., Faiver, Ingersoll, O'Brienn, & McNally, 2001; Griffith & Brian, 1999). Similar to other forms of cultural awareness, relating effectively with another person on issues of spirituality becomes very difficult if not impossible if the therapist has not developed clarity and comfort with her or his own spirituality. Faiver and colleagues described awareness with regard to religion and spirituality as an awareness of one's own beliefs combined with open-mindedness to other beliefs. To this definition we would add that it is helpful if the therapist can develop a genuine interest in the beliefs of her or his clients as well as a comfort in exploring the overlap of religious and spiritual values with other cultural and contextual variables.

Religious and spiritual perspectives vary from orthodoxies of major international religions, such as Catholicism, Islam, Hindu, and Buddhism, to much less structured perspectives including those of various indigenous peoples, such as the Navajo peoples, to nonreligious-based approaches to spirituality, such as the humanist and moralist approaches. Affective acceptance of religious and spiritual diversity requires the counselor to be, at minimum, versed in her or his own views and beliefs in religion and spirituality while simultaneously open to learning new views and beliefs. It is also quite common to find that the clients' use and focus on spirituality and religiosity will vary because of other cultural variables. For example, Furnham and Forey (1994) found that women are more likely than men to seek alternative therapeutic help.

Zinnbauer and Pargament (2000) presented four helping orientations that counselors use with regard to religious and spiritual issues in psychotherapy. These approaches are rejectionism, exclusivism, constructivism, and pluralism. An overt focus on how we approach others' religiosity and spirituality is necessary because no therapeutic relationship is value free regardless of the counselor's efforts to maintain a value-free stance and because counseling has been found to be inherently value laden (Bergin, 1980; T. A. Kelly, 1990).

Rejectionism is an approach that is focused on denial of the importance of religious and spiritual realities commonly fundamental to the majority of our clients. Belief in the existence of a god, spirits, heaven, reincarnation, resurrection, and holy land are examples of the types of spiritual realities that rejectionists deny. From this perspective, expressions of spirituality and religiosity are interpreted as evidence of underlying mental illness instead of taken simply as expressions of spirituality and religiosity. These counselors focus on helping their clients to work beyond the supposed defenses, delusions, and magical thinking of such to a more rational and ego-oriented manner of living. As examples of this approach, Zinnbauer and Pargament (2000) included the psychoanalytic concept that religion is little more than a defensive primitive idealization, the cognitive-behavioral approach that equates religious thinking with irrationality and disturbed mental and emotional functioning, and the existential description of religious beliefs as ways to avoid responsibility and decision making and defenses against anxiety about death and dying. Zinnbauer and Pargament criticized this approach to religiosity and spirituality as (a) deterring a counselor's ability to develop an effective therapeutic alliance with religious clients, (b) creating a general wariness of therapists because of expectations that the clients' values and religious beliefs will be altered and demeaned in counseling, (c) misrepresenting religiosity and spirituality as counterproductive to mental wellness, and ultimately (d) disrespectful to cultural variance in clients.

In direct contrast to the rejectionist approach is the exclusivist approach to religious and spiritual issues. *Exclusivism* is based on a fundamental belief in the reality of a religious or spiritual dimension of existence for all peoples. Exclusivists tend to have strong beliefs that they do not readily reconcile with beliefs of others that are different. They believe that there is a set of absolute realities that are true and applicable to themselves as well as all people. These realities are generally based on orthodox translations of religious texts. Emanating from this belief set is the assumption that one set of values and worldviews is ultimately correct and thus most conducive to mental and emotional health. Exclusivism can function much like religious zealotry in that the exclusivist is resolute to help the client also believe in a specified solitary "true" religious or spiritual worldview. The exclusivist sees the counselor's role with clients who believe differently as one of responsibility to bring the client to also believe in the same religious values and percepts as the counselor. Zinnbauer and Pargament (2000) criticized this approach as being (a) ethically unsound in its overt rejection of different values and beliefs as well as proselytizing of the counselor's values and beliefs, (b) judgmental and rejecting of others from different religious backgrounds and different denominations in the same religious vein (e.g., Catholic and Baptist), and (c) ignorant of the fact that both religious and nonreligious varieties of coping play a role in mental health and in coping successfully with challenges.

The constructivist approach refutes the existence of an absolute reality while recognizing that individuals have the ability to create their own personal realities and meanings out of life. *Constructivism* is based on the assumption that all belief systems are ultimately constructed by individuals and collectives on the basis of their varying social contexts. The focus of constructivists is primarily on the quality of the client's constructions as evaluated by its internal consistency and coherency as well as its functionality in helping the client adapt to her or his context. Constructivists intentionally work within the belief systems of their clients, intentionally incorporating the worldviews of each client. Zinnbauer and Pargament (2000) highlighted a few concerns about use of the constructivist approach: (a) Authenticity may become a concern when the beliefs of the constructivist counselor vary significantly from those of the client, thus harming the quality of therapeutic alliance; and (b) clarity of definition of wellness and pathology may become tenuous, as definitions of propriety are sometimes based on religious values that run contrary to commonly accepted cultural norms (e.g., the view of children having rights independent of their parents).

The pluralist approach allows for multiple interpretations of reality based on various religious and spiritual perspectives. *Pluralism* is based on recognition of the existence of an absolute reality but affords numerous and even conflicting belief systems as appropriate in defining it. The pluralist believes that many spiritual paths can be valid in the human striving for spiritual fulfillment and that the same spiritual reality can be expressed within different cultures and by different people in diverse ways. Pluralistic perspective clarifies that no single religious system is able to fit all religious or spiritual reality as each different system has a limited slant on the truth. In this way, the pluralistic counselor may maintain personal religious beliefs while simultaneously appreciating the different beliefs of her or his clients. These differences are not seen as detrimental to the therapeutic alliance as they each play a role in defining the same ultimate reality. The pluralistic approach requires both the counselor and client to be cognizant of her or his own individual spiritual and religious history, worldview, and values. Therapeutic goals are codefined from a shared belief in an absolute reality with flexibility for differing cultural interpretations and perspectives.

Similar to the advice of Zinnbauer and Pargament (2000), we recommend that counselors develop the ability to use either the constructivist or pluralist approach to client spirituality and religiosity. The approach that fits you best will depend largely on your own spiritual and religious stance. Those who have no specific religious or spiritual leanings will likely be most comfortable with the constructivist approach, whereas those maintaining a set of religious beliefs and values will likely be more comfortable working from the pluralist approach. Either approach requires the counselor to be aware of her or his own spiritual and religious beliefs and values and maintain openness to those of the client.

A culture-centered perspective enhances a person's spiritual completeness by linking culturally different spiritual perspectives of the same Ultimate Reality. Spiritual dimensions are partially defined by each different perspective of many different cultural groups. The goal should be to acknowledge each group's limited and imperfect attempt to describe the Spiritual Infinite rather than being the exclusive captive of any one limited perspective. Clients define themselves and their realities on the basis of spirituality and religiosity from any number of sources. We need to become aware that for many cultures, the healing process is infinitely intertwined with spiritual wellness. To many people, psychological distress is basically related to a sense of spiritual entanglement that requires "straightening." Empathic counselors and therapists will select approaches to counseling from a ground of flexibility and broad awareness of the varying importance of spirituality in the process. The counselor with ICE will also be able to work with creativity and flexibility that allows for a blending of conventional and more alternative methods of helping (D. W. Sue et al., 1996).

The following are a few questions that might be used in exploration of the role of religion and spirituality in your clients' identity, as paraphrased and adapted from Archer and Waterman (1993, pp. 327–329):

- Do you have a religious preference?
- On a 7-point scale, with 7 being *extremely important* and 1 being *not important*, how important are your religious beliefs to you?
- Do your parents have a religious preference, and if so, how important is it to them?
- Does your spouse have a religious preference? How does your spouse feel about your religious beliefs?
- Are there any differences between your beliefs and those of your spouse or parents?
- Do you currently attend religious services? If so, how often? Have you in the past?
- What are your reasons for attending the services?
- How do you feel while you are engaged in activities related to your religion?
- Do you find yourself getting into religious discussions? If so, what point of view do you take?

Exhibit 5.1 is designed to highlight how people of different cultures experience a different truth from the perspective of their cultural values.

ASSUMPTION 8: AMBIGUITY, ALTHOUGH INCONVENIENT, HAS POTENTIALLY POSITIVE VALUE

Social scientists have increasingly come to the realization that ambiguity is not necessarily an enemy to mental health. Many have hypothesized that knowledge itself is much more integrative and interactive than it is static. Kitchener and Brenner (1990) defined wisdom as a synthesis of knowledge from divergent points of view. Meacham (1990) hypothesized that a key aspect of wisdom is a consciousness of one's own unreliability and an awareness of what one does and does not know. Labouvie-Vief (1990) highlighted the importance of an efficient and evenhanded dialogue between logical forms of thinking and more illogical forms of processing. In response to 25 years of science, life, and practice, Gelatt (1989, 1991) changed his theoretical perspective from a fully rational approach to decision making (Gelatt, 1962) to an embracing of ambiguity he called *positive uncertainty*. This approach focused on the value of maintaining an open mind accepting and even embracing inconsistency and uncertainty and using the nonrational thought and intuition in the process of making decisions. The focal rationale for this perspective is based on the postmodern philosophy that reality is not objectively measurable but instead the subjective creation of each individual from her or his given frame of reference.

The following three guidelines of this approach are useful for highlighting the manner in which therapists may begin to embrace ambiguity en route to developing ICE. These guidelines focus on information, process, and choice. The value of embracing uncertainty is emphasized throughout.

1. "Treat your facts with imagination, but do not imagine your facts" (Gelatt, 1989, p. 254). The basic premise behind this guideline is that decision processes would be completely unnecessary if we had constant and consistent access to all the information. The process of decision making is based on the need to collect, evaluate, and respond to information. The problem with a solely rational approach to doing this is based on three issues. First, the reliability of facts is limited as they become obsolete quickly. Society is going through such a rapid amount of change that knowledge on any issue has a short tenure. What we learn today can become obsolete tomorrow and then be seen as little more than misinformation. Second, increased information often brings increased uncertainty. Information can be garnered at such great speed today that it inherently outpaces our ability to fully process it. It is not uncommon for the most learned scholars to state that the greatest thing they have learned is that they really do not know anything. Third, as information is sent and received by people with subjective perspectives and varying worldviews, it becomes modified at both ends of the transaction. Thus, no information is truly objective and devoid of bias. As therapists, we will benefit from the knowledge that what we actually know is ultimately ambiguous and the tip of the iceberg of what is actually truth. As we become comfortable with our uncertainty about that which we know, we can develop an attitude of enthusiasm for collecting other new and different information and opinions. Such an approach affords us with the ability to embrace the fact that there is always more to learn and respond with creativity and imagination.

2. "Know what you want and believe but do not be sure" (Gelatt, 1989, p. 254). If we become too fixed on what we want, we can miss out on the opportunity to discover new and better things to want. Evidence to this end includes the fact that many of the

greatest inventions were discovered by accident. Examples of this include the accidental inventions of the microwave oven, Silly Putty, Velcro, the Slinky, Vaseline, and the yo-yo. In the case of the microwave oven, in 1942, Percy Le Baron Spencer was working with radar equipment at Raytheon when he noticed that a candy bar had melted in his pocket. The story follows that the second thing Spencer held in front of the equipment was a bag of unpopped popcorn. It is clear that Spencer, and ultimately the world, was served by his creative responding to unexplained happenstance. The process of making decisions should not only be a process for achieving goals but also be one for discovering them. An approach to life as it unfolds around us devoid of a rigid holding to a set of beliefs can lead to creative responding and powerful discovery. Our beliefs have a tendency to function as glasses through which we look at the world. On this metaphor, rigid holding to beliefs can leave us living a life with blinders on, blocking our ability to see fantastic new opportunities. Our creativity, imagination, and positive coping are best served when we have embraced the ongoing process of including new information and arranging and rearranging it in our mind's eye.

3. "Be rational, unless there is a good reason not to be" (Gelatt, 1989, p. 255). This guideline emphasizes a holistic approach to science in which a balance is created between what is considered to be rational and what is intuitive. Knowledge and logic function most effectively when counterbalanced with creativity and flexibility. A natural result of this combination is inconsistency in choice. It is likely impossible to be flexible and inventive without demonstrating a certain amount of inconsistency. When balancing our environs in this manner, flexibility calls for a capability to respond to change as well as a capability to foster change. The future is much less predictable than it is created. Embracing dichotomies affords us the ability to invent the future instead of allowing someone else to invent it for us.

The debate activity in Exhibit 5.2 is designed to help bring affective acceptance and develop skills relative to positive uncertainty.

Vignette for Debate Activity

Martha, a 21-year-old high school dropout, was kicked out of her father's home at age 16. She survived the first 3 of the past 5 years by living with friends and working odd jobs. In the past couple of years, she found herself becoming increasingly dependent on others, as she has developed an addiction to crack

EXHIBIT 5.2
Dichotomous Thinking Versus Positive Uncertainty Debate

Directions: Divide the class into four groups. The groups are all presented the debate scenario listed in the text and are then asked to prepare different arguments from the perspective of their group affiliation.

1. Dichotomous Thinking Group A: Responsibility of the Individual
   This group is to prepare an argument on why all responsibility falls on the individual in the vignette.
2. Dichotomous Thinking Group B: Responsibility of Society
   This group is to prepare an argument on why all responsibility falls on society, based on the vignette.
3. Positive Uncertainty Group
   This group is to prepare an argument on how responsibility is not inherently an "either/or" issue, on the basis of the vignette.
4. Debate Evaluation Group
   This group will prepare to evaluate the merits of the debate of each group. Part of this group's preparatory discussion should include how they will evaluate the debaters' arguments without allowing bias to enter into the process.

cocaine. Over the past 2 years, her living environment has varied from homelessness to living with friends to living in a crack house. Martha has turned to using her sexuality to support her addiction in the past year. Martha recently had a baby boy from an unknown father who was born addicted to crack.

Question for the Debate

On whom does the responsibility for the care of the baby boy stand?

Discussion Questions for the Debate Activity

1. How did you feel when you were put in the position of taking a particular stand on this issue?
2. Did anyone develop a new perspective through this activity? If so, what is it, and how did you develop it?
3. What other types of issues might be well served by a "positive uncertainty" perspective?
4. How might positive uncertainty help counselors develop better ICE?

FINAL THOUGHTS ON AFFECTIVE ACCEPTANCE

Each of the eight assumptions presented in this and the previous chapter is important to the development of the kind of awareness necessary to develop ICE. We would like to add that as counselors seeking to become culturally aware, one should also do the following. First, one needs to become familiar with cultural and language differences and how these differences create contexts for others that are different than for themselves. As discussed in this and the previous chapter, many variables come into play in the quality of experience of each person with whom therapists come in contact. Awareness of the relevant biases, prejudices, and the systemic responses built out of them allow counselors opportunity to become effective and empathic.

Second, counselors and therapists who are culturally aware are also concerned for the welfare of culturally different clients. There are many issues and situations that our culturally different clients confront and are confronted with on a regular basis that may be very different from our own experiences and contexts. In chapters 6 and 7, we cover applications of ICE that demonstrate that culturally inclusive professionals respond to the welfare needs of clients through empowerment, prevention, and advocacy efforts.

Third, an awareness of multicultural issues is directly related to an ongoing desire to learn about, understand, and become sensitive to the experiences and perspectives of people of different cultures and contexts. This requires ongoing efforts to learn, flexibility regarding personal beliefs and expectations, and a passion to connect with clients where they are. Although many therapists have historically strived to meet their clients in the middle on these variables, this has not always worked in the clients' favor. Such expectations can too easily become culturally impositional, as many therapists define wellness on the basis of their own cultural background and biases. The section in this chapter on the importance of internal spiritual resources (Assumption 7) focused on four different types of approaches used in responding to the cultural differences of religion and spirituality (rejectionism, exclusivism, constructivism, and pluralism). These four approaches somewhat parallel those offered in the section focused on exploring cultural similarities and differences.

Fourth, as we become increasingly aware of the perspectives of our clients, it is important that we are also able to articulate our own cultural backgrounds effectively. Such articulation should only be carried out in a manner that avoids any perception of imposition of values on our clients. The ability to articulate our own backgrounds is important because we need to navigate the territory of both similarities and differences we have in common with our clients.

As we develop increasing multicultural competence, we must recognize that there will always be limits to our cultural expertise. When one observes the multitude of cultures and intersections of cultures, it is easy to see that it is not possible for any one person to know everything. Multicultural competence is more of a journey than a destination. Cultures are constantly evolving as they interact and adjust to changes in a complex world.

6

INTELLECTUAL UNDERSTANDING: RACE, GENDER, RELIGION, AND SPIRITUALITY

As we clarified in chapter 3, a key to becoming a therapist with inclusive cultural empathy (ICE) is the development of intellectual understanding of relevant multicultural issues. To develop intellectual understanding, the therapist needs to increase both knowledge and comprehension of specific similarities and differences between her- or himself and the client(s) within each counseling relationship. To do this, the therapist must possess specific knowledge and information about each particular group with which he or she is working and develop a good understanding of the sociopolitical system's operation in the United States with respect to relevant marginalized groups. The therapist must also be aware of institutional barriers that prevent some diverse clients from using mental health services and maintain clear and explicit knowledge of how the generic characteristics of counseling and therapy affect the counseling relationship with each client.

As the therapist comes to the previously discussed understandings, she or he must now identify gaps in her or his knowledge and then actively pursue filling them. Although therapists cannot hope to accumulate all relevant knowledge to every possible client's culture and context, they can still aspire to the complex task in an active and ongoing manner. In this chapter, we provide a template to evaluate knowledge relevant to developing inclusive cultural empathy. We do this through a set of key cultural identity constructs.

KEY CULTURAL IDENTITY CONSTRUCTS

To value the full range of differences and similarities that contribute to the quality of the dynamic balance of the therapeutic relationship, culturally inclusive therapists need to develop an understanding of a set of key identity constructs. Although each construct is important on its own, they all effectively overlap and interact. T. L. Robinson and Howard-Hamilton (2000) referred to this phenomenon as *convergence*. A person's key identity constructs converge in different ways on the basis of one's experiences, contexts, interactions with the converging identities of others around, and one's resulting beliefs and emotions. Culturally inclusive therapists have a clear understanding of each construct independently as well as the multiplicity of ways that they can and do converge. A therapist using a basic empathy approach, as defined in chapter 1, will likely overlook many of these variables and thus not be able to provide an adequate quality of empathy.

The key cultural identity constructs in ICE include the following:

- race,
- language,
- religion and spirituality,
- gender,
- familial migration history,
- affectional orientation,
- age and cohort,
- physical and mental capacities,
- socioeconomic situation and history,
- education, and
- history of traumatic experience.

We do not assume that this is an all-inclusive list of cultural identity constructs, but for the purposes of teaching ICE, the list appears to be sufficiently broad. To increase awareness, we define and discuss seven of the key cultural identity constructs with relevant key concepts as they relate to varied learned assumptions and experience. Following a discussion of the importance of salience, this chapter focuses on the constructs of race, gender, and religion. Chapter 7 focuses on affectional orientation, age, physical and mental capacity, and class and socioeconomic status.

THE IMPORTANCE OF SALIENCE

The prominence of any key cultural identity construct varies for every individual on the basis of experience, time (i.e., age, cohort, and era), and other contextual variables. This is because every key cultural identity construct can also serve as a status identifier in society. Thus, for some individuals, their status in society and accompanying self-definition will be based on one or two primary key cultural identity constructs, such as race and gender, whereas others will base their self-definitions on other constructs, such as physical ability and sexuality.

T. L. Robinson (1999) argued that identities are socially constructed, possess rank in society, and are constructed hierarchically in society on the basis of a set of dominant discourses. Although Robinson focused primarily on dominant discourses across race, affectional (sexual) orientation, gender, ability, and class, we expand on this hypothesis to include religion and age. This list is of course not all-inclusive, but it does focus on the majority of dominant discourses in Western society. People who diverge from the preferred and established standard on each of the various identities commonly experience devaluation and oppressive discourse and action aimed at punishing such deviation. For example, in U.S. society, being White is generally more valued than being a person of color, males are preferred to females, heterosexuals in closed relationships are considered morally superior to those in other forms of affectional relationships, Christians are favored over non-Christians, and so forth. These discourses are identified in varying forms, from more visible to less visible (see Figure 6.1). Exhibit 6.1 is designed to evaluate each individual's view of salience during self-definition.

Race	Ethnicity	Language	Religion/spirituality
Sex/gender	Family migration history	Sexual affectional orientation	Age/cohort
Physical/mental capacity issues	Socioeconomic situation and history	Education	Trauma history

Figure 6.1. Key identity constructs.

EXHIBIT 6.1
Exploring Identity Salience

Directions: Put the following key identity constructs in order of importance or salience to you when you are sitting in a classroom of your peers. Your job here is to decide which variables are most important when you self-define. Be sure that no two constructs can have equal ranking.

Arrange the key identity constructs as they apply to you, adjusting them based on how you believe you may see yourself interfacing with others in the following scenarios. Be sure to think about how you might feel in each circumstance and the factors that play into how you perceive yourself and how you feel others might perceive you.

_____ Imagine that you are having a picnic with your family and closest friends.
_____ Imagine that you get into a car accident that leaves you permanently wheelchair bound.
_____ Imagine that you have just had a child who was born mentally retarded.
_____ Imagine that you are faced with the task of negotiating a good deal on a major automobile repair. The mechanics that you encounter are all Latino and male.
_____ Imagine that you are driving through an upper-middle-class neighborhood alone. You notice that a police vehicle has been following closely for blocks.
_____ Imagine that you relocate your home to a region where the majority of the people around you are a different religion from your own (e.g., Islamic, Mormon, Catholic, Baptist, or Buddhist).
_____ Imagine you have a teenager who appears to have begun a serious relationship with a person who is the same sex.
_____ Imagine you get transferred in your work to a predominantly Islamic nation.

Identity Salience Discussion Questions
1. Given each of the above new contexts, what, if any, of the variables changes and why?
2. What contexts affect the order of salience and why?
3. If the salience of the variables nearly never changes for you, why do you think this is so?
4. Do you think that this is the case for all people? If not, what might encourage deeper understanding of how salience affects some people more than others?

As the therapist gets to know the client, it is crucial for her or him to remember a few key issues with regard to salience. First, individuals will rank order the key cultural identity constructs somewhat differently, even if those individuals grew up in the same household, family, and context. No two people are truly culturally identical. We all respond to a multitude of variables that ultimately affect the salience of the key cultural variables. A key issue that plays into our self-definition is that of experience. For example, one of the authors knows of two Filipino American brothers who both grew up in a lower-middle-class home on Oahu, Hawaii. A significant difference between the two brothers is that one of them spent years at battle in Vietnam, whereas the other was able to remain stateside throughout the war. Although on most variables both brothers define themselves similarly, in reference to experience with trauma, the Vietnam veteran defined himself first as a Vet and then would list himself by other variables. For this individual, in most contexts, no variable appears to be more important to him than having survived this very traumatic and life-altering experience.

Second, the relative importance of cultural variables will change in response to changes in our contexts. We do not all perceive ourselves the same way in every context. Instead, we tend to perceive ourselves in relation to others around us. Part of how we rank the relative importance of the variables that define us is how we feel others around us respond to and define us. For example, you do not likely interface with the world the same way when having a picnic with your family as you do when you are alone in a new city in a different region of the country or the world. With your family, the relative familiarity of environment, similarity of background with those around you, and safety in being where others understand you will likely affect which variables are most salient at that moment. However, the differences you experience in a new place with people different from you may make certain key cultural contexts more salient than they were at the picnic with your family.

Finally, relative salience of key cultural variables will likely remain in flux for each individual, sometimes shifting more than once in a given day. No matter how each of us self-defines, the way others choose to define us can play a role in how we self-define at any given moment. For example, a friend of one of the authors pointed out that, as an African American, the relative salience of race and ethnicity for him varies in direct response to where he is at any given moment. If he is in a relatively racially integrated environment, his race and ethnicity will move down in salience as opposed to when in an environment that is relatively White. He pointed out that feeling as if all eyes are on him makes him more aware of why the people around feel a "need" to be watchful. He explained that every time he goes through certain White neighborhoods, he feels as if he has to be extra careful to not draw attention to himself for fear of how a policeman may overreact. We thus do not necessarily have stagnant identities on every variable, despite the fact that we may have a core cultural identity.

RACE

The construct of race has been interpreted by scientists as varying in number from as few as 3 (Caucasoid, Mongoloid, and Negroid) to as many as 200 distinct categories throughout history. Although it has undergone numerous definitions, a prevailing and overarching definition of race can be defined as "an isolated inbreeding population with a distinctive genetic heritage" (Healy, 1997, p. 309). The complete mapping of the human genome has afforded us with the ability to scientifically assess genetic differences in racial distinctions. The most current genetic research has demonstrated that more genetic diversity exists between individuals within a given racial category than between groups construed as racially different (Cornell & Hartmann, 1998). A study of 1,056 individuals from 52 populations replicated previous findings, clarifying that "within-population differences among individuals account for 93 to 95% of genetic variation" whereas "differences among major groups constitute only 3 to 5%" (Rosenberg et al., 2002, p. 2381). Thus, the use of distinctions along racial lines appears to be more of a sociocultural phenomenon than a biological fact. Race is ultimately a phenomenon that distinguishes people on the basis of simplistic phenotypic variance such as skin color, facial features, and hair to distinguish group association.

Despite the evidence surrounding the biology related to the construct of race, race continues to play a significant role in the lives of the majority of people throughout the world. This issue is particularly relevant in the United States, where race has long been used to shape mindsets and opportunities. As Cornel West (1993) stated, "To engage in a serious discussion of race in America, we must begin not with the problems of black people but with the flaws of American society—flaws rooted in historic inequalities and longstanding cultural stereotypes" (p. 1). For example, leading sociologists have long argued that the systemic efforts such as the long-term elimination of job opportunities for skilled and semiskilled workers in urban areas is the force most responsible for the growth of the African American underclass in America's inner cities (Wilson, 1987). Numerous studies also provide mounting evidence that African American men and women experience increased levels of psychological distress as a result of reported experiences of discrimination and prejudice (Klonoff & Landrine, 1999; Klonoff, Landrine, & Ullman, 1999; Landrine & Klonoff, 1996; Moradi & Subich, 2003; Utsey & Ponterotto, 1996). It is very likely that similar experiences occur for most other people of color in the United States.

T. L. Robinson and Howard-Hamilton (2000) argued that attitudes about race and multiculturalism may be associated with variance in moral development, with racism, defensiveness, and denial associated with lower moral development, and celebration of multicultural variance associated with higher moral development. This continuum of moral development is not dissimilar from the Racial and Cultural Development model of D. W. Sue and Sue (2003), in which human beings are described as developing from mere social conformity in the hierarchical and oppressive viewpoints on race, to more of a multiperspective viewpoint, in which one is aware in an integrative fashion.

Attitudes about race ultimately exist on a moral continuum, with every individual interacting with others located differently along this same continuum. Culturally inclusive therapists will likely be most effective at experiencing and communicating empathy if they have developed further along this continuum. The more effective the therapist is at viewing race through a developmental lens as an identity construct, the more likely he or she will be able to meet clients where they are in their experience as racial beings in a world of varied developmental responses to race.

As race is merely a social construction, why is understanding the way it interfaces in society key in developing empathy with the experience of so many people? This may be because racial distinctions have long been used as a method to differentiate, distinguish, separate, segregate, and oppress (West, 1993). Race is used in decisional processes by bankers, adjudicators, law enforcement, educators, parents, policy writers, and so forth. People make assumptions about others based on perceptions of race and ethnicity in most daily interchanges. Over the past few decades, it has become apparent that racially prejudiced attitudes have evolved from a more unconcealed and hostile approach to one that is more subtle and ambivalent (Brief, Dietz, Cohen, Pugh, & Vaslow, 2000). Even though research has documented a decline in self-reported racist attitudes, practices of racial discrimination appear to continue in the workplace (Maass, Castelli, & Arcuri, 2000). African Americans, for example, have experienced an extensive history of disadvantages in occupational settings when compared with European Americans that continue through current times (Bound & Freeman, 1992; King, 1992).

Constructions of race and the biases that accompany them play a role in a counselor's ability to properly engage therapeutically with clients. Research has demonstrated that reported lower multicultural competency tends to be associated with strong negative racial attitudes in counselors (Constantine, 2002; Constantine, Juby, & Liang, 2001).

An important factor to assess in any therapeutic relationship is the experience that clients have in relation to individual, institutional, and cultural forms of racism, as discussed in chapter 4. Although discussing racism is commonly an unsettling experience for many people, it plays a key role in the origins and history of the United States, and thus is key to developing ICE. Experience with racial bias in some forms is nearly universal for non-White people in the United States. Culturally inclusive therapists will maintain a keen eye to the possibility of any or all forms of racism playing a role in the experience of their clients. A key variable to keep in mind is the various forms of unintentional racism as a result of White privilege, as discussed in chapter 4.

Another key issue of experience and context regarding race is that of racial identity development. There are likely as many forms of racial identity development as there are societal constructions of race. One of the more influential models is D. W. Sue and Sue's (2003) racial and cultural identity development (R/CID) model, which integrates the experiences of people of all racial backgrounds into a five-stage model: (a) conformity, (b) dissonance, (c) resistance and immersion, (d) introspection, and (e) integrative awareness. These stages can be summed up as moving from an ethnocentric perspective to a multicultural perspective focused on ending racial inequity and all forms of racism.

Another influential model of racial identity development is Cross's (1991, 1995) nigresence model. This model describes African American racial identity development as a maturation process in which external negative self-images based on experiences of marginalization are replaced with positive internal conceptions in five stages: (a) preencounter, (b) encounter, (c) immersion and emersion, (d) internalization, and (e) internalization–commitment. The final stage includes a focus on eradicating racial oppression for all oppressed people throughout the remainder of one's life. Other key racial identity development models include Poston's (1990) biracial identity development model, Helms's (1984) White racial identity model, and Ruiz's (1990) Latino/Hispanic American identity development model. Each model appears to be subsumed within D. W. Sue and Sue's (2003) R/CID model. We recommend reading D. W. Sue and Sue's text for further learning in relation to racial identity development.

Race Census

The following information is intended to increase reader knowledge around the issue of the use of race labels by the U.S. government. First read the definitions of race and ethnicity as clarified by the U.S. Census Bureau (Lowenthal, 2000; U.S. Census Bureau, 2001a), then review the race and ethnicity categories in selected U.S. censuses (see Table 6.1). Once you have done this, consider the discussion questions that follow in Exhibit 6.2.

U.S. Census Definitions

The following are definitions of race and ethnicity as clarified by the U.S. Census Bureau.

Race: A classification of people into groups based on physical, cultural, or social characteristics. Ideas about race, such as how many categories to use, who belongs in which category, and what the differences mean, have changed over the years, both in popular usage and in official statistics. Beginning in 1997, all forms from the federal government, such as the Census forms, allow people to report more than one race. The racial categories now include White; Black, African American, or Negro; American Indian or Alaska Native; Asian; Native Hawaiian or other Pacific Islander; or "Some other race."

Ethnicity: The cultural practices, language, cuisine, and traditions—not biological or physical differences—used to distinguish groups of people. Hispanic origin is an example of ethnicity.

TABLE 6.1

Race and Ethnicity Categories in Selected U.S. Censuses

Category	Census				
	1860	1890[a]	1900	1970	2000[a]
Race	White Black	White Black	White Black (Negro descent)	White Negro or Black	White Black, African American, Negro
	Mulatto[a]	Mulatto[a] Quadroon Octoroon			
			Indian	Indian Indian (American)	American Indian or Alaska Native
		Chinese Japanese	Chinese Japanese	Chinese Japanese Filipino Korean	Chinese Japanese Filipino Korean Asian Indian Vietnamese Other Asian
				Hawaiian	Native Hawaiian Guamanian or Chamorro Samoan Other Pacific Islander
				Other	Some other race
Hispanic ethnicity				Mexican Puerto Rican Cuban Central/ South American/ Other Spanish (None of these)	Mexican, Mexican American, or Chicano Puerto Rican Cuban Other Spanish/ Hispanic/ Latino Not Spanish/ Hispanic/ Latino

Note. In the 2000 Census, respondents were allowed to select more than one race. Questions about Hispanic origin were asked of a sample of Americans in 1970 and of all Americans beginning with the 1980 census. From "America's Racial and Ethnic Minorities," by K. Pollard and W. O'Hare, 1999, *Population Bulletin, 54*(3), p. 9. Copyright 1999 by the Population Reference Bureau. Reprinted with permission.
[a]In 1890, the term *mulatto* was defined as a person who was three-eighths Black, a person who was *quadroon* was one-quarter Black, and person who was *octoroon* was one-eighth Black.

EXHIBIT 6.2
Race Census Discussion Questions

1. What is your general reaction to the definitions and the selected race and ethnicity categories in Table 6.1?
2. What do you feel is the current role of race and ethnic categories in society?
3. What do you think is the logic behind the government listing "Hispanic" as a separate category of ethnicity from race?
4. What are your responses to the use of terms like "mulatto," "octoroon," "Negro," and "Hispanic"?
5. How do you feel about the use of different terms in different eras to denote categories of people?
6. What are your thoughts about the expansion of racial and ethnic categories over time (from three to dozens)?
7. What groups of people remain excluded or relegated to the "other" category even in the modern census? (For example, how are people from Brazil accounted for?)
8. How do the terms used by the U.S. government reflect the values of the society it represents?
9. How does language shape our realities?
10. What are some other examples of the power of language in influencing social realities?

U.S. Census Categories

Race and ethnicity categories in selected U.S. censuses include the following.

American Indian or Alaska Native: A person having origins in any of the original peoples of North and South America (including Central America) and who maintain tribal affiliation or community attachment.

Asian: A person having origins in any of the original peoples of the East Asia, Southeast Asia, or the Indian subcontinent, including Cambodia, China , India, Japan, Korea, Malaysia, Pakistan, the Philippine Islands, Thailand, and Vietnam.

Black, African American, or Negro: A person having origins in any of the Black racial groups of Africa. It includes people who indicate their race as Black, African American, or Negro or provide written entries such as African American, Afro American, Kenyan, Nigerian, or Haitian.

Native Hawaiian or other Pacific Islander: A person having origins in any of the original peoples of Hawaii, Guam, Samoa, or other Pacific Islands.

White: A person having origins in any of the original people of Europe, the Middle East, or North Africa. It includes people who indicate their race as White or report entries such as Irish, German, Italian, Lebanese, Near Easterner, Arab, or Polish.

Some other race: Includes race responses not included in the regular race categories given. Respondents providing write-in entries such as multiracial, mixed, interracial, or a Hispanic/Latino group are included in this category.

GENDER

Although often used interchangeably, the terms gender and sex have very different meanings. *Sex* is the system of sexual classification based on biological and physical differences, such as primary and secondary sexual characteristics, which create the categories "male" and "female." In between these constructs exist more ambiguous sexual characteristics properly referred to as *intersex*. More properly defined, an intersex person is one who is born with genitalia or secondary sexual characteristics of indeterminate sex or that combine features of both sexes. A more archaic and less preferred term for intersex people is "hermaphrodite."

Gender, however, is a system of sexual classification based on the social construction of the categories "men and boys" and "women and girls" as two polar constructs. In between these constructs exists any combination of gender, with "androgyny" located at the center. Figure 6.2 illustrates these concepts. The term *androgyny* refers to two concepts: (a) the blending of masculine and feminine characteristics or (b) a person who is perceived as neither masculine nor feminine (Bem, 1974). Thus androgynous traits are those that either have no gender value or have some aspects generally attributed to the opposite gender.

A person's gender does not inherently match a person's sex. For example, a female person can gender identify as a male, or a male person can gender identify as a female. Also, the current practice for people who are born intersex is to have their gender selected for them by their parents or doctor(s). They may also undergo medical procedures to adjust their sex to match the selected gender. There is a movement in the United States, supported by the American Counseling Association, to eradicate the use of any such medical procedures on intersex people until they are of the age of consent. This is to say that one can be sex female and gender male or sex male and gender female. Although people tend to self-define in gender the same way they self-define in sex, this norm is much more of a sociocultural expectation than a biological imperative. This is because sexual identity is more objective in nature whereas gender identity is more subjective.

Sex:	Female	↔	Intersex	↔	Male
Gender:	Women	↔	Androgynous	↔	Men
	Girls				Boys

Figure 6.2. Sex and gender on continuums.

Much as White privilege and accompanying forms of racism affect people on the basis of perceptions of race, gender preference and expectations color the experience of people on the basis of gender and sex. U.S. society has long been androcentric, or biased in the favor of people gendered and sexed male. *Androcentrism* is the practice, conscious or otherwise, of placing male human beings or the masculine point of view at the center of one's view of the world and its culture and history. Androcentrism is a form of a broader phenomenon commonly referred to as sexism. *Sexism* is the belief that women and men are inherently different, with men being superior to women. The gender role stereotypes discussed previously are born out of sexist belief patterns. A more extreme form of androcentric sexism is misogyny. The term *misogyny* derives from Greek with *misein* meaning "to hate" and *gyne* meaning "woman." Misogyny is often seen as a form of political ideology wherein an exaggerated aversion toward women is cultivated with the underlying goal of justifying and reproducing the subordination of women by men.

Gender roles are behaviors, attitudes, values, emotions, beliefs, and attire that a particular cultural group considers appropriate for males and females on the basis of their biological sex. Gender roles are composed of several elements. A person's gender role may be expressed through clothing, choice of work, interpersonal interaction style, types of personal relationships, and other factors. The term *gender role* has been used interchangeably with that of *sex role*, although the latter term is now considered outdated.

Gender role stereotypes are socially determined models that contain the cultural beliefs about what the gender roles should be. This differs from the concept of gender role in that it tends to be the way people feel "others" should behave. Resulting paradigms of traditional gender role socialization that influence the opportunities offered girls and women are sets of rigid gender role stereotypes or traditional attitudes about women and men (Blazina & Watkins, 2000; Mintz & Mahalik, 1996). Traditional attitudes regarding the roles of women have been characterized as women being subordinate and maintaining roles in private settings and men being dominant and maintaining public roles (Henley, Meng, O'Brien, McCarthy, & Sockloskie, 1998). Examples of these stereotypes include well-documented orthogonal traits that are associated with males and females and maintained through interpersonal, institutional, and cultural means (Broverman, Vogel, Broverman, Clarkson, & Rosenkrantz, 1972; Deaux & Lewis, 1983; Rosenkrantz, Vogel, Bee, Broverman, & Broverman, 1968; Spence & Helmreich, 1978). Stereotypical characteristics of females include an ability and propensity to be devoted to others, interdependence, accommodating, supportive, cooperative, and aware of others' feelings. Stereotypical characteristics of males include self-confidence, dominance, autonomy, and emotional aloofness.

Gender role stereotypes play an active role in the opportunities and services rendered to girls and women in society. For example, in the year

2000, working women were paid about 72 cents for every dollar working men were paid, a differential 2 cents per dollar worse than in 1996 (U.S. Census Bureau, 2001b). Women face many external and internal barriers to optimal career outcomes. These barriers include educational and workplace discrimination, socioeconomic disadvantage, prejudice related to gender, occupational stereotyping, sexual harassment, a paucity of mentors and role models, low outcome expectations, multiple role conflicts, underestimation of capabilities, and constrictive gender role socialization (McLennan, 1999; McWhirter, Torres, & Rasheed, 1998).

Such gender bias appears in many forms and settings, including education. Research has produced consistent evidence that boys in school generally receive more constructive feedback from their teachers as well as more consideration and praise than do girls. Boys are called on by name more often and are asked more complex and abstract questions than are girls. Ultimately, boys receive more defined attention (positive as well as negative), thus enhancing their performance, whereas girls are more likely to become marginalized and relatively invisible members of the classroom (Marshall & Reinhartz, 1997; D. Sadker, 2000; M. Sadker & Sadker, 1994).

According to statistics from the World Health Organization (2003), women experience different patterns of psychological distress than men. The worldwide overall common conditions of women's lives appear to be related to these patterns. Women suffer victimization of trafficking and prostitution, interpersonal violence and sexual abuse, greater psychological trauma, greater poverty, and greater family separation than do men (Bemak et al., 2003). These experiences bring a sense of hopelessness, ongoing exhaustion, fear, anger, and less economic independence (World Health Organization, 2003).

Restrictive, sexist, and inflexible gender role expectations and stereotypes often result in a sense of devaluation or overcontrolled restriction in many women, creating an experience referred to as *gender role conflict* (O'Neil, Helms, Gable, David, & Wrightsman, 1986). To be culturally inclusive, counselors need to be aware that women experience more stress than do men as a result of gender role conflict. Research suggests that reported experiences of prejudice and discrimination are related to greater levels of psychological distress for women (Corning, 2002; Landrine & Klonoff, 1997; Landrine, Klonoff, Gibbs, Manning, & Lund, 1995; Moradi & Subich, 2002).

As is clarified in Figure 6.3, the agents, or members of the dominant category of people in the case of gender, are men and gender-identified as men. People who are born female or have their gender selected for them as female bear the brunt of the underlying andocentrism and sexism inherent in Western society. Females have historically experienced numerous forms of discrimination and inequity throughout the ages. They have long been the victims of sexual harassment and aggression, gender discrimination in job opportunities and in equity in wages, unequal educational opportunities,

Race	Gender	Affectional orientation	Physical/ mental ability	Age	Religion/ spirituality	Class/ socioeconomic status
Visible and Invisible Identities						
Whites	Males	Heterosexuals Closed relationships	Able- bodied	Middle aged	Christian	Middle class
People of color	Females	Gay men Lesbians Bisexuals Open relationships	Persons with disabilities	Young Elderly	Jews Muslims Buddhists Unitarians Hindus Atheist/agnostic	Lower class

Consequences of Dominant Discourses

↕	↕	↕	↕	↕	↕	↕
Racism	Sexism and gender bias	Homophobia and sexual prejudice	Ableism	Ageism and adultism	Religious prejudice	Class elitism

Figure 6.3. Dominant discourses and their consequences.

as well as countless limitations as defined by gender role expectations (Bank & Hall, 1997; Kaufman, 1995; Reasons, Conley, & Debro, 2002; Schor, 1992). Despite institutional attention to the numerous ways in which females are disadvantaged by educational and institutional policies, very little attention has been focused on the ideological, economic, and social forces underlying them (Stromquist, 1997). This lack of focus on the underlying causes of such bias serves to perpetuate the discrimination and suffering that women experience on a regular basis.

A challenge for many in society is the fact that most cultures are very prescriptive regarding gender role expectations. Individuals who choose to not follow typical gender role expectations are commonly referred to as *transgendered*. The term *cisgendered* has been gaining popularity among transgendered populations in the past decade. Cisgendered refers to people who possess a gender identity and perform a gender role that society considers appropriate for their sex. This new term appears to have been developed under the hypothesis that categorizing everyone will clarify a difference between equal alternatives, whereas singling out the minority group implies some deviance, immorality, or defect on the part of the labeled group. The term *heterosexual* appears to have similar social justice–oriented roots, creating a label for people who are affectionally oriented to people who are not the same sex, when previously labels existed only for those who did not fit in to this more dominant category. As gender and sexual orientation are separate concepts, androgynous people may consider themselves straight, gay, bisexual, asexual, or none of these. This is also true for people who are intersex, male, or female.

Our experiences and upbringing have a great deal to do with our perceptions and expectations of others based on gender. There is research evidence that adolescents with employed mothers have less stereotyped perceptions of female gender roles than do adolescents whose mothers are full-time homemakers (Huston & Alvarez, 1990). Adolescents who are more atypical in their gender identity tend to report a much greater amount of stress than those who gender identify in a cisgendered manner (Yunger, Carver, & Perry, 2004). Furthermore, research has indicated that men who experience difficulty expressing affection to other men also tend to endorse more stereotypical attitudes toward women (D. T. Robinson & Schwartz, 2004).

Biases such as those previously mentioned can be translated into therapeutic relationships. For example, the amount individuals conform to gender role stereotypes appears to influence therapists' assessments of their clients (Morrow, 2000; Wisch & Mahalik, 1999). Counselors tend to pathologize their clients if they act in manners inconsistent with societal expectations for men and women (Robertson & Fitzgerald, 1990). In a society in which males enjoy preferential bias and privilege, female clients are more likely to experience both unintentional and intentional gender oppression in the course of the therapeutic relationship if the therapist does not make an active effort to overcome biases. Counselors need to develop a solid knowledge base of issues of gender bias and oppression to develop ICE for people of all sexes and genders.

Exhibit 6.3 is designed to examine one's awareness of gender bias. The exhibit uses children's movies, books, and cartoons as examples.

RELIGION/SPIRITUALITY

As the previous chapter included coverage of the basic issues underlying the development of religious and spiritual awareness, this chapter focuses more on the importance of developing understanding of some of the ways in which differences in religion might serve a more divisive and damaging role for some clients.

Religious Discrimination

Religious discrimination has long been a significant issue in societies throughout the United States and the world. As the Christian faith predominates in the United States, a general bias toward as well as preferential treat-

EXHIBIT 6.3
Gender Bias in Children's Movies, Books, and Cartoons

Select and evaluate two children's movies, children's books, or children's cartoon series. Collect data regarding the following:

Number of characters depicted	Male	Female
Roles depicted	Male	Female
Aggressive		
Rescuing others		
Submissive		
Passive		
Being rescued		
Comic roles		
Domestic roles		
Positions of authority		
Emotional		
Concerned with physical appearance		
Physically fit		
Overweight		
Professional occupation		
Service occupation		
Other (describe)		

Gender Activity Discussion Questions
1. Are males and females represented with equal frequency in children's media?
2. In what roles are females and males likely to be portrayed? What attributes do they share?
3. Is there a difference in terms of which characters play more active or passive roles?
4. What clothing do the characters wear?
5. What role does the physical attractiveness of the characters play?
6. How is attractiveness defined for female characters? For male characters?
7. What are children being taught about "appropriate" gender roles for boys? For girls?
8. What conclusions can you draw about gender stereotyping in children's media based on your observations?
9. On the basis of your observation, what suggestions would you have for parents concerned about exposing their children to gender stereotypes?

ment of Christians is common, although such bias is generally not noted by Christians. Such bias appears in the form of language used for the holidays (Merry Christmas instead of a more inclusive statement such as Happy Holidays) to terms used to describe places of worship (church and chapel instead of synagogue, mosque, or some more inclusive term). The general rule of thumb on religious discrimination is that those who are not of the religious majority in a given country or region often experience various forms of religious discrimination and even persecution.

Religious freedom for people of all religious and spiritual persuasions is not a reality in most of the world today (Wood, 2004). In 2001, the United Nations drafted a declaration clarifying that religious persecution and discrimination continue to be a significant international problem and urged nations to adopt measures to ensure people belonging to religious minorities have equal access to basic human rights, such as education without discrimination and rights of equal treatment under the rule of law (Maran, 2002). It is a sad fact that the United States delegation walked out of this very same conference as a result of a disagreement over the inclusion of "Zionism as racism" in the conference deliberations, and thus played a role in the United Nations not ratifying the declaration.

Although religious bias and discrimination come in many forms, few forms are as historically noteworthy as anti-Semitism. Anti-Semitism is the systematic discrimination against, hatred, denigration, or oppression of Judaism, Jews, and the cultural, religious, and intellectual heritage of Jewish people. Anti-Semitism is also a persistent form of racism. The term itself was coined in the 1870s by Wilhelm Marr, an Austrian anti-Jewish journalist, who emphasized racial, economic, social, and political stereotypes instead of religious difference, as in previous periods in history.

Jews have historically referred to people who are not Jewish as *Gentile*. Gentile is a term derived from the Latin term *gens*, meaning "clan" or a "group of families," and the Latin term *gentilis*, meaning "pagan." Although the term has been historically used to describe people who are not Jewish, it has fallen out of favor in recent decades to be replaced by the term *non-Jew*.

Anti-Semitism has taken many forms throughout history. Beginning in the historical era BC, Jews were forced to emigrate and were enslaved. From the early Christian era forward, Jews suffered loss of religious rights, forced conversion to Christianity, exclusion, segregation into "ghettos," expulsion, massacres, political and economic restrictions, as well as various forms of scapegoating leading to the Holocaust. In the process of all of this oppression, Jews have been the recipients of the bias associated with countless stereotypes, many which have lasted for centuries.

Anti-Semitism has ongoing dire effects on Jewish people. In a qualitative study of Jewish participants, Friedman, Friedlander, and Blustein (2005) found that two thirds of the consistent universal themes of American Jewish identity were results of religious prejudice. All participants in this study reported the consistent experience of feeling marginalized and an ongoing awareness of religious discrimination in their daily lives. Jews in the United States today report feeling less fearful of attacks and stigmatization than they did half a century ago, but they also appear to be less conscious of their heritage and more prone to internalized anti-Semitism (Langman, 1999). Despite these reports, there is continuing evidence of anti-Semitism in society, although the face of anti-Semitism may be undergoing an international transformation (Fischel, 2005).

Within the field of counseling, multicultural researchers and theorists have historically not focused on Jewish people, their culture, or their context (Fischer & Moradi, 2001). It has been hypothesized that this has been caused by anti-Semitism throughout membership of the helping profession (Kiselica, 2003; Weinrach, 2002). This lack of focus could also be due, in part, to the inaccurate presumption that Jews are not an ethnicity but are a religious sect. Jewish people are also commonly classified as "White" despite broad racial diversity within the ethnicity (Rosen & Weltman, 1996).

Religious intolerance and oppression take many forms in society. In the recent decades, anti-Islamic oppression has been growing throughout the United States. For example, the Council on American-Islamic Relations (CAIR; 2002) reported over 700 discriminatory acts against Muslims in the year following the September 11, 2001, terrorist attacks. Muslim people also commonly experience numerous forms of discrimination. Another report by CAIR (2001), with data collected prior to 9/11, demonstrated a wide array of discrimination, including denial of religious accommodations (37%), job termination (13%), unequal treatment (8%), verbal abuse (8%), denial of employment (7%), and denial of access to public facilities (5%). Workplace discrimination appears to be a significant issue for Muslims, with 50% of the reported cases occurring at work.

Religious discrimination and oppression appear to be on the rise in general in the United States. The U.S. Equal Employment Opportunity Commission reported an increase in complaints of religious bias at work in the late 1990s (Hansen, 1998). The news reports of religious discrimination in the United States appear to be increasing into the 2000s as well. For example, it was reported that the U.S. Department of Justice intervened in a case alleging religious discrimination of a sixth grader who refused to remove a headscarf worn for religious reasons (Hurst, 2004). The student was expelled for not obeying a district policy that prohibits students from wearing any type of headgear, including hats, caps, and scarves. No exceptions were made for headgear worn for religious purposes.

Therapists who seek to develop ICE need to become knowledgeable on the various ways in which religious minorities suffer from discrimination and oppression. It is safe to assume that, in general, the people with agent status in U.S. society are Christian, on the basis of the relative domination of Christian religions. The targets tend to fall into the categories of people who practice non-Christian religions and those who practice no religion. It is important to note here that many people who consider themselves agnostic or atheist also perceive themselves as recipients of religious discrimination.

Contemplating Religion in Family Life

The following was designed to assist in exploration of issues associated with ways in which religious oppression manifests itself. Think about different means through which religion might be used to control or oppress family members either intentionally or unintentionally.

Consider the following possibilities:

1. Children are often raised within a given faith without being afforded the freedom to explore other religions or decide whether their first religion isn't a "fit" with them. Many children are made to feel guilty if they look into other religious or spiritual options than those of their families of origin well into adulthood.
2. Vows and other wording in religious wedding ceremonies can serve to reinforce a subservient role for women in marital and family relations (e.g., "man and wife" or "honor and obey").
3. Women and men experience differential sex role expectations regarding behavior and attire based on religious pressure. For example,
   - the woman's role is perpetuated as being centered on the home (some would prefer the term *restricted* or *confined*) and is structured to make the home comfortable for male members of the family (e.g., be a good homemaker), and
   - more orthodox religions might restrict women to specific attire while not making comparable restrictions on men (e.g., Is a necktie equal in restrictiveness to a dress?).
4. Individuals experience pressure to limit their associations and affiliations based on religious similarities and differences. For example,
   - people experience pressure regarding the importance of fostering and maintaining friendships with others who are of the same religious affiliation,

- children experience pressure and expectations regarding "appropriate" dating and marital relationships and can include issues of what religion the other is as well as what gender, and
- children experience pressure and expectations regarding school attendance at religiously affiliated institutions.

5. Are you able to think of other examples?

CONCLUSION

This chapter focuses on ways that one might explore the key identity constructs of race, gender, and religion on the path to developing the intellectual understanding necessary to become truly culturally inclusive. Chapter 7 focuses on other key identity constructs necessary for this development.

7

INTELLECTUAL UNDERSTANDING: EXAMINING OTHER KEY CULTURAL IDENTITY CONSTRUCTS

To develop the intellectual understanding necessary to become culturally inclusive in empathy, it is important to develop an ability to understand ourselves and others as human beings with converging identities within context. This chapter focuses on four key identity constructs that are often overlooked and misunderstood. These constructs are affectional (sexual) orientation, age, physical and mental capacities, and class and socioeconomic status.

AFFECTIONAL ORIENTATION

In the United States, the majority of people publicly self-identify as heterosexual. It has been reported that 97% of women and 96% of men in the United States identify themselves as heterosexual, 2.1% of women and 3.5% of men identify themselves as homosexual, and 0.9% of women and 0.6% of men identify themselves as bisexual (Reasons, Conley, & Debro, 2002).

The relative minority status of being nonheterosexual places individuals in position to experience biased attitudes and oppression. Over one third of homosexual men and women report having been victims of interpersonal violence, and up to 94% report some type of victimization related to their affectional orientation (Fassinger, 1991; National Gay and Lesbian Task Force, 1990). Violence against gay men appears to be the most predominant form of sexuality-based interpersonal violence in the United States, making up 75% of known incidents of hate crimes against lesbian, gay, bisexual, and transgender individuals (U.S. Department of Justice, 2002). A key word to note in this statistic is "known" as this clarifies that the data do not include unreported sexuality-based violence.

Readers may note that this section is titled *affectional orientation* instead of the more traditional term *sexual orientation*. The preference of using the term *affectional orientation* over that of *sexual orientation* comes from the fact that a person's orientation goes beyond sexuality. A person's orientation is defined by the type of person with whom he or she is predisposed to share personal affection or with whom he or she bonds with emotionally. Sexual attraction plays a role in affectional orientation but is not the complete relationship. The term affectional orientation is therefore more inclusive of all interpersonally affective relationships than is the term sexual orientation.

Homophobia and Sexual Prejudice

George Weinberg introduced the term *homophobia* in 1967 to indicate "the dread of being in close quarters with homosexuals" (Weinberg, 1972, p. 4) or more broadly a conscious or unconscious adoption and acceptance of negative attitudes and feelings about people who are homosexual or homosexuality. These attitudes and fears result in harassment, prejudice, discrimination, or acts of violence against sexual minorities. These attitudes are commonly based on false assumptions, such as the assumption that homosexuality is learned. Such assumptions may be related to negative feelings toward sexual minorities. For example, individuals with the strongest negative affect toward people who are homosexual are those who assume that homosexuality is a learned trait (Aguero, Bloch, & Byrne, 1984).

Homophobia has been hypothesized to serve four functions based on the psychological benefit they bring to the homophobic person (Herek, 1986, 1987). In the *experiential schematic* function, adverse contact with a particular individual who is homosexual functions to reinforce negative attitudes about homosexuality and people who are homosexual. The cause of this negative contact is attributed to characteristics of the people who are homosexual instead of to any personal attributes or biases that may have colored the interactions. The *social expressive* function of homophobia is based on the approval individuals win from peers and other significant individuals for the adoption of antihomosexual postures. The *value expressive* function allows individuals to affirm their own identity by expressing personal values deemed important, such as conservative religious ideologies that are against homosexuality. The *defensive* function of homophobia is avoidance of personal insecurities and anxieties associated with sexuality and gender roles through the characterization of sexual minorities as suitable recipients of denigration and attacks.

Researchers have become disinclined to use the term *homophobia* as it implies a phobic reaction to lesbians and gay men akin to the American Psychiatric Association's (2000) *Diagnostic and Statistical Manual of Mental Disorders* (4th ed., text rev.) terminology, and it is not as inclusive as more modern terminology (Haaga, 1991; Herek, 2004). The term *sexual prejudice* was proposed to replace the term *homophobia* by Herek (2000), with the intention to incorporate "all negative attitudes based on sexual orientation, whether the target is homosexual, bisexual, or heterosexual" (p. 19). Herek stressed that sexual prejudice is "almost always directed at people who engage in homosexual behavior or label themselves gay, lesbian, or bisexual" (p. 19). Research suggests that sexual prejudice is associated with antigay behaviors including violence and intimidation (Haddock & Zanna, 1998; Van de Ven, Bornholt, & Bailey, 1996) as well as anger in response to homosexuality (Ernulf & Innala, 1987; Van de Ven et al., 1996).

Sexual prejudice appears to be strongest among men, as evidenced by the high prevalence of violence toward gay men by men (U.S. Department of Justice, 2002). The sexual prejudice and violent reactions of men to men who are homosexual appears to be based on a confluence of factors. These factors include adherence to traditional gender roles (Kilianski, 2003; Parrott, Adams, & Zeichner, 2002; Polimeni, Hardie, & Buzwell, 2000), an exaggerated masculine ideology (Mosher & Sirkin, 1984), perceived threats to masculinity (Parrot et al., 2002), peer influence and thrill seeking (Franklin, 2000), and unwanted sexual arousal triggered by exposure to homoerotic cues (H. E. Adams, Wright, & Lohr, 1996).

Sexual prejudice develops in a society that embraces heterosexism. *Heterosexism* is a belief in the superiority of heterosexuality or people who are heterosexual resulting in a systematic process of privilege of people who are heterosexual over those who are not. This privilege is based on the notion that heterosexuality is both normal and ideal in society (Dermer, Smith, & Barto, in press; Herek, 2004; Palma & Stanley, 2002). Heterosexism is evidenced in the exclusion, by oversight or intention, of nonheterosexual persons in policies, procedures, and proceedings. The message underlying heterosexism in society is that all nonheterosexual feelings and behaviors are outside of the norms of society and thus abnormal or deviant. Such beliefs ultimately lead to discrimination, prejudice, and oppression of all people who do not fit within heterosexual norms (Dermer et al., in press).

Heterosexism manifests itself in two forms: cultural heterosexism and psychological heterosexism (Herek, 1990). Cultural heterosexism is the stigmatization, repudiation, subjugation, or defamation of sexual minorities within societal institutions ranging from churches to the law. Psychological heterosexism is the personal internalization of the worldviews underlying cultural heterosexism resulting in antigay, antibisexual, and antitransexual prejudice.

There are countless examples of cultural and institutional bias against sexual minorities throughout society. The following are a few examples:

- U.S. Senator and former Senate Majority Leader Trent Lott stated that homosexuality is a sin comparable to sex addiction, alcoholism, and kleptomania.
- The U.S. Supreme Court ruled that expelling a gay scoutmaster was within the Boy Scouts of America's constitutional rights. The organization formally banned both people who are homosexual and people who are atheist from their organization.
- The state of Colorado passed a constitutional amendment banning the institution of any laws entitling any person to claim discrimination on the basis of sexual orientation in 1992. This law was overturned in the U.S. Supreme Court in 1996.
- Southern Baptists denounced President Bill Clinton for his order proclaiming June as Gay and Lesbian Pride Month (Baker, 2002).

Effects of Bias on People

Although it can be challenging, it is possible for people to overcome deeply ingrained biases such as heterosexism. As we clarified previously, men are more likely to have negative attitudes and emotions about homosexuality. If a male therapist is striving to overcome heterosexist attitudes, he may find it most helpful to simultaneously work on overcoming traditional gender role attitudes. Traditional gender role attitudes have been found to be greater predictors of homophobia than gender (Kerns & Fine, 1994; Stark, 1991). In fact, there are a number of ideological stances that are associated with negative attitudes about homosexuality. When seeking to overcome heterosexism and sexual prejudice, therapists should keep in mind that they are associated with not only more traditional attitudes about gender roles but also more conservative religious ideologies, greater sexual guilt, greater negative attitudes about sex, and likelihood to express authoritarian beliefs. Other factors related to negative attitudes about homosexuality are less under the control of individuals (Greenlinger, 1985; Herek & Glunt, 1993; Marsigilio, 1993; Seltzer, 1992; Stark, 1991; VanderStoep & Green, 1988). Such factors include residing in the South or Midwest of the United States, being raised in a small town, being male, being older, or being less well educated (Britton, 1990; Bruce, Schrumm, Trefethen, & Slovik, 1990; Herek, 1984; Herek & Glunt, 1993; Seltzer, 1992).

Therapists wishing to learn more about issues surrounding sexual minorities can learn a great deal from the Association for Gay, Lesbian, and Bisexual Issues in Counseling (http://www.aglbic.org) and the American Psychological Association's Division 44: Society for the Psychological Study of Lesbian, Gay, and Bisexual Issues (http://www.apa.org/divisions/div44/). There are a number of excellent texts available as well, including *Overcoming Heterosexism and Homophobia: Strategies That Work*, by James T. Sears and Walter Williams; *How Homophobia Hurts Children: Nurturing Diversity at Home, at School, and in the Community*, by Jean M. Baker; and *The Therapist's Notebook for Lesbian, Gay and Bisexual Clients*, by Joy S. Whitman and Cyndy J. Boyd.

Exhibit 7.1 is designed to increase knowledge toward developing inclusive cultural empathy (ICE) regarding the experience of being a sexual minority. The questions posed encourage people who are heterosexual to examine the language used to talk with sexual/affectational minorities.

AGE

Age and perceptions of age can convey important social meanings to the self and others. The dominant culture of the United States has long maintained stereotypic and frequently negative perceptions of older adults (Busse, 1968; Kite & Johnson, 1988). Common language used in society reflects these negative and stereotypic biases. Derogatory phrases such as "all used up," "over the hill," and "old biddy" designate old age as a period of ineptitude and impotence (Nuessel, 1982). This language is reflective of the phenomenon of ageism. *Ageism* can be defined as prejudice and accompanying systematic discrimination based on chronological age toward older adults (Butler, 1969). Ageism is based on a set of beliefs, attitudes, and observations about the aging process that define older people as no longer able to be productive because of advancing age.

Certain meta-analyses on ageism provided strong evidence that older individuals are generally perceived less favorably than those who are younger (Gordon & Arvey, 2004; Kite, Stockdale, Whitley, & Johnson, 2005). Some have argued that ageism may be one of the most prevalent biases in Western culture today, possibly more prevalent than racism and sexism (Butler, 1995; Levy & Banaji, 2002; Palmore, 2001).

Much like race, class, and gender, age is a socially constructed factor along which privileges and disadvantages are institutionalized in society. For example, in 1993, an article published in *U.S. News and World Report* created a great stir in the United States when it disclosed that older Americans are routinely mistreated by the U.S. health care system, referring to a widespread medical bias against older people (Podolsky & Silberner, 1993). According to the article, despite the fact that all Americans over age 65 are covered by

EXHIBIT 7.1
Affectional Orientation

The following questionnaire was designed by Martin Rochlin (1982) to encourage people who are heterosexual to look into the language used to talk with sexual minorities. As you read the following questionnaire, think about how it might feel to be a sexual minority and be asked questions such as these on a regular basis.

Heterosexual Questionnaire
1. What do you think caused your heterosexuality?
2. When and how did you first decide you were a heterosexual?
3. Is it possible your heterosexuality is just a phase you may grow out of?
4. Is it possible your heterosexuality stems from a neurotic fear of others of the same sex?
5. Isn't it possible that all you need is a good gay lover?
6. Heterosexuals have histories of failures in gay relationships. Do you think you may have turned to heterosexuality out of fear of rejection?
7. If you have never slept with a person of the same sex, how do you know you wouldn't prefer that?
8. To whom have you disclosed your heterosexual tendencies? How did they react?
9. Your heterosexuality doesn't offend me as long as you don't try to force it on me. Why do you people feel compelled to seduce others into your sexual orientation?
10. If you choose to nurture children, would you want them to be heterosexual, knowing the problems they would face?
11. The great majority of child molesters are heterosexuals. Do you consider it safe to expose your children to heterosexual teachers?
12. Why do you insist on being so obvious and making a public spectacle of your heterosexuality? Can't you just be what you are and keep it quiet?
13. How can you ever hope to become a whole person if you limit yourself to a compulsive, exclusive, heterosexual object choice and remain unwilling to explore and develop your normal, natural, healthy, God-given homosexual potential?
14. Heterosexuals are noted for assigning themselves and each other to narrowly restricted, stereotyped sex roles. Why do you cling to such unhealthy role-playing?
15. How can you enjoy a fully satisfying sexual experience or deep emotional rapport with a person of the opposite sex, when the obvious physical, biological, and temperamental differences between you are so vast? How can a man understand what pleases a woman sexually or vice versa?
16. Why do heterosexuals place so much emphasis on sex?
17. With all the societal support marriage receives, the divorce rate is spiraling. Why are there so few stable relationships among heterosexuals?
18. How could the human race survive if everyone were heterosexual like you, considering the menace of overpopulation?
19. There seem to be very few happy heterosexuals. Techniques have been developed with which you might be able to change if you really want to. Have you considered trying aversion therapy?
20. A disproportionate number of criminals, welfare recipients, and other irresponsible or antisocial types are heterosexual. Why would anyone want to hire a heterosexual for a responsible position?
21. Do heterosexuals hate and/or distrust others of their own sex? Is that what makes them heterosexual?
22. Why are heterosexuals so promiscuous?
23. Why do you make it a point of attributing heterosexuality to famous people? Is it to justify your own heterosexuality?

EXHIBIT 7.1
Affectional Orientation (*Continued*)

24. Could you really trust a heterosexual therapist or counselor to be objective and unbiased? Don't you fear he or she might be inclined to influence you in the direction of her or his own leanings?

Questions for Discussion and Thought
- Did any of the questions seem absurd to you? If so, why?
- How do you think these types of questions feel to people who are sexual minorities?
- How did it feel to be in the shoes of a sexual minority while reading these questions?
- Is homosexuality a form of deviance requiring explanation in any way in which heterosexuality isn't?
- What does reading these questions tell you about what we say about interpersonal sexuality?

Note. Adapted from "Heterosexual Questionnaire," by M. Rochlin, 1982, *M: Gentle Men for Gender Justice, 8,* p. 9.

federal health insurance under Medicare, there were numerous studies demonstrating a systematic failure to prevent, detect, or treat health problems of older patients as aggressively or as well as for younger patients. This report was backed by a review of numerous studies documenting this very problem (Lebowitz & Niederehe, 1992). Little has been done to change this phenomenon over more than a decade since this article was published. For example, older adults have been repeatedly found to receive less aggressive medical treatment in both outpatient and inpatient settings for a wide range of medical services (Belgrave, 1993; Bell, Micke, & Kasa, 1998; Bowling, 1999).

Older adults appear to be underserved in the area of mental health as well. They have historically made up a very small proportion of the caseloads of mental health workers, are generally underserved in outpatient settings, and have long been the recipients of general reluctance to serve by mental health professionals (Gatz & Smyer, 1992; Hillerbrand & Shaw, 1990; Kastenbaum, 1963; VandenBos, Stapp, & Kilburg, 1981). These difficulties in service exist despite the preponderance of evidence that older clients respond positively to therapeutic interventions (e.g., Scogin & McElreath, 1994). It is important to note that biased behavior and attitudes against older adults among mental health practitioners might be intertwined with biases against people who have poorer health overall (Braithwaite, 1986; James & Haley, 1995). These forms of negative stereotypes and attitudes against those in poor health were first documented and labeled *healthism* by Gekoski and Knox (1990).

Research has provided evidence that perceived age discrimination is associated with harm to psychological well-being among older adults (Garstka, Schmitt, Branscombe, & Hummert, 2004). More specifically, age discrimination has been shown to have negative effects on employee satisfaction of older adults in the workplace (Hassell & Perrewe, 1993; McMullin & Marshall, 2001; Orpen, 1995). This is particularly evident in the fields of acting and computer technologies, as well as jobs requiring manual dexterity, such as the garment industry, in which older adults have a harder time finding work despite their qualifications.

Counselors who seek to develop ICE must increase their knowledge of age-based (ageist) biases in society as well as in therapeutic practice. In Western societies, ageist attitudes appear to be stronger and more prevalent in men than in women and strongest among young adults (Fraboni, Saltstone, & Hughes, 1990; Kalavar, 2001; Kite et al., 2005; Rupp, Vodanovich, & Credé, 2005). Young male counselors should therefore pay particular heed to the likelihood that they may be more susceptible to ageist attitudes and biases. Of course, female counselors can also develop these same problems and thus must also be vigilant. Exhibit 7.2 is designed to help professionals develop better ICE in relation to ageism.

The young are also susceptible to age bias. The term used to identify this form of bias and oppression is *adultism*. Adultism is bias against and oppression of young people through attitudinal, systematic, and cultural discrimination. Although this concept is relatively new to the social sciences and thus not very carefully studied to date, there is preliminary evidence that such oppression also plays a role in Western society (Rupp et al., 2005). Examples of adultism include stereotypes about young people (lazy, mean, angry, self-absorbed, silly) and failure to include young people in decisions made at home, in the classroom, in developing Individual Education Plans (IEP), in school boards, in community agencies, in city councils, and in drafting legislation. As a more specific example of this form of discrimination, the U.S. federal law requires that IEP teams include parents, a Special Education teacher, a person who can interpret evaluation results, a school system representative, and a transition services agency representative (when transition is discussed). The actual student is not required to be present with the exception of transition meetings. The U.S. Department of Education recommends that the members of an IEP team include the student as well. Unfortunately, inclusion of children in key decisions about their lives is not yet uniformly practiced.

A key difference to consider when comparing adultism and ageism is the relative permanence of the lower status in society. Older adults will never be able to regain the status they had when they were middle-aged adults, but younger people will inevitably move into this higher status category. It is likely that these differential expectations of status mobility may affect emotional and cognitive responses to age discrimination and bias, with the younger group generally handling the bias better than the older. This may explain why social scientists continue to focus on ageism much more than they do adultism. Nonetheless, counselors should also consider issues of age discrimination and bias against the young as they seek to develop ICE.

EXHIBIT 7.2
Learning to Grow Old

Objective

To understand the constraints faced by the culture of older adults.

Procedure

The group is given a list of 25 items and they are each asked to identify the top 10 priorities for them personally from this list. They should pick those priorities most essential to their "quality of life." The priorities are as follows:

1. Helping others/community involvement
2. Exercise
3. Self-respect
4. Health
5. Happiness and inner peace
6. Mobility
7. Pets
8. Independence
9. Hobbies
10. Sports
11. Safety/security
12. Music and the arts
13. Faith/religious/spiritual development
14. Love/opportunity to love
15. Family/relationships with relatives
16. Sex/intimate relationships
17. Friends/relationships with friends
18. Work/gainful activity
19. Humor
20. Travel
21. Creativity/self-expression
22. Finances/financial security
23. Freedom/choices
24. Wisdom/intellectual development
25. Shopping

When everyone has identified their 10 priorities, tell them that 10 years have passed and they will have to give up 3 of these priorities because of aging. When they have crossed off 3 of their "best" priorities, then tell them that 20 years have passed and they will have to give up 3 more priorities. When they have crossed 3 more priorities off the list, then tell them that 30 years have passed and they will have to cross off 3 more priorities. This leaves them with only 1 of the 10 priorities left.

In debriefing, you may want to compare the similarities and differences among group members regarding the one remaining priority. You will also want to have the members tell how they felt giving up their quality of life. What were the consequences of having to give up these priorities that were so meaningful? Ask them if they thought the answer would be different if they were to do the exercise over again.

Insight

Growing old is a process of narrowing your priorities.

Note. From *Culture-Centered Counseling Interventions: Striving for Accuracy* (pp. 291–292), by P. B. Pedersen, 1997. Thousand Oaks, CA: Sage. Copyright 1997 by Sage. Adapted with permission.

To focus on issues of adultism and stereotypes about young people, consider asking yourself the following questions:

1. How do I communicate with young people? Do I "talk down" to them or do I try to talk to them with more balance in power?
2. Can I remember what it is like to be 4? 8? 13? 16?
3. How much time do I take to know many young people? What is important to them? What are they thinking about?
4. Am I willing to create time, space, and support for young people's ideas at home, at school, and in the community?
5. Do I respect the ideas and thoughts of people younger than me? How often do I put their ideas into practice or at least consider them when making decisions and forming opinions?

PHYSICAL AND MENTAL CAPACITY ISSUES

According to a census report, approximately 20% of the U.S. population (54 million people) are disabled (McNeil, 2001). Thirty-three million of these people, or 12% of the U.S. population, are considered to have a severe disability. These numbers provide evidence that the people who have disabilities are the largest minority group in the United States. People who are disabled tend to have a more difficult time getting work than those who are able-bodied. For example, Kruse (1998) found that twice as many people with disabilities who are unemployed live in poverty than those without disabilities who are unemployed.

Ableism is a system of discrimination and exclusion that oppresses people who have mental, cognitive, emotional, and physical disabilities. This system is based on strongly held beliefs perpetuated by the public and private media about health, productivity, attractiveness, and the value of human life. These beliefs function in combination to create an environment that is commonly hostile, unfriendly, or unyielding to people whose mental, physical, and sensory abilities are not within the scope of what is currently defined as socially acceptable (Rauscher & McClintock, 1996).

Physical violence against people with disabilities has been widespread and has often operated under the auspices of the state, including even forced sterilization. A sadly powerful example of violent bias against the disabled is the story of Tracy Latimer, a young girl with cerebral palsy. In 1993, Tracy was murdered by her father because he found her "suffering" to be unbearable (Kafer, 2003). Saxton (1998) argued that the legacy of violence toward the physically disabled can be traced in the widespread assumption that all pregnant women want to screen their fetuses for possible disabilities and would choose abortion if any such "defects" were found.

Although we are forced to use the term *disability*, it is important to acknowledge the profoundly important feelings and emotions that society has attached to that and other similar terms to label special populations. Stone (2005) was sensitive to the meaning of words and to the importance of relationships in serving people with disabilities. On the one hand, there is a "culture of disability" in which people with a disability share a unique perspective with one another, acknowledge implicit rules for interaction, use a preferred vocabulary to express meanings, and have other markers of a cultural group that are less familiar to people who do not have a disability. This unique perspective is celebrated and acknowledged by the community of people with disabilities as a legitimate group in its own right, without reference to or judgment by those groups or individuals who do not "belong." On the other hand, there is a treasure of information in Stone's book about similarities and differences in how disability is viewed and managed across the country cultures of China, Jamaica, Korea, Haiti, Mexico, the Dominican Republic, and Vietnam. From a global perspective, disability can be viewed both as a separate culture and as a special perspective within other cultures.

Stone (2005) presented many new ideas. The book is focused primarily on new immigrants as a minority typically controlled by the majority culture. Many problems of language, housing, employment, understanding, and being understood by service providers come up that are magnified when the minority groups are served by majority-group providers. Stone sought to train majority providers to be more accurate, meaningful, and appropriate in their service.

Stone (2005) emphasized the importance of providing services as an educational process in which the target population is not referred to as a patient or client but more likely as a student or a consumer, emphasizing the person's role as a user of services. Another important distinction is in the use of "culture brokering" as a process of facilitating and mediating between the culture of the consumer and the host culture of the majority group provider. The importance of service providers becoming directly involved in the helping process, rather than maintaining objectivity and distance in the pretense of neutrality, is rapidly gaining credibility as service providers become more activist and less passive when confronted by social injustice.

Exhibit 7.3 defines and lists the principles of universal design and is provided to evaluate one's awareness of physical and mental capacity issues.

CLASS AND SOCIOECONOMIC STATUS

The three key cultural cornerstones of multicultural theory, research, and practice are race, gender, and social class (Pope-Davis & Coleman, 2001). Although most people in the United States do not like to talk about or acknowledge the existence of social class (Mantsios, 1998), it is one of the

EXHIBIT 7.3
Physical and Mental Capacity Issues

Read the following definition of universal design and the principles of universal design, then contemplate or discuss the questions that follow.

Definition
- Universal design is an approach to the design of products, services, and environments to be usable by as many people as possible regardless of age, ability, or situation.
- Universal design is a relatively new paradigm that emerged from barrier-free or accessible design and assistive technology. Barrier-free design and assistive technology provide a level of accessibility for people with disabilities, but they also often result in separate and stigmatizing solutions, for example, a ramp that leads to a different entry to a building than a main stairway.
- Universal design is intended to present broad-spectrum solutions that help everyone, not just people with disabilities.
- Universal design is built on recognition of the importance of how things look. For example, although built-up handles is an approach to making utensils more usable for people with gripping limitations, some companies introduced larger, easy-to-grip, and attractive handles as a feature of mass-produced utensils. They appeal to a wide range of consumers.

Principles of Universal Design
1. Equitable use
   The design is useful and marketable to people with diverse abilities.
   Guidelines include the following.
   a. Provide the same means of use for all users: identical whenever possible; equivalent when not.
   b. Avoid segregating or stigmatizing any users.
   c. Provisions for privacy, security, and safety should be equally available to all users.
   d. Make the design appealing to all users.

2. Flexibility in use
   The design accommodates a wide range of individual preferences and abilities.
   Guidelines include the following.
   a. Provide choice in methods of use.
   b. Accommodate right- or left-handed access and use.
   c. Facilitate the user's accuracy and precision.
   d. Provide adaptability to the user's pace.

3. Simple and intuitive
   Use of the design is easy to understand, regardless of the user's experience, knowledge, language skills, or current concentration level.
   Guidelines include the following.
   a. Eliminate unnecessary complexity.
   b. Be consistent with user expectations and intuition.
   c. Accommodate a wide range of literacy and language skills.
   d. Arrange information consistent with its importance.
   e. Provide effective prompting and feedback during and after task completion.

4. Perceptible information
   The design communicates necessary information effectively to the user, regardless of ambient conditions or the user's sensory abilities.
   Guidelines include the following.
   a. Use different modes (e.g., pictorial, verbal, tactile) for redundant presentation of essential information.

EXHIBIT 7.3
Physical and Mental Capacity Issues (*Continued*)

b. Provide adequate contrast between essential information and its surroundings.
c. Maximize "legibility" of essential information.
d. Differentiate elements in ways that can be described (i.e., make it easy to give instructions or directions).
e. Provide compatibility with a variety of techniques or devices used by people with sensory limitations.

5. Tolerance for error
The design minimizes hazards and the adverse consequences of accidental or unintended actions.
Guidelines include the following.
   a. Arrange elements to minimize hazards and errors: most used elements, most accessible; hazardous elements eliminated, isolated, or shielded.
   b. Provide warnings of hazards and errors.
   c. Provide fail-safe features.
   d. Discourage unconscious action in tasks that require vigilance.

6. Low physical effort
The design can be used efficiently and comfortably and with a minimum of fatigue.
Guidelines include the following.
   a. Allow user to maintain a neutral body position.
   b. Use reasonable operating forces.
   c. Minimize repetitive actions.
   d. Minimize sustained physical effort.

7. Size and space for approach and use
Appropriate size and space is provided for approach, reach, manipulation, and use regardless of user's body size, posture, or mobility.
Guidelines include the following.
   a. Provide a clear line of sight to important elements for any seated or standing user.
   b. Make reach to all components comfortable for any seated or standing user.
   c. Accommodate variations in hand and grip size.
   d. Provide adequate space for the use of assistive devices or personal assistance.

Questions for Thought or Discussion
1. Of the activities you have participated in today, which would have been difficult or impossible? If you
   • were in a wheelchair,
   • had a physical impairment such as blindness or deafness,
   • could not speak or read English,
   • had to carry a supplemental tank of oxygen, or
   • were a person with a learning disability.
2. How well is the world around us designed with the needs of all in mind?
3. What are the values underlying the principles of universal design?
4. In what ways should these values inform the work of counseling?
   a. How can counselors focus on career issues in a way that is in the best interest of all students?
   b. It has been suggested that effective counselors empower their clients who have disabilities by fostering inclusion in the broader workforce and in society. How can we do this as counselors?

Note. From *The Principles of Universal Design,* by the Center for Universal Design, 1997, Raleigh: North Carolina State University, College of Design. Retrieved August 26, 2007, from http://www.design.ncsu.edu/cud/about_ud/udprinciples.htm

more significant dimensions in our lives (Fitzgerald & Betz, 1994; Fouad & Brown, 2001). Despite the importance of this variable, it has been quite understudied as it relates to counseling and psychology (Brown, Fukunaga, Umemoto, & Wicker, 1996; Frable, 1997; W. M. Liu et al., 2004; T. L. Robinson & Howard-Hamilton, 2000). There is evidence, however, that social class is a significant variable in efficacy of various forms of counseling (Carter, 1991; Luzzo, 1992; Nicks, 1985).

Classism is the systematic oppression of poor people and those who work for wages by those who have more wealth and access to control over the necessary resources by which other people make their living. Classism is maintained by a system of beliefs that ranks people according to economic status, status of their job, level of education, and "breeding." Classist assumptions are that the working class is less articulate and intelligent than those of the upper class. Classism serves as a mechanism to keep people down or "in their place." Classism in society defines the norms in society on the basis of the upper middle class and the wealthy. All that is "normal" or "acceptable" is based on the attitudes, beliefs, and behaviors of the relatively wealthy. It is not uncommon for most counselors to accept this standard as the norm and thus buy in to the myth that the grand majority of the country is middle class.

There is a lack of clear agreement on how one determines which class a person is in. As the data we present subsequently clarify, if it is defined by who has control over the majority of the wealth in society, at least 80% of the U.S. population is middle class, working class, working poor, or impoverished. This is despite the fact that the grand majority of U.S. citizens prefer to self-label as "middle class" under the assumption that they have the same status in society as the upper middle class. Although a majority of people refer to themselves as middle class, most do not enjoy the privileges afforded to the upper 20% of society. Another concept key to understanding classism in society is that of elitism. *Elitism* is an assumption of superiority and privilege based on beliefs and attitudes that a particular group of people are those who deserve to be in charge and whose views ultimately matter most. In this way, elitists see themselves and others supposed to be like them as having privilege over others who do not equal their abilities or attributes.

The elitism underlying classism is maintained, in part, on the maintenance of a set of social myths in U.S. society. Mantsios (1998) wrote of four prevailing and contradicting myths that are maintained in society through the media and other institutions.

Myth 1: The United States is essentially a class-free society. All people are equal under the law and all have equal access to education, health care, and opportunity.

Myth 2: The United States is fundamentally a middle-class nation. Most Americans are in the middle class, and the middle class is growing.

Myth 3: Everyone in the United States is getting wealthier.

Myth 4: Everyone in the United States has an equal chance to succeed financially or to live the "American Dream."

Many counselors hold tight to these myths, working under the supposition that their clients do not experience hardships based on social class differences any more than those that they face. However, the myths fall apart when confronted with the realities of social class differences. To increase readers' knowledge of the realities of social class in the United States, the following are some facts that fly in the face of these myths.

There are numerous class differences in U.S. society, the middle class is not growing, and the wealthiest are getting wealthier. Approximately 31 million American people, or about 11%, live in poverty (U.S. Census Bureau, 2001b). In the United States, 1% of the population own 47% of the wealth, and the next 19% of Americans, often referred to as the "upper middle class" (higher paid professionals like lawyers, doctors, bankers, managers, or heads of corporations) own 44% of the wealth. The remaining 80% of the population share ownership over only 10% of the wealth (U.S. Census Bureau, 2001b). In the past three decades, the wealth distribution has moved increasingly in the favor of the upper 1%, as in 1973, the richest fifth of the nation owned 44% of the wealth (Cassidy, 1998). In this way it is clear that the richest are getting richer and all others are getting poorer. In effect, 94% of the total wealth in the United States is controlled by merely 20% of U.S. households (Reasons et al., 2002).

We do not all have an equal chance to succeed financially. As a result of intergenerational transfer of class, the class we are born into greatly affects the financial opportunities we will encounter. The strongest predictor that a person will be very wealthy is whether or not he or she was born very wealthy, and the strongest predictor that a person will be impoverished is whether or not he or she was born impoverished (Rubinstein, 1993).

Poverty creates multiple dilemmas in the lives of those who are impoverished. According to the U.S. Census Bureau (2001b), of those people living in the lowest 20% of income, 38% regularly have trouble meeting at least one basic need, and 25% have ongoing difficulty with more than one basic need. Further working against the interest of those of lower social status is the fact that a person's social status appears to be directly related to the likelihood that he or she will be successful in education (De Lone, 1978; Sewell, 1971). More specifically, growing up impoverished appears to be related to both academic failure and problematic behavior (Duncan & Brooks-Gunn, 2000; Linver, Brooks-Gunn, & Kohen, 2002; McLoyd, 1998). This relationship appears to hold true today, as SAT test scores correlate strongly with relative family income (e.g., College Entrance Examination Board and Educational Testing Service, 1996; see Table 7.1).

TABLE 7.1
Average Combined Scores by Income on the SAT

Family income	Median score
More than $100,000	1,129
$80,000 to $90,000	1,085
$70,000 to $80,000	1,064
$60,000 to $70,000	1,049
$50,000 to $60,000	1,034
$40,000 to $50,000	1,016
$30,000 to $40,000	992
$20,000 to $30,000	964
$10,000 to $20,000	920
Less than $10,000	873

Note. From *1996 College-Bound Seniors Profile Reports by State.* Copyright © 1996 The College Board, http://www.collegeboard.com. Reproduced with permission.

Socioeconomic status difference is the great connector of the majority of the significant oppressions in society. A survey of U.S. Census Bureau (2001b) data quickly clarifies that race and gender interact in powerful ways. For example, White-headed households are less likely to live in poverty than non-White households regardless of living situation. Furthermore, households led by females with no male present demonstrate even further discrepancies. Those female-headed households that are Latino and African American are two times as likely to live in poverty as White female-headed households (U.S. Census Bureau, 1995). Table 7.2 demonstrates that the various key cultural identity constructs all interface with that of social class in a powerful manner. From this table, it becomes clear that Latinos and African Americans are more than twice as likely as those of the total U.S. population to

TABLE 7.2
Percentage of Total U.S. Population Reporting Not Having
Enough Food in Household by Selected Characteristics:
October 1995 Through January 1996

Group	%
Hispanic (of any race)	11.7
Lowest 20% of households by income	11.2
Black non-Hispanic	9.3
Children under age 18	7.3
Total population	4.8
Age 60 or older	1.9
Highest 20% of households by income	0.8

Note. Data from the U.S. Census Bureau, 1993, Panel of the Survey of Income and Program Participation, October 1995–January 1996.

report that they do not have enough food to eat on a regular basis (U.S. Census Bureau, 1996).

As social class plays such a dominant role in the lives of so many of our clients, it is imperative that we put time into developing accurate knowledge about it. Counselors seeking to develop ICE must be versed in the emotional, mental, and social costs of poverty in society at large as well as with those whom we serve. Many counselors tend to overlook the role that social class plays in the lives of their clients. Instead they assume equivalent daily stress as well as comparable overall opportunities between themselves and their clients, when class differences belie these assumptions. All too often, counselors approach the therapeutic relationship under the assumption that their clients simply have to make better decisions, see things differently, or experience better motivation, when in fact the counselors' viewpoint is tainted with classist, elitist, and culturally encapsulated assumptions.

Exhibit 7.4 is designed to help readers and students develop their knowledge with regard to the role that social class plays in clients' lives. The emphasis of this activity is to focus learning on the institutionalization of classism.

CONVERGENCE AND SALIENCE

Although all key cultural identity constructs can and often do converge, race has a tendency to be one of the most salient variables to people of color owing to both historical and current dominant discourse. Because race is a generally visible identity construct, people commonly respond to others on the basis of assumptions, biases, and stereotypes perpetuated through historical discourse. In the United States, it is not uncommon for White people not to see race as a key cultural identity construct for themselves because they experience White privilege, as discussed in chapters 4 and 6. Those without this privilege are generally much more aware of this construct as a key factor in their identity. It is also common that other highly salient cultural identity constructs that converge with race are some of the more visible ones, such as gender and ability. These more highly visible identities can cause an experience such as that discussed in chapter 4, in which the university professor translates her experience as an African American woman in academia as paying a "double tax" on a daily basis.

FINAL THOUGHTS ON INTELLECTUAL UNDERSTANDING

The key cultural identity construct of class or socioeconomic status plays a significant role in the manner that it converges with that of race when it comes to impact on the family and individual. The key cultural identity

EXHIBIT 7.4
Social Class Pyramids

Preparing for the Pyramid Activity

For this activity, you will need a picture, drawing, or model of a pyramid. Have the students look at the pyramid as a geometric figure for a moment. Then ask the group the following:

- Is it easy to move or change the shape of a pyramid?
- Is it easy to tip over or turn it over?
    (Typical answers include "It's sturdy," "It's solid," "Most of the weight is on the bottom," and "It would be hard to move, tip over, or turn over.")
- Assuming social class in the United States is structured like a pyramid, is it easy to move or change its shape? Turn it over?
    (Typical answers include "It looks pretty set up," "It seems solid," "Most of the people are on the bottom," and "It's hard to move or change it.")

Explain the following:

> Like the other oppressions, this structure of classism is kept in place by institutions. An *institution* is a persistent structure that is built to shape how people live, grow, and learn. Institutions define how communities develop and function and may function to bring people together or to keep people separated.

Instructions: Pyramid Activity

Have students form groups of 4 to work on the following pyramids project. Give each group butcher paper and markers as well as a copy of the brainstorm questions (see below) for this activity. When groups are formed and materials distributed, have each group draw a large pyramid on the paper. For the project, assign one of the following institutions to each group of students, who in turn will write the institution name as a title on their page.

- Government
- History texts
- Educational systems
- Real estate/housing/land ownership
- Business/jobs/corporations
- Criminal justice/prison system
- Media/entertainment industry
- Banks/financial institutions
- Organized sports

Have each group brainstorm and write answers into and around their pyramids for the following questions. (For examples, see "Examples of Possible Answers for Pyramids Activity" discussed subsequently.) Students are to write down all answers they can think of.

Conduct the activity as a fast-moving brainstorm, moving the teams quickly through each question. Circulate among groups to assist where necessary.

Brainstorm Questions: Pyramid Activity

1. Who is at the top in this pyramid? This can include those people or organizations who have the most wealth within the institution (e.g., highest paid people who work in the institution) as well as who the institution most supports, protects, and keeps wealthy (e.g., who the institution benefits or works for most). Write your answers at the apex of the pyramid.
2. Who is at the bottom of this pyramid? This can include both who is poorest (lowest paid or nonpaid people who work in the institution) and who the institution most excludes, makes invisible, or keeps poor. Write your answers across the bottom of the pyramid.

EXHIBIT 7.4
Social Class Pyramids (*Continued*)

3. How are the people who are lower in the pyramid exploited by being made to work for, serve, or provide profit for those who are at the top? Write answers across the middle of the pyramid.

4. What ways does the institution function to hide or cover up social class differences or distract people from seeing social class differences (i.e., that we are not all on a level playing field)? Write answers along right and left sides of the pyramid.
For the last two questions, have groups turn papers over. On the other side, draw a circle. Fill the circle with answers to the following questions:

5. What are possible ways this institution could (and even does) work *against* classism, to promote equality?

6. Write in any examples of people or movements you can think of who have resisted class separation in this institution: people from history or people you know.

Discussion: Pyramid Activity

• Have students report their findings from the various groups.
• What is one new insight you have gained from this activity?
• How do you feel that classism relates to racism?
• How do you feel that classism relates to sexism?
• How do you feel that classism relates to ableism?
• What are some issues that various groups might have better considered?

Examples of Possible Answers for Pyramid Activity (Government and History Texts)

Following are samples of answers that the group might generate for the institutions in this activity.

Government
The top:
• The wealthy (inheritance laws); chief executives and legislators (congress people, senators, representatives); wealthy financial contributors to political campaigns; industry lobbies (e.g., pharmaceutical, airline, agribusiness, and tobacco industries).

The bottom:
• The poor, low-income people without access to legislators; noncitizens such as new immigrants, temporary workers, undocumented workers; disenfranchised people (people not allowed to vote, e.g., young people, people with criminal records, noncitizens).

The exploited:
• Unequal taxation (lower taxes, tax shelters, and tax breaks for wealthy); the ability to spend money unfettered on lobbying and campaigns considered free speech (the wealthy have more access to this form of free speech than the poor, government funds from taxpayers diverted from social service and education toward defense, law enforcement and protection of property and business).

Distract, hide, or cover up social class differences:
• Voting system gives the appearance of full choice and equal participation of all citizens in government; the three-part government system (executive, legislative, judicial) is supposed to guarantee "checks and balances" that prevent any one group of people from controlling the government for their own interests.

Government working against classism:
• Voter registration drives and changes to laws to make registering easier for the working poor; citizen advocacy groups; the government as an employer prescribing equal access and employment for women, People of Color, and others; Bill of Rights

(*continued*)

EXHIBIT 7.4
Social Class Pyramids (*Continued*)

for all citizens; "New Deal" legislation during the U.S. Great Depression to create jobs and promote greater equality and less differential between the rich and the poor; legal constraints against invasion of privacy; government regulation of industries to prevent unfair labor practices, environmental destruction.

Within-system resistance:
- Alternative, community-based, or "town hall" local forms of government; "people's" movements on behalf of all groups targeted for oppression; ongoing citizen movements to reform and improve government; "civil disobedience": actions, usually nonviolent, that citizens take to violate or protest laws they consider to be unjust.

History Texts
The top:
- Kings, rulers, military leaders, statesmen, "founding fathers."

The bottom:
- The poor, working class, soldiers, the conquered, the enslaved, immigrants, women, "the people."

The exploited:
- Women, people of color, the working class, immigrants, laborers, and accomplishments of masses of people ignored or made invisible.

Distract, hide, or cover up social class differences:
- "Heroes" version of history (history is written by the victors); description of development of the United States as a "class-free" and "melting-pot" society.

History books working against classism:
- The purpose of studying history is to find out the truth. History is continually revised and rewritten to find out "what really happened."

Within-system resistance:
- "People's" history emphasizing popular resistance, movements for women (her-story), immigrants, people of color, workers; oral histories (interviewing people who have direct experience) to uncover viewpoints and voices of people otherwise made invisible.

constructs of race, ability, age, and gender all should be considered within the context of class and socioeconomic status. In 2000, 25% of female-headed households, 22% of African Americans, and 21% of Latinos lived in poverty; in addition, 16.6% of all children lived in poverty, whereas 90% of all people over the age of 18 did not (U.S. Census Bureau, 2000). When categories are combined the numbers change, much in the same manner as the "double tax" previously mentioned. For example, in 1996, 32.6% of all female-headed households lived in poverty, but 50.9% of all Latino female-headed families lived in poverty (Lamison-White, 1997). It is thus important to consider relative privilege based on the salience of the key identity constructs that converge for each person with whom we work if we strive to have the intellectual understanding necessary to be culturally empathic.

8

INTEGRAL SKILLS:
HEARING OUR CULTURE
TEACHERS THROUGH EMPATHY

Helping professionals who seek to develop inclusive cultural empathy (ICE) will build on their awareness of assumptions and knowledge of identity constructs to develop the skill of "hearing" or imagining what clients are feeling and thinking but not saying as they hear the voices of their culture teachers in their internal dialogue. ICE provides access to the emotions and thoughts that clients cannot, or choose not to, articulate in therapy. Some of these messages will be positive and others will be negative. In our opinion, the more therapists are accurately aware of their client's negative and positive thoughts, the more likely it is that therapists will perceive the client's cultural context accurately (Pedersen, 2000b). Having accurate awareness and meaningful knowledge is a necessary but not sufficient condition for having appropriate skills. However, the greater the number of cultural differences between therapist and client, the more difficult it will be to imagine the client's internal dialogue.

An important skill for ICE is the ability to perceive affective and cognitive data behind the client's behaviors. If you are aware of the need for understanding context in order to interpret behaviors, and you gather specific knowledge about the contexts that shape behavior, then you are well on your way to developing this skill. Once you can perceive feelings and thoughts, the next step is to reflect back both sets of messages without stereotyping, judging, or classifying, so that the client gets an authentic view of her or his situation. This process requires the helping professional to go beyond her or his own feelings and thoughts. Then the therapist can sort out the information from the client's perspective and generate accurate labels for the client's thoughts and feelings in a way that makes sense for the client (Goldstein & Michaels, 1985; Keefe, 1976). Finally, the therapist synthesizes all the facts and variables into a pattern and selects an appropriate intervention strategy based on that pattern. The most inclusive intervention strategy is that which allows the client to define her or his ideal outcome as well as the boundaries for achieving that outcome.

In this and the following chapter we teach you how to use internal dialogue as a tool for understanding a client's belief system, where it comes from, how it works, and how it feels. We review the clinical literature on internal dialogue and self-talk and give detailed examples of how to reflect feelings and meanings through inclusive, culturally sensitive ways. Finally, we return to the concept of balance in ICE first developed in chapter 3 and show you how to help clients leverage their internalized voices to find life balance.

PURPOSE OF INTERNAL DIALOGUE

Professionals using ICE skills will learn to hear or imagine what clients are feeling and thinking but not saying. Why might a client leave potentially relevant feelings and thoughts unsaid when working with a helping professional? Perhaps the client does not like the counselor or feels uncomfortable with the experience of being "helped" but does not wish to hurt the counselor's feelings. Or, perhaps the client fears that voicing negative feelings and thoughts will only exacerbate the issue he or she is trying to resolve. Many times, however, clients' inner thoughts, both positive and negative, are not rational and coherent statements, and they may be inextricably intertwined with emotions. If expressed aloud, these thoughts and emotions may not conform to anyone's accustomed forms of meaning and semantic structure.

Models of Internal Dialogue

One way counselors can learn the skill of hearing inner dialogue is by using or adapting the triad training model (TTM; Pedersen, 2004). This training paradigm involves a role play in which the client's role is conceptualized as, and played by, three people: the client, a "procounselor," and an "anticounselor." The pro- and anticounselors' job is to make clear—literally, to voice—the positive and negative thoughts and feelings of the client during the counseling experience. The TTM is described in more detail later in the chapter. First, we review the research on internal dialogue, its purpose, and its usefulness in counseling and psychotherapy.

Little is known about the cognitive process of self-awareness and self-consciousness. Self-verbalization was formerly considered to be nonfunctional and a sign of immaturity, but with a better understanding of the link between inner speech and self-awareness, it is being given more importance (Vygotsky, 1987). As mentally ill persons sometimes hear voices, individuals who are not mentally ill, including respected leaders and a great variety of the general public, may also hear voices (Liester, 1996). This inner or private speech is typically in terms of a dialogue with two sides, identities or interactors participating, one typically in a positive and the other typically in a negative role. The inner voices are not typically evenly or equally balanced in terms of the positive and negative messages.

We assume that our internal dialogue mediates our understanding or comprehension of the outside world. Self-statements influence behavior in the same way that statements by others do. Clients and counselors in therapy need to monitor their own thinking and interacting both with others and within themselves. These assumptions seem to square with clinical approaches such as cognitive behavior change, in which clients are encouraged to change the "scripted nature" of their behavior (Beck, 1996; Ellis, 1987; Meichenbaum, 1986; Pedersen, 2000b).

Mindfulness Meditation Exercise

It is necessary to be both present and aware of our own thoughts and internal dialogue. Mindfulness meditation is a strategy that we have used to help our awareness of self and others. Mindfulness or mindfulness meditation is not a new concept. Buddhists have practiced it for over 2,500 years. Similar practices can be found throughout the histories of most cultures. The practice involves becoming aware or gaining insight by living in the present moment. Mindfulness is the process of placing the mind firmly in the present and keeping it absorbed in the task that is being performed.

ICE practitioners need to be fully present to gain understanding and appreciation of the complex combination of variables that create each individual. This process further allows for the creation of a context that is safe for the client. A psychological climate or place of understanding is created that is devoid of all judgment. Researchers have shown that when a person is in a mindful state, others in the room are also affected positively (Goleman, 2003).

There is no wrong way to do meditation other than to not do it. The process involves setting aside 10 to 40 minutes each day to sit quietly and become aware of all that is going on around your world. Concentrate on your breathing, and learn to breath deeply and slowly. As thoughts enter into your mind, let them go and return your focus to breathing. The following is one way to begin a practice of mindfulness meditation.

Create a quiet place and repeat this same routine each day at the same time. You can sit on the floor or in a chair as long as you can keep your back straight and your breathing effortless. Make sure that your hands are supported and your neck is comfortably positioned.

Learn to see things as they really are. Watch your breath for several days and you will begin to pay close attention to your sensations. You will realize that you are obsessed with cravings—food, warmth, all sorts of desires—as well as aversion to unpleasant things. Then you realize the impermanence of it all. Everything changes. The pain in the knee moves to the neck. One obsession replaces another, and another.

Take a couple of slightly deeper breaths, and allow your body to relax. Feel your shoulders ease, your face soften. Feel a sense of letting go of the day, and bring yourself into this here and now. Close your eyes.

Experience the contact of your body with the floor. Imagine giving the whole of your weight to the ground, just letting the ground support you. Try to have a sense of the weight of your torso falling directly down the pelvis into the earth.

Imagine that the more completely you give up the gross weight of your body, the lighter the body feels and the more easily energy can move in the body. So there is a feeling of the weight of your body being held by the earth, and at the same time you can feel the subtle energy in your body rising upward. There is an opposite yet complementary movement of weight and energy in your body.

So let your body settle into its posture, allowing your shoulders to relax, checking your belly and buttocks for any holding of energy, relaxing your face. Have a sense of your body becoming quiet, becoming still . . . of the space that your body takes up . . . and of the space around your body.

Now without any special effort, start to take notice of your breath. We don't need to grab at it—it is not going anywhere. It is always just there, waiting for us patiently to notice it. So we begin to notice it.

Follow it down your body, into the space inside your body. Notice how your body responds to the breath, the movement low down in your belly, the gentle expansion and contraction of your chest at the sides of your back.

As you sit with this breath coming and going, be aware of how you feel. Let the breath bring you in a simple and direct way to yourself, your feelings, at this moment. What is the tone of your being—light or dark, happy or sad, dull or excited? Just have a general sense of your self, your basic emotional state. Acknowledge your feelings.

Come back to the breath, coming and going. There is plenty of room for your feelings in the breath; allow them, like the breath, just to come and go.

Now begin to count the breaths, counting at the end of each outbreath, just marking the breath. Count to yourself; make the counting just strong enough to stay with the breath. If you lose count, start again at "one." It doesn't matter. The breath is still there, waiting for your attention. Just sit with the breath in this way for a few minutes.

Now we are going to make a small change. The breath is just the same, coming and going, but now we count at the beginning of the breath, just before we draw the breath in. So we are anticipating the breath by an instant. Count "one"—breathe in, breathe out; count "two"—breathe in, breathe out. . . . Let the breathing be easy, just follow it.

Keep your body relaxed, your face soft, not straining to stay with the breath; just come back to it whenever you feel your mind wandering and moving away. Just use the counting to help you keep an eye on your mind. If you lose count, start again at "one." Never mind how it happened, just start again. So you are counting in sets of 10, just staying with the breath a few minutes.

Now let the counting fade into the breath; let it go. Here you are, just with the breath; there is nothing else in the whole world that you need to do just now. Just follow the breath. It does not matter if you lose it—it is always there, waiting for you to come back to it.

Just like watching the great ocean upon the shore, coming and going, feel the breath wash over you, and then withdraw. Feel the whole of the breath, each breath becoming the next. The great tide of your breath inside you—feel it in the body, filling the body, bringing life and energy into the body. Just you and the breath, coming and going. . . . Stay with the breath for a few minutes.

Now, while experiencing the whole of the breath, begin to notice the first sensation you experience as you draw in the breath—where the breath first "breaks" against your body. You're looking for a subtle sensation in your nostrils or at the back of your throat, wherever you first feel the breath as it enters your body.

Keeping your face relaxed, begin to gather your attention around this point, noticing more and more this detail of your breath. It is a constantly changing sensation, so it cannot be pinned down. If you try to take hold of it you will lose it. Attend to it, appreciate it, let it go. Don't force your attention but look for a sense of enjoying the sensation as it comes and goes with the breath. Spend a few minutes enjoying this sensation.

Now come back to the whole of the breath. Be aware of your body, be aware of the ground beneath you. Slowly become aware of the room around you and any sounds inside and outside the room. Have a sense of the outside world, and in your own time allow your eyes to open wide and your body to move.

Good cognitive therapy does not reduce the client's thinking to categorized irrational belief systems but rather tries to understand why that particular client appraises events in that particular way. Cognitive therapy seeks to understand both where the person is coming from and her or his idiosyncratic way of appraising events. Sometimes the person's thoughts and emotions about an event may appear irrational to the counselor but, given her or his way of seeing the world, the response may actually be entirely rational when seen from the client's perspective.

Once the counselor, and ultimately, the client can articulate those thoughts and feelings that were once strictly internal, the data can be leveraged for therapeutic change. Morin (1995) examined the characteristics of an effective internal dialogue for the mediation of self-awareness as a problem-solving task. Self-talk served to focus attention on the task, foster constant self-evaluation, and take the perspective of others. Morin (1993) suggested that two social mechanisms leading to self-awareness can be reproduced by self-talk. First, engaging in dialogues with oneself and fictitious persons permits the internalization of others' perspectives, and addressing comments to oneself about oneself as others might do leads to the acquisition of self-information. Second, self-observation is possible only when there is a distance between the individual and any potentially observable self-aspect as through self-talk, which conveys self-information through words in a continuous communication loop.

An individual's perception of another's perception of her- or himself is called a *metaperception*. The symbolic interactionists (Langer & Wurf, 1997) contend that metaperceptions are based on social feedback, going outside the self, whereas social cognitivists say metaperceptions are formed by self-perception, going inward. Dyadic social experience includes both a direct view of the self and a view of the other and a view of the other's view of the self. We not only look at ourselves but also look at others looking at ourselves. Langer and Wurf (1997) researched the importance of verbal and nonverbal feedback indicating both processes are important and noted,

> Results indicated that the feedback and the self are both important interactively: when the verbal element of the message is congruent with self-conception nonverbal sensitivity occurs, and metaperceptions are based on both the verbal and nonverbal components; when the verbal element of the message is self-incongruent, the evaluative implications of the nonverbal feedback do not matter. (p. 2)

A variety of strategies are available for incorporating internal dialogue into therapist training or direct service therapy processes as discussed in

Pedersen (2000b). Of these approaches, self-instruction is probably the best known, but others such as structured learning and psychodrama are available as well. The positive effects of including attention to self-talk in the counseling process are clearly documented and are adaptable to a variety of therapy styles. The notion of multiple selves as a kind of "inner family" is useful when applied to family therapy and systems theory. Hickson and Kriegler (1996) documented this inner-family process among clients in South Africa. This family metaphor provides a useful link of research on internal dialogue as it applies to direct service and to training for ICE skills.

THE TRIAD TRAINING MODEL AS A WAY TO PRACTICE HEARING INTERNAL DIALOGUE

Although we cannot know exactly the client's internal dialogue, we can assume that some of these messages are negative in their orientation, whereas other messages are positive in their orientation. The TTM gives counselors and other helping professionals a chance to experience hearing both sets of messages out loud during a simulated interview. The role of the client is played by three individuals. The client in the role play will be culturally different in some way from the counselor, whether the difference is nationality, ethnicity, age, gender, or another identity construct. The client, the procounselor, and the anticounselor are coached on how to provide continuous direct and immediate feedback on the counseling process (Pedersen, 2000b). The anticounselor seeks to explain the negative messages a client from that culture might be thinking but not saying, whereas a procounselor seeks to explain the positive messages in the client's mind. These thoughts tend to be infused with emotion as well as rational argument and are intended to evoke or provoke emotional reactions in the counselor. Although either an anticounselor or a procounselor may be used without the other, their combined influence is to "hear" the client's internal dialogue or hidden messages in both its positive and negative aspects.

Many sources of resistance to counseling across cultures consequently become explicit and articulate, even to a culturally different counselor, providing the foundation for ICE. The client's hidden messages articulated in the TTM also provide an abundance of other information the counselor will need. Although more research is needed, additional data on the TTM are being collected to determine its specific strengths and weaknesses in a variety of settings (Pedersen, 2000b), the hope being that trainees, having been exposed to the effect of cultural differences in role play, can generalize from these experiences to increase their expertise in attending to cultural details with real clients.

The setting of the simulated interview, the resource persons involved in the role play, and the type of debriefing that follows all deserve attention for the TTM to work well. First, the simulated interview needs to occur under conditions that the counselor and client consider "safe." For example, if the role players can be protected from real-world consequences of what they say in role, the role players are likely to feel safer. The simulation needs to reflect actual events in realistic ways and should be spontaneous and not scripted. The interview should be brief (8–10 minutes) to avoid overwhelming the counselor with information during or after the interview.

The person playing the role of the client should be in some way culturally different from the counselor. Resource persons selected as procounselor and anticounselor should, ideally, share one or more features of cultural identity with the client whose voices they are to represent, or at least have sufficient experience with that particular culture to allow them to speak authentically. Pro- and anticounselors should possess a vocabulary sufficiently wide to be able to articulate a range of positive and negative emotional and cognitive messages. Training of resource persons will increase their ability to respond immediately, use explicit descriptions, and be able to come up with positive or negative feedback for the counselor at any and all points during the interview. Learning the procounselor and anticounselor roles is best done by experiencing a series of role plays with debriefing feedback so that they "learn by doing" the role play itself.

The person playing the role of counselor should be able to move the interview along while simultaneously listening and responding to the procounselor and anticounselor. This can be a difficult skill to learn. We have found that feedback and improvement strategies can be more easily communicated during debriefing when a videotape of the entire interview is available.

In describing the TTM, it is important to understand the role of the procounselor and the anticounselor. These roles articulate the client's perspective within its cultural contexts, thus providing the counselor an opportunity to see the problem as something more than a diffuse abstraction. When the problem itself is embodied in the procounselor and anticounselor, the counselor can more easily empathize with the client's pro- and antiperspectives. The anticounselor is deliberately subversive in attempting to exaggerate mistakes by the counselor during the interview. The counselor and anticounselor are pulling in opposite directions, with the client judging which is "more right." The anticounselor articulates the negative, embarrassing, and impolite comments that a client might not otherwise say. The anticounselor attempts to distract the counselor, which trains the counselor to focus more intently on the client. These strategies force the counselor to become more aware of the client's perspective and examine her or his own defensiveness. As mentioned before, the anticounselor is trained to point out a counselor's inappropriate interventions immediately during the interview itself. The advantage of this approach is that it allows the counselor to recover from the mistake in the real time context of the interview rather than later and therefore practice recovery skills.

There are several things that an anticounselor might do in the interview to articulate the negative aspects of a client's internal dialogue. The anticounselor can build on positive aspects of the problem and the client's ambivalence; distract or sidetrack the counselor; attempt to keep the conversation superficial; attempt to obstruct communication between the counselor and client, physically and psychologically; annoy the counselor, forcing the counselor to deal with defensive reactions; exaggerate differences between the counselor and client to drive them farther apart; demand immediate and observable results from counseling; communicate privately with the client; identify scapegoats to encourage the counselor's and client's unrealistic perspectives; or attack the counselor's credibility and request that someone more expert be brought in.

These hidden messages of a client's negative internal dialogue are seldom addressed directly in counselor training. The TTM encourages the direct examination of hidden negative messages during the interview, circumventing the defensive "spin" that might otherwise attempt to explain the mistake after the fact. This helps the counselor develop skills for dealing with those negative messages during the actual interview process.

The procounselor attempts to articulate the hidden positive messages that might also be included in a client's internal dialogue. The procounselor helps both counselor and client articulate the counseling process as a potentially helpful activity. The procounselor functions as a facilitator for the counselor's effective responses. The procounselor understands how cultural differences between client and counselor may be affecting the interview process and is thus able to provide relevant background information to the counselor during the interview. The procounselor is not a cotherapist but an intermediate resource person who can guide the counselor through suggesting specific strategies and information that the client might otherwise be reluctant to volunteer. In these ways, the procounselor can reinforce the counselor's more successful strategies, both verbally and nonverbally.

The procounselor is a resource person to consult when the counselor is confused or in need of support. He or she makes explicit any information about the client that might facilitate the counselor's success. Rather than the counselor having to work alone, the procounselor provides a partner for the counselor to work with on the problem. The procounselor helps the counselor stay on track and avoid sensitive issues that might increase client resistance. The feedback a procounselor provides helps the counselor avoid mistakes and build on successful strategies.

The procounselor builds on positive and constructive aspects of the counseling interview through encouragement and support to the counselor, who may feel under attack by the anticounselor. The procounselor might provide that support by restating or reframing what either the client or counselor said, relating client or counselor statements to the basic underlying problem, offering approval or reinforcement to the client or the counselor when they are cooperating, reinforcing and emphasizing important insights that need to be discussed and expanded, reinforcing client statements as the client becomes more cooperative in the interview, or suggesting alternative strategies to the counselor when another strategy is not working.

In real counseling interviews, it usually takes several sessions to move from rapport building to problem solving because, at first, clients will not likely be able to or want to voice all the positive and negative inner dialogue. Having the pro- and anticounselors' feedback during simulated interviews allows the role-played client to move more rapidly toward honest feedback. This immediate availability of honest feedback accelerates the transition from rapport building to problem solving, so all involved in the simulation can get a feel for what that transition looks like in a short amount of time. The more role plays practiced, therefore, the more exposure counselors will have to this process of hearing internal dialogue and the transition from rapport building to problem solving. We believe it is in precisely this transition that ICE begins to grow and be nurtured.

Exhibit 8.1 provides an example of a role play using the TTM. The excerpt of the transcript from a simulated interview allows the reader to try out the model and determine its usefulness in local settings.

DEBRIEFING

The two primary culture-centered skills that were demonstrated in the interview in Exhibit 8.1 were (a) seeing the problem from the client's perspective and (b) increasing the counselor's ability to be nondefensive. When the counselor was confronted with the Black stereotype, which she later said was very off-putting, she did not respond defensively but rather included that perspective in her understanding of the client's perspective. In C13, the client brought up the topic of cultural differences as an explicit topic. In C26, the topic of "saving face" was introduced as a cultural phenomenon. In T48, the counselor demonstrated nondefensive behavior.

The TTM lends itself to use in group settings such as graduate classes as well as professional training and continuing education or clinical supervision groups. As mentioned earlier, it can also be used by one or more clinicians at their own practice site, as long as adequate training can be provided to resource people.[1]

---

[1]Videotapes demonstrating the triad training model are available through Microtraining Associates, Inc., 141 Walnut Street, Hanover, MA 02339, (888) 505-5576 (phone/fax).

EXHIBIT 8.1
Example Transcript Excerpt From a Triad Training Model
Simulated Interview

The following brief transcript of a Black female therapist working with a Japanese American female client provides a sample of how the procounselor and anticounselor interact with the counselor and client. In the transcript, C represents the client, T represents the therapist, P represents the procounselor, and A represents the anticounselor. The letter indicates the role and the number indicates the numerical order of statements made by the person in that role.

Interview 1: Black Female Therapist
C1: Hi, my name is Noella, and I will be playing the role of the client coming in for the first session for a presenting problem.
A2: Hi, my name is Leanne, and I will be playing the anticounselor, and my role today will be to bring forth the negative thoughts and stereotypes that may be found in the minds of the client and the counselor.
P3: Hi, my name is Melody, and I'll be playing the role of the procounselor. My main job today is to provide insight into the positive thoughts and concerns for the client and therapist.
T5: Hello, Noella, my name is Shelly, and what brings you in today?
P6: Good start.
C7: Hi, Shelly. I've been feeling really depressed and anxious lately because of problems that my family has been giving me because of my impending move.
A8: Depressed . . .
T9: Depression and anxiety, that's what you're feeling right now.
C10: Yeah, it's a heavy feeling that I have in my body and I was hoping you could help me gain some insight into what's going on right now.
T11: Well, can you tell me a little bit more about what's going on, how you're feeling right at this moment?
A12: You don't understand. . . . She's Black!
C13: Well, before we kind of get into that, I just wanted to kind of bring to light the issue being that we're from different cultures.
P14: Good, and that's a concern.
C15: If I could maybe . . . maybe you could express that issue and address that.
T16: I'm African American. What is your ethnic background?
C17: I'm Japanese American.
T18: I would imagine there are differences and similarities between our two cultures.
P19: We're both women.
C20: Yeah, I can imagine that. But you know that this is my first session, I'm a little uneasy and a little nervous.
A21: I'm uneasy . . .
P22: Build on that.
T23: Well, we'll take our time, I suppose. Can you give me a sense of your experience as the Japanese American woman?
P24: Great. Excellent. Good job.
A25: She doesn't understand . . .
C26: I'm glad that you asked that question because I've been having some really hard problems, you know, with issues of guilt and saving face, being that I'm going to be moving away to a different town.
P27: Saving face.
C28: To a different town, and my parents have been saying to me, being the eldest daughter, that you're a role model to your younger brother and sister, and how could you be leaving the family, and dividing everybody up, and you're doing this for yourself. You're being very selfish.

(continued)

A29: Selfish.

T30: So I'm hearing . . . there are a few things that are standing out for me. Saving face.

P31: Great.

T32: That's something very different from my experience, I think. So saving face, can you tell me more about what it's like and what it feels like to save face?

P33: Excellent.

C34: Well, as far as I know, it's kind of like bringing honor to your family and that you represent your entire family. Not only yourself as an individual and that's a burden.

A35: Lots of pressure . . .

P36: You can't express yourself.

T37: It is a burden and there is a whole lot of pressure to represent the family. Lots of pressure. And so the burden and pressure, I imagine, is very difficult to find your own voice 'cause there are so many others that you have to speak for.

P38: Exactly.

C39: I'm glad that you said that. To be able to speak my voice and to have that position in the family because I felt that my parents have always taken precedence and their wishes and needs have always overshadowed my own.

A40: You're so independent.

T41: I imagine the saving faces . . . my culture doesn't have that as a notion. We've . . . at least my strength has been to be independent and I imagine that's the difference between our experiences. In terms of saving face, do you feel that at certain times, like when you're anxious, you need to save face?

C42: I think a lot of that comes from the anxiety.

P43: She guesses??

A44: She's speaking for you.

C45: That the pressure over my family is always following me wherever I am. It's kind of like there's a weight that I feel on my shoulders, and I think that's been adding to all this anxiety and reluctance I have been having.

A46: Too much anxiety . . .

P47: She trusts you, she's opening up.

T48: I wonder if there is some anxiety to even speak with me?

P49: Good, great.

C50: Yeah . . . Being that this is my first counseling session, I really didn't know what to expect.

A51: You're uncomfortable.

C52: I have to admit I'm a little uncomfortable, I'm glad that you're a woman, being that we have that commonality.

P53: You're making progress.

A54: There you go again softening it up!

P55: Commonality.

T56: It sounds like you're attuned to what's going on for you, and that you're willing to share.

Note. From *Pedersen's Triad Training Model: Five Vignettes of Culturally Different Counselors Interviewing a Single Client,* by P. Pedersen and J. Brooks-Harris (videotape and manual), 2005. Framingham, MA: Microtraining and Multicultural Development Press. Copyright 2005 by Paul B. Pedersen. Adapted with permission.

Debriefing after completion of a triad training simulated interview can involve not only analysis of the videotape but also analysis of transcripts. Going to this level of analysis can allow counselor educators and others interested in improving cultural understanding in helping relationships to look at counseling technique through the lens of social psychology theory. Analyzing transcripts such as the one shown in Exhibit 8.1 will allow researchers to identify implicit as well as explicit cultural bias in both the general definition of the problem and the specific definitions of problems. Strous (2003) published data on the use of the TTM to articulate problems in multicultural contexts of South Africa. Trainees can also learn to discern which differences articulated in the simulated interview are individual differences and which ones are patterned or cultural differences. Yet another way of charting the counseling process with data from simulated triad interviews is to look at how the balance of power and resistance changes over the course of the interview.

A useful process for looking at balance of power among problem, counselor, and client comes from social psychology research on triads (Pedersen, 2000b). We encourage helping professionals to learn, practice, and teach the TTM using an eclectic application of theoretical approaches. Doing this will illustrate how different theoretical approaches can influence the power balance and facilitate formation of client–counselor coalitions. If the goal of a simulated interview is establishing ICE, then empirical instruments can be developed that will evaluate the triad model's effectiveness in specific conditions. Counseling goals can also be behaviorally defined in terms of how liberated the client becomes or how much the client's autonomy is increased, rather than merely how well the client's cultural differences were accommodated by the counselor. We discuss the empowering impact of ICE in chapters 10 and 11 of this volume.

OTHER INTERNAL DIALOGUE TRAINING MODELS

In addition to the TTM, several other approaches have emerged that focus on training counselors to hear the client's internal dialogue (Pedersen, 2000b). The goals and objectives of these alternative training models are similar to those of the TTM but the methods are quite different. The four models presented here are all role-played training interviews, although others have further adapted these training approaches for use in direct service.

The bicultural contextualizer (BCC) was developed by Chalsa Loo (see Pedersen, 2000b) to increase the cultural sensitivity of counselors on ethnic identity issues. In addition to the counselor and client, there is a third person who explains the counselor and the client messages in their appropriate cultural context. Sometimes the BCC resembles a cocounselor and sometimes a coclient as the BCC helps both counselor and client deal with areas of vulnerability. This clarification helps the counselor develop empathy skills. Usually the BCC interventions are short and specific to give more time to the counselor and client. The BCC provides a guide for counselors working with bicultural and multicultural clients, highlighting the client's thoughts and the thoughts of others in the client's cultural context.

The anticlient and proclient model was developed by Martin Strous in South Africa (Strous, 2003) and puts the focus on the counselor's inner dialogue as it shapes the therapeutic alliance. The anticlient triad design that is proposed is a role personification of antagonistic or unhelpful feelings the counselor has toward counseling a culturally different client. The anticlient brings up feelings, thoughts, and attitudes that are insensitive to the client's cultural background. The proclient brings up positive thoughts, feelings, and attitudes that demonstrate areas of common ground and shared interest between the counselor and client.

The anticlient input brings up thoughts that prevent empathy from developing even when the counselor is aware of the client's culture. Growing up under the apartheid ideology might influence counselors to be primarily concerned with classifying people according to cultural categories rather than recognizing their essential personhood. A major finding of Strous's (2003) research was that "White therapists' discomfort, fear, guilt, and guardedness around Blacks might impede both their empathy and spontaneity in interracial contexts" (p. 111). The proclient, however, tries to create a safe place for the client and counselor to explore their shared interest, sometimes raising racial issues directly while disregarding negative racial stereotypes.

Margo Jackson developed a stereotype reversal in counselor training (see Pedersen, 2000b). Stereotype reversal is designed to help the counselor's perspective-taking ability with culturally different clients, recognize the counselor's own racial bias, and attend to stereotype-disconfirming information. An anticounselor becomes a third voice in the stereotype reversal method to restructure the client's statements as if the social norms were reversed. This confrontation results in cognitive restructuring by the counselor to experience stereotyping themselves. The objective is to identify perceptual blind spots and misattributions by the counselor that limit the counselor's effectiveness.

James Cole (Pedersen, 2000b) introduced a proactive approach to reducing prejudice. The focus is to hear the internal voices of clients by putting the counselor into the role of "concerned listener" and the client into the role of "sharing person" while a third person plays the role of "distracter." The polarity of helper–helpee is removed so that both can meet with equal power. The objective is not to solve problems for disenfranchised clients but to help the counselor build empathy with that client as an equal. The counselor learns to listen more effectively. Following each training interview, there is a debriefing process in which the role players and other observers share their perspective of the interview.

A central theme running through all the training methods thus far reviewed is that of bringing inner dialogue to the surface. We postulate that this skill is central to developing ICE. When inner dialogue is spoken aloud, clients are empowered to challenge not only the counselor's proposed solutions or strategies but the very definition of the problem itself, and even the definition of the helping relationship. Counselors are likewise empowered to ask more pertinent questions. We discuss empowerment more extensively in chapters 10 and 11. It is our hope that, by using training models such as those reviewed in this chapter to learn ICE skills, the counseling relationship will come to be viewed as inevitably multicultural.

REFLECTION OF FEELINGS

As mentioned earlier in this chapter, internal dialogue is often made up of feelings intertwined with meanings. Feelings are the affective and frequently the more explicit, observable, and emotional aspects of a problem. Meanings are the cognitive and usually more implicit, hidden, and intellectual aspects of a problem. Although these aspects are often combined, it is useful to separate them (Cormier & Cormier, 1991). Once you have developed the general skill of hearing internal dialogue, you can further refine that skill by learning to attend to meanings separate from feelings. Although separating feelings from meaning may sound like a simplification, it can bring incongruency to light as well as help the client identify the culture teachers whose influence affects patterns of emotion and cognition. Once this is done, you can then take one further step by learning how to unite feelings and meanings to see how they each contribute to the organic life of problems. Although most of the books on counselor skill training separate reflections of feelings from reflections of meaning, this chapter deals with them both as symbiotic or interrelated with one another.

Reflection of feelings is accomplished by giving the client feedback on which feelings are being displayed in the interview, whether or not they were intended. Having their feelings reflected back to them helps clients feel understood and facilitates communication. Reflecting back feelings without adding any of the counselor's own self-reference feelings or judgments helps clients feel safe, and therefore helps them take the risk to express more of their positive and negative feelings. Safety may also reduce nonproductive anger or strong feelings on other topics. Voicing more feelings helps clients discriminate and distinguish between mixed feelings and become more specific in identifying and labeling feelings, which in turn helps clients take control of and manage feelings, propelling them toward more important counseling goals.

Making implicit feelings more explicit means finding a way to express them with words. Frequently people have mixed feelings and are not sure themselves about what they feel. Unless those feelings are clarified in the counseling interview—a process that may be complicated when there are many cultural differences between counselor and client—confusion of feelings can interfere with the helping process and goal setting. Sometimes the interviewer may infer certain feelings, but unless the inference is verified out loud, misunderstandings may build on one another. After making a tentative statement about the interviewee's feelings, it is important to find out whether that feeling was accurately identified.

In this section we first provide a brief review of how various theoretical orientations deal with client feelings and reflect them. Next, we offer two exercises to help therapists increase their emotion vocabulary and use that vocabulary to improve their attending skills. Third, we describe the steps involved in reflecting feelings during a real counseling or therapy session and list several cautions.

Theoretical Perspectives on Reflection of Feelings

Reflection of feelings in counseling and psychotherapy is dealt with in a variety of different ways by different theoretical perspectives. Clark (2007) reviewed the primary sources for these different perspectives on reflection of feelings.

For example, Adlerian therapists do not focus directly on feelings but rather on the beliefs that led to those feelings. Feelings are the result of—rather than the cause of—thoughts and beliefs. Feelings result from the way a person thinks and lead to the way the person acts. Adlerians would approach feelings through the clients' thoughts.

Behaviorism also deemphasizes feelings or emotional processes, assuming that feelings follow behaviors and if the counselor can change the behaviors the feelings will follow. In their discussion of empathy, Kanfer and Goldstein (1986) indicated that affective dimensions in behavior therapy are important in modifying cognitive and behavioral events.

The existentialists view feelings as facilitative, helping put the client in touch with reality. Feelings such as anxiety, for example, can motivate the client to change. The existentialist counselor might help a client become one with her or his feelings. For example, such a counselor might say that a certain level of anxiety is a normal part of life and should not be eliminated. Feelings would be reflected as a friendly resource of energy for change.

Rational emotive therapy (RET) helps clients eliminate their irrational feelings (Ellis, 1962). The feelings are reflected back to put the client in control of which feelings they want to increase or decrease. The counselor works as a teacher to help the client learn ways to take control of their feelings and change their lives through more rational thinking.

Person-centered approaches to therapy help the client explore a wider range of feelings to accept and explore them. The first stage of therapy is helping the client identify, explore, and express their feelings in a safe setting. Clients have the right and the ability to discover their own feelings, and the counselor's task is to provide a facilitative relationship.

The psychoanalytic perspective sees feelings as symbolic of deeper thoughts, beliefs, and ideas that control the client. The feelings are a resource or a pathway to understand the client better. The client is encouraged to transfer feelings about others to the counselor so that the feelings can be made more conscious. The feelings themselves are less important than the state of mind they symbolize.

Reality therapy deals with the whole person, helping the person get what he or she wants by negotiating goals within the constraints of reality. The counselor functions as a teacher leading the client to insights about how actions and thoughts can control feelings rather than be controlled by feelings. The counselor works with clients by first establishing a relationship of trust and support where reflection of feelings would be a useful skill.

Each model that uses a version of positive or negative internal dialogue or both demonstrates a different emphasis. At the same time, each example also demonstrates a similarity in emphasizing the importance of positive and negative voices for building empathy with a client in a real or role-played setting.

Exercises to Improve Emotion Vocabulary and Attending

To build accuracy in naming feelings, we offer two vocabulary exercises. Individuals can use each exercise on their own, in the classroom, or in a variety of other situations.

Each person has a list of preferred words that exactly describe and focus the feelings we experience. If you can find a letter that you have written to a friend, go through the letter and underline all the words describing an emotion or a feeling in the letter. You will probably find that you use a relatively small collection of emotion or feeling words. Frequently, people have mixed feelings and are not sure themselves about what they feel. This confusion, when combined with a lack of vocabulary to name feelings, can interfere with an interview. Therefore it is useful to identify and expand that pool of "feeling" words.

For the first exercise, identify at least 10 different synonyms of each of the following 10 emotions: *love, happiness, fear, anger, contempt, mirth, surprise, suffering, determination*, and *disgust*. Then, see if you can come up with several metaphors you could use to discuss each of those feelings ("Love is like . . ."). Having an expanded list of emotion words and metaphors at your disposal will help you focus on feelings the client might be experiencing but not expressing directly. For example, if clients are feeling fearful but their culture teachers tell them it is unacceptable to talk about fears, a counselor with a rich reserve of emotion words and metaphors can come up with alternative ways for the client to talk about fear without specifically naming it as such. This type of vocabulary-generating exercise can be used at any time, even during a counseling session.

The next exercise is called *nested feelings*. It is designed to help you evaluate your own ability to identify another person's feelings accurately (Pedersen, 2004). When another person is speaking, it is important to note (a) the specific expressed emotional words used by a client, (b) the implicit emotional words not actually spoken, (c) nonverbally expressed emotions, and (d) mixed and often discrepant verbal–nonverbal emotional cues. Even when you practice such careful attending, however, not everyone will welcome your interpretation of their feelings.

To practice nested feelings, ask someone to talk for 3 or 4 minutes about a situation they have experienced that resulted in strong feelings, whether positive or negative or mixed. While the person is speaking, use a rating sheet to score the extent to which the storyteller experienced various feelings, both at the time of the event and as telling the story. Ask the storyteller to use the rating sheet presented in Exhibit 8.2.

EXHIBIT 8.2
Rating Sheet for Scoring Emotional Content of a Story and Emotions Felt While Telling a Story

A "10" high score indicates a great deal stronger feeling. A "1" low score indicates very little or none of the feeling.

Feeling	How strong was the feeling at the time the event happened?	How strong was the feeling at the time the story was told?
Love		
Happiness		
Fear		
Anger		
Contempt		
Mirth		
Surprise		
Determination		
Disgust		
[Other]		

Note. From *110 Experiences for Multicultural Learning* (pp. 119–120), by P. B. Pedersen, 2004, Washington, DC: American Psychological Association. Copyright 2004 by Paul B. Pedersen. Adapted with permission.

After the storyteller and listener(s) finish filling in the rating sheet, ask the storyteller to read her or his score on all the relevant feelings. Listeners can then score themselves in terms of how accurately they were able to predict the storyteller's stated feelings. This exercise can be practiced informally, using a friend or colleague as the storyteller, or adapted for the classroom or clinical supervision, or even adapted for use in direct service.

How to Reflect Feelings Back to the Client

Cormier and Cormier (1991) described steps for learning how to reflect feelings, identify the emotional tone of an interview, and rephrase the client's feelings in an articulate way.

1. Listen for feeling or affect words in what the client says. Feelings might also be revealed through nonverbal behaviors.
2. Reflect the feelings back to a client in your own words. The reflected words need to reflect both the feeling itself and the intensity of the feeling.
3. Reflect the feelings back to a client by taking a basic sentence stem that may be visual ("It looks like . . ."), auditory ("It sounds like . . ."), or kinesthetic ("It feels like . . ."), whichever best reflects the way that client would talk.
4. Describe the situation in which the feelings occurred, thereby reflecting back your awareness of when and why those feelings occurred.
5. Check out how effective you were and verify the accuracy of your reflection of feeling.

For example, imagine you had four different clients who each presented for therapy because of a family issue. Each client differs from the other and from you in various key cultural identity constructs. The language they use to express emotions is rooted in those cultural constructs. As you read each imaginary client's self-introduction presented in Exhibit 8.3, ask yourself how you might execute Steps 1 through 5 with each client. How will the interview progress after introductions (Hofstede, Pedersen, & Hofstede, 2002)? For a full elaboration of the four synthetic cultures and an additional exercise, see Appendixes A and B.

When you read the introductions in Exhibit 8.3, did you envision the client's nonverbal behaviors? How would you respond to the nonverbal behaviors? To which client would you feel most and least comfortable reflecting feelings? How would your strategy for reflecting feelings differ for each of the four clients? For further details and examples of how to reflect feelings, readers may wish to consult sources such as Ivey and Ivey (2007), which discuss component microskills in detail.

EXHIBIT 8.3
Example of Clients' Self-Introduction

ALPHA Client 1

I am very fortunate to be so well cared for by my family and by persons such as yourself. I try to be conscientious in obeying the rules and respecting my betters, but my family must not be pleased with what I am doing since they sent me to you. I hope you will help me so that I can make a better contribution in the future. I promise to be a good and worthy client, following any advice you give me.

BETA Client 2

Life certainly is full of surprises, and most of them are not good. Here I sit wasting my time doing God only knows what while I could be somewhere else. If I only knew what my family wanted, I could do it, but they don't know themselves what they want. I wonder if you have any idea yourself. I know this much, things can't keep going as they have been.

GAMMA Client 3

Well, I came here, so what do you have in mind for me? I don't enjoy playing games so just tell me what you want and let's get on with it. You should be able to teach me some new strategies so I can get along better with my family, if you're any good. We don't have to like one another to work together you know.

DELTA Client 4

Isn't that a crock? Me coming here to see you? I'm the one who has been successful in our family and now they send me to see a shrink like I'm some kind of wimp. You sit there looking at me with that loosey-goosey look in your eye, what the hell do you know about anything? I'll tell you this, if you don't prove yourself this session, there's no way in hell I'm coming back!

Note. Both the synthetic cultural designation (Alpha, Beta, Gamma, Delta) and the therapist–client role are indicated for each client. For a full elaboration of the four synthetic cultures and an additional exercise see Appendixes A and B (this volume).

Several cautions are in order when using the empathy skill reflection of feelings. For example, the counselor also has feelings in the interview that might facilitate or get in the way of counseling. Having feelings is normal as long as the counselor is able to monitor those feelings so that they do not distort the counseling message. It is useful for the counselor to listen and "self-interpret" the anti and pro voices about what the counselor is saying in the interview. The same skills used to detect client feelings can also help detect the counselor's own feelings. Look for discrepancies, changes in topic, changes in body language, distractions, and other danger signs. In some cultures self-disclosure of your own feelings can be helpful as a model of risk taking, but in other cultures it destroys your credibility completely.

In addition, Brammer (1988) recommended that counselors be particularly careful about encouraging emotional expression when

- the client has a severe emotional disorder.
- the client is under such pressure that he or she may respond with more intensity than he or she can control.

- the client has a history of emotional crises getting out of hand.
- the client is strongly and explicitly against exploring feelings.
- the counselor is not sure how to help people deal with their feelings.

REFLECTION OF MEANINGS

Think about an interaction you had with someone whose beliefs and values were different from your own. How did your beliefs and values differ? How did you discover those differences? How long did it take to discover the differences? What did the interaction feel like (e.g., confusing, stimulating, fun, hurtful)? Differences in beliefs and values can profoundly affect even casual interactions, so when the element of helping enters the equation the potential for misunderstanding may be even greater. The purpose of reflecting meaning is to explore the values and beliefs underlying the interview. Two people may experience the same event—such as an interview—but it may have a different meaning for each of them. The search for meaning is an important goal for most people, and even when the meaning is not explicitly mentioned in the interview, reflecting back that implicit meaning can be a useful skill for interviewing.

The functions of reflecting meaning are to help interviewees interpret their feelings and actions accurately, to explore values or goals, and to understand deeper aspects of an interviewee's experience. It will not be appropriate to explore these deeper meanings in all interviews, but it will be important for the interviewer to have the skill to perceive the meanings nonetheless.

Theoretical Perspectives on Reflection of Meaning

Frankl's (1963) work on logotherapy built a whole theory of counseling on the search for meaning and purpose in life. Logotherapy is rooted philosophically in existentialism, which describes "meaninglessness" as the primary problem of our age. Theoretically, then, many of the clients who seek counseling do so to resolve the problem of meaninglessness. Counseling helps clients find meaning and purpose in several ways. Frankl used the skill of reflection to help clients discover positive meaning in even negative events. Direct reflection might, however, result in continued focusing on the negative, especially if the client already "hyperreflects" about the problem too much.

Ivey (1988) made a similar point in his advocating a "positive asset search" as a counseling skill. Identifying positive assets gives the interview an optimistic emphasis and helps the client identify positive assets to increase personal power through the interview. Without denying the reality of negative aspects, the counselor might identify the thoughts, feelings, and behaviors that have a positive loading for the client, find positive features even in a serious problem, and reframe negative self-statements. Highlighting these assets helps enhance the client's development, identify sources of support, and promote positive change for the client.

Ellis (1962) developed RET to reeducate clients by removing irrational beliefs through persuasion, direction, and logical argument with clients. According to this theory of therapy, counseling helps clients accept their imperfect selves and prevent illogical beliefs from controlling their lives. Meaning is reflected to identify and remove self-defeating beliefs and irrational thinking, and usually proceeds in the following way: (a) identifying the activating event, (b) intervening to rationally reframe the beliefs about that event, and (c) changing the consequences of the event toward more rational conclusions. A skilled counselor changes the consequence not by changing the event but by changing the beliefs about that event. Changing beliefs requires a reflection of meaning about the event. RET is likely to be less successful in cultures that value dependency more than independency and self-sufficiency.

Meichenbaum's (1977) *Cognitive–Behaviour Modification* uses self-instruction for changing the way a client thinks. Clients monitor their own internal dialogue and understand how they perceive themselves as well as how they are perceived by others. The therapist identifies thoughts that may be maladaptive. When these maladaptive thoughts are reflected back to the client, and the client learns new ways to cope and solve problems, positive change occurs. Meichenbaum's cognitive restructuring requires that (a) clients observe themselves and their own behavior, (b) clients learn a new internal dialogue that is less maladaptive, and (c) clients learn new skills for constructive coping. Reflection of meaning helps the counselor understand the client and build a relationship, identify new alternative meanings to facilitate coping, interpret culturally ambiguous messages, and help the client transfer new meanings to the real world.

Carl Rogers (1975) is best known for his reflection of feeling, but like other humanists and existentialists, the reflection of meaning also becomes an important way to help the client fully encounter reality. According to Rogers (1986), congruent, accepting, and empathic counselors reflect both feeling and meaning not as a technique but as an extension of the counselors themselves on a "shared journey" with the client toward positive growth.

Cormier and Cormier (1991) discussed cognitive modeling as a means of reflecting meaning through five steps of self-instructional training. First, the counselor performs the task while reflecting out loud about what is being done. The client then performs the same task following the counselor's model and getting verbal feedback. Next, the client repeats the task while reflecting out loud about what is being done. Then the client whispers the instructions while modeling the task again. Finally, the client repeats the task while monitoring the process through internal dialogue. Many other behavioral approaches for monitoring cognitive processes, such as structured learning (Clark, 2007), follow a similar sequence of events in skill building.

How to Reflect Meaning Back to the Client

Once the client's feelings have been accurately identified, the helping professional can proceed to reflect back the client's beliefs and values as they relate to the situation at hand. Reflecting meanings and feelings separately can help the counselor and client identify when two or more culture teachers may be sending conflicting messages (Pedersen & Ivey, 1993). The steps include the following:

1. Interpret the meaning of feelings displayed by the interviewee.
2. Explore alternative interpretations of what is being said.
3. Explore a priority of interpretations of explanations.
4. Verify whether the reflection of meaning was accurate.

For an example of this process, first read this imaginary client's self-introduction:

> I am very fortunate to be so well cared for by my family and by persons such as yourself. I try to be conscientious in obeying the rules and respecting my betters, but my family must not be pleased with what I am doing since they sent me to you. I hope you will help me so that I can make a better contribution in the future. I promise to be a good and worthy client, following any advice you give me.

In reflecting feelings, the therapist might ask if the client, let's call him Jack, is feeling guilty that he may not be reciprocating the care offered him by his family. If Jack verifies that he is indeed feeling guilty, then the therapist can later help him to explore the beliefs and values underlying that feeling. For example, the therapist could ask Jack to explain what he means by "make a better contribution in the future." Does he believe he has unique abilities he could contribute to his family life (e.g., earning a professional degree at an out-of-state institution)? Does his proposed contribution cross the boundaries of what his family considers to be a worthy contribution (e.g., working in the family business)? Could the guilt actually be coming from a clash of values between Jack and his family or other culture teachers?

COMBINING FEELING AND MEANING: A BALANCING ACT

Once you and your client feel confident that the feelings and meanings being voiced are accurate interpretations of the client's internal dialogue, you can build from simple reflection to synthesizing those reflections into possible solutions for the client's problem. Or, to state it in a way that accounts for cultural viewpoints that may not strictly dichotomize "problems" and "solutions," reflecting feelings and meanings can help you formulate a balance of positive and negative emotions and cognitions.

Balancing the positives and negatives is more than reconciling dissonance, which seeks to avoid, change, ignore, or transcend dissonance. The reflection of a meaningful balance can be described as a tolerance for inconsistency and dissonance (Pedersen, 2000b). This more complicated definition of balance means finding and reflecting both pleasure and pain rather than merely resolving conflict to increase pleasure. The reflection and restoration of this balance is a continuous and not an episodic process, reflecting the organic metaphors of holistic systems. For example, Chinese perspectives on the importance of balancing yin and yang have continued to be relevant for many centuries. Problems, pain, and otherwise negative aspects of our experience make an essential contribution to the ecological analysis of multicultural psychology.

For practitioners developing ICE, finding balance means identifying incongruent feelings and meanings without necessarily resolving the conflict. Healthy functioning may require maintaining multiple conflicting but culturally learned roles without resolving the dissonance. Accurately voicing the client's internal dialogue will help the client and counselor identify which culture teachers are the most helpful and which ones balance contrasting viewpoints. For example, if a client can "hear" the positive implications of an otherwise negative experience, or anticipate potentially negative implications from an otherwise positive experience, then he or she will feel more power over the managing of balance in the interview. Ultimately, ICE in action will increase the client's perceived power over time and across different situations and social roles. The therapist's main task then is to maintain a harmonious rapport with the client and adjust her or his influence to facilitate a client's growth and development.

CONCLUSION

A person's internal dialogue is important to her or his psychological health. If opposing ideas provide a dialogical basis for thinking, then even optimal thinking will include both positive and negative ideas. Focusing on a client's negative or even nonproductive thoughts and feelings may be important and require more work than merely building positive perspectives.

Synthesizing Egan's (1986) list of suggestions for the use of empathy, we offer some general tips to keep in mind when helping a client hear her or his own culture teachers:

- Set aside your own biases and judgments.
- Listen for the core message in what the client says.

- Listen for both verbal and nonverbal messages.
- Respond fairly frequently but briefly.
- Be flexible and tentative to give the client room.
- Be gentle and keep focused on primary issues.
- Respond to experiences, behaviors, and feelings alike.
- Move toward exploring sensitive topics.
- Check out if your empathic response was on target.
- Determine if your empathic response is helpful.
- Note signs of stress and the reason for being stressed.
- Keep focused on helping the client.

The goal of establishing a cognitive and emotional balance is a measurably appealing goal for counseling. Rather than focus only on increasing positive coping or reducing dysfunctional emotions and cognitions, counselors can conceptualize counseling as striving toward a healthy and meaningful balance of positive and negative thoughts and feelings, even though that balance may be asymmetrical. ICE therefore allows counseling to become a process of gradual oscillation between extremes until a balance is established in which clients can reduce dependence on their problem and the counselor and experiment with alternative ways of thinking, feeling, and behaving.

This chapter discussed the skills of reflecting feelings and meanings to hear a client's internal dialogue, or the voices of the client's culture teachers. In the following chapter, we address several sets of microskills that facilitate learning of the larger ICE skills.

9

INTEGRAL SKILLS: MICROSKILLS FOR INCLUSIVE CULTURAL EMPATHY

Inviting the client's culture teachers into a therapy session or other type of helping interaction can make for a cacophony of voices, especially when culture is defined broadly to include the constructs discussed in chapters 6 and 7: ethnographic (nationality, ethnicity, race, etc.), demographic (age, gender, place of residence, etc.), status (social, economic, educational, etc.), and affiliations (formal and informal). As we have mentioned before, we consider every helping professional's work to be inherently multicultural. Giving voice to culture teachers also invites mistakes on the part of the helper, especially when there are many cultural differences between helper and client. In this chapter we outline several microskills that we have found, through our clinical experience, to be the sturdy scaffolding surrounding the development of the inclusive cultural empathy (ICE) skills described in the previous chapter (e.g., attending, reflection of feeling, reflection of meaning, etc.). The focus of these skills is on recovering from the inevitable mistakes that occur in the process of building ICE. Examples of competencies that can be learned through the triad training model (TTM) from chapter 8 are discussed to help the reader see the connection between the TTM and learning ICE competencies.

MISTAKES AND RECOVERIES

Imagine, if you can, what someone would be like who always did a perfect job and never made any mistakes in working with clients. Would you want to go to such a person for help? We would much rather spend time with someone who was willing to take some chances but who could recover from their mistakes. The irony is that if you are confident that you can recover from any mistake you might make, it is likely that you will be less apprehensive about making mistakes in the first place! Instead of looking at the mistake as a catastrophe, look at the mistake as an unfreezing event, in the perspective of force-field theory, where there is a brief opportunity for positive as well as negative change to take place, depending on how well you recover.

Recovery skills are frequently overlooked as a teachable and learnable skill area for inclusive empathy. It is therefore important to identify those microskills that might contribute to a helping professional's ability to recover. Each individual will develop her or his own repertoire of recovery skills that work well for them but perhaps not as well for others, building on that individual's natural management style. Some of the more obvious recovery skills include the following.

- Changing the topic: The counselor can redirect the interview appropriately following a controversial interaction.
- Focusing: The counselor can refocus the interview on the basic problem instead of on the controversial issue.
- Silence: The counselor is able to tolerate periods of silence in the interview that can convey as much meaning as talking if rightly understood.
- Role reversal: The counselor can solicit consultation from the client as a resource for generating solutions and alternative responses to the crisis.
- Challenging: The counselor confronts the client with her or his own perception of what is really happening in this crisis.
- Referral: The counselor is able to refer the client to another counselor in a culturally appropriate way and at an appropriate time.
- Termination: The counselor is able to terminate the interview prematurely in a culturally appropriate way.
- Arbitration: The counselor brings in a third person or "culture broker" to mediate the dispute in a culturally appropriate way.
- Metaphorical analysis: The counselor identifies the crisis as a microcosm of a larger macro situation and uses the crisis to gain insights about the larger picture.
- Positioning: The counselor identifies an area of unmet need or opportunity not yet recognized by the client and builds on it to the client's advantage.

The primary source for learning more about these microskills is Ivey and Ivey (2007), in which microskills are organized into a pyramidlike structure from less to more difficult. This resource cites over 300 empirical studies in which microtraining was found to be superior when measured against other training methods. Another resource for microskills in multicultural environments is Pedersen and Ivey (1993), which looks at how the microskills can be adapted to fit a variety of different cultural groups.

To learn effective recovery skills, it is important to develop three basic abilities. The first is the ability to articulate the problem from the client's own culturally biased viewpoint. Second, it is important to recognize resistance relating to cultural differences between the counselor and client in specific rather than in general terms. Otherwise, the danger is that you will either not know that you have made mistakes or you will know that you made mistakes but not know what those mistakes were. Third is the ability to recognize when the counselor feels threatened, distracted, or defensive and to overcome these tendencies. Contact with a culturally different client can cause these feelings in the counselor. When the counselor becomes defensive, the rapport with the client is diminished and the mistake escalates. Each of the three fundamental abilities will contribute to the counselor's effective recovery skills.

ARTICULATING THE PROBLEM FROM THE CLIENT'S PERSPECTIVE

Seeing the problem from the client's perspective, rather than imposing the counselor's perspective on the client, may involve the following.

- Paraphrase: The counselor gives back to the client the essence of past verbal statements by selective attention to the content of what the client is saying.
- Summarization: The counselor reflects a client's feelings over a longer period of time and describes repeated patterns of the client's behavior across situations.
- Concreteness: The counselor's statements are less vague or ambiguous and more concrete and specific.
- Immediacy: The counselor matches the client's statements by using the same time perspective—whether past, present, or future—as the client used.
- Respect: Explanatory statements by the counselor about self or others are considered to represent respect whereas negative statements or put-downs indicate an absence of respect.
- Genuineness: There is an absence of mixed verbal and nonverbal messages.

- Positive regard: The counselor gives selective attention to positive aspects of self or others or to the demonstrated belief that people can change and manage their own lives effectively.
- Tracking: The counselor is able to follow accurately and even anticipate what the client will say next.

RECOGNIZING CLIENT RESISTANCE TO THE HELPER OR HELPING PROCESS

Resistance occurs when the client starts to feel negatively about the counselor or the process of counseling. It is important to recognize resistance related to cultural differences between a counselor and a client in specific rather than in general terms. When resistance arises, it is important to identify and deal with it before proceeding to discuss problem management, otherwise those negative feelings of resistance will sabotage the discussion. The following microskills will help the counselor improve her or his abilities to recognize specific types of resistance.

- Stress-coping insight: The counselor is able to describe and anticipate the client's response to a particular problem.
- Values conflict: The counselor is able to identify both similarities and differences in values between the counselor and client.
- Questioning: The counselor is able to use either open or closed questions in a culturally appropriate way.
- Directions: The counselor is able to tell the client what to do in a culturally appropriate way.
- Confrontation: The counselor is able to provide negative feedback to the client without making the client angry.
- Interpretation: The counselor is able to rename or relabel the client's behaviors as seen from other perspectives.
- Focus on topic: The counselor identifies the subject of the client's underlying topic of interest or problem.
- Focus on group: The counselor is aware of the client's natural support systems and helps the client identify others who can be resources.
- Mirroring: The counselor is able to reflect and adjust voice tone, body position, or other aspects of communication style so that the counselor is in synchrony with the client.
- Self-awareness: The counselor has an explicit awareness of what he or she is doing from the client's viewpoint.

Recognizing resistance requires the counselor not to take things personally but to focus first of all on the task of building inclusive empathy. The natural tendency is to put a negative interpretation on ambiguous behaviors of the client and to become defensive, as though the counselor was under attack. Once the counselor has become defensive, any attempt to recover becomes more difficult and small problems become big problems.

OVERCOMING DEFENSIVENESS TOWARD CLIENTS

Interaction with clients who are culturally different is frequently ambiguous and can cause even a skilled counselor to become less sure of her- or himself, leading to defensive behavior. It is important for the counselor to avoid the distraction of defensive behavior and to focus on the client's basic message, which may not be intended as a personal attack on the counselor. If the counselor allows her- or himself to be distracted by becoming defensive, the rapport with a culturally different client is likely to diminish.

Skills for diminishing defensiveness or helping the counselor control the impulse to feel threatened in multicultural situations include the following.

- Sense of humor: The counselor is able to facilitate rapport by seeing the humor in a mistake when culturally appropriate.
- Self-disclosure: The counselor is able to disclose information about her- or himself in a culturally appropriate way.
- Evaluation: The counselor is able to accurately interpret the client's expression, manner, or tone of response to get at hidden agendas.
- Description: The counselor is able to describe the client's perspective without evaluating it as either good or bad.
- Spontaneity: The counselor is able to be spontaneous rather than strategic in responding to the client.
- Receptivity: The counselor is able to accept advice or help from the client in a culturally appropriate way.
- Admitting to being defensive: The counselor is able to openly admit to her or his own defensive behaviors in a nonapologetic way.
- Apologizing: The counselor is able to accept responsibility for making mistakes and apologize appropriately.
- Planning: The counselor is able to develop and explicate a plan of action to the client for their time together.
- Manipulation: The counselor is able to bring the client to accept what the counselor perceives as being in the client's best interest.

One source of counselor error is failing to recognize that two people may display the same behaviors but mean different things by them, or display different behaviors but mean the same thing. Several of the microskills mentioned previously allude to this fact, so we expand on it at some length here, providing examples of ICE approaches to establishing the shared positive expectations between and among people. Conceptualizing cultural differences can help counseling professionals interpret behaviors accurately in terms of the expectations and values expressed in those behaviors. If two people are accurate in their interpretation of each other's positive, "common-ground" expectation, they do not always need to display the same behavior. The two people may agree to disagree about which behavior is appropriate and continue to work together in harmony despite their different styles of behavior. Practice with the TTM (discussed in chap. 8) can help counselors raise their threshold for nondefensive reactions. The TTM makes explicit the negative and positive internal dialogue of the counselor and client to include the hidden messages as well as explicit verbal messages of counseling. ICE uses the TTM as well as other approaches to demonstrate inclusion in the counseling context.

People who have used the TTM reported that they are better able to articulate the problem from the client's viewpoint after a series of training interviews with the procounselor–client–anticounselor teams (Seto, Young, Becker, & Kiselica, 2006). Participants also reported that they are better able to identify specific sources of resistance in the counseling interview, on the basis of immediate and continuous feedback from the procounselor and anticounselor. Participants further reported becoming less defensive after training with the anticounselor and less threatened by working with culturally different clients. Finally, participants indicated the importance of developing recovery skills after they have said or done the wrong thing, as pointed out by the anticounselor or procounselor. The framework for charting increased competence of ICE is provided in the developmental, three-stage awareness–knowledge–skill format.

DEVELOPING MULTICULTURAL COMPETENCIES WITH THE TRIAD TRAINING MODEL

Structured experiences, such as provided by the TTM, can help create favorable conditions for cross-cultural contact, provide a safe setting to rehearse new strategies, provide a quick and efficient means of expanding awareness with a minimum of consequences, maintain focus on aspects of awareness, provide research opportunities in controlled settings with unambiguous roles, and provide the opportunity to clarify objectives. Those who oppose structured experiences for developing multicultural awareness point out that many cultures are unfamiliar with or opposed to role-playing structured experiences and that the required degree of openness is culture specific, as is the direct communication of meanings. Participants from hierarchical cultures wherein status is especially important may have difficulty participating in a setting in which everyone is treated equally. Some structured experiences present simplistic views of other cultures and might lend themselves toward superficial stereotypes of other cultures if debriefing is not properly done.

As one example of structured experiences for learning multicultural awareness, the TTM has been used as an in-service training model for counselors working with a variety of different populations. These settings include training foreign student advisors to work with foreign students, training counselors to work with clients from other ethnic minority groups, training counselors to work with alcoholics and clients who are drug dependent, training counselors to work with clients who are disabled, training counselors to be more sensitive to gender-based attitudes, training military personnel to negotiate differences between rank and service branch, and training prisoners at a federal prison to work with social workers in the cultural context of prison (Pedersen, 2000b). The range of possible applications extends to any situation in which the culturally learned values, beliefs, or expectations of the counselors are likely to be different from those of their clients, requiring the counselor to develop a more inclusive perspective. The TTM allows in-service trainees to make mistakes in the relatively safe context of a simulated interview with clients from the target culture. The counselor trainees receive immediate, direct, and continuous feedback from clients through the procounselor and anticounselor during the role-played interview itself. These "trainers" are members of the very population the counselors are being trained to serve later.

D. W. Sue (1980) field-tested the anticounselor and procounselor versions of the TTM with students at California State University, Hayward. The anticounselor version was judged more effective in achieving self-awareness, developing cultural sensitivity for contrasting cultural values, and understanding political or social ramifications of counseling. The anticounselor version was also more effective in giving participants an awareness of their cultural values and biases and engendering cultural sensitivity to other ethnically defined groups. The procounselor version was more effective in helping students obtain specific knowledge of the history, experiences, and cultural values of the client's ethnic group. Students were more comfortable with the procounselor version, whereas the anticounselor version was more anxiety provoking. When asked to rate which model was more effective for learning about multicultural counseling in the shortest period of time, however, the anticounselor version was seen as superior. The anticounselor brought out issues of racism, bias, and conflicting values through immediate feedback to the counselor trainee, whereas the procounselor tended to facilitate acquisition of awareness, knowledge, and skills more gently.

Murgatroyd (1995) described a program using the TTM to prepare counselors at the University of New Orleans. First, the model helped trainees understand and explore the presenting problem of role-played clients. Second, it made negative thoughts toward counseling and the counselor more explicit. Students were divided into two groups. The six students in Group 1 had completed from 9 to 18 credits of graduate study in counseling, whereas the six students in Group 2 had completed at least 24 credits. Third, it aided in understanding the "payoffs" a problem offers to the client.

> The model facilitates a faster and deeper exploration of presenting problems for group one counselor trainees. For group two trainees, the model heightens the developmental issue of dependency versus autonomy. They struggle with an authority of positive and negative voices which in turn allows them an opportunity to work through their developmental task and become more mature in their identity. (p. 22)

Murgatroyd (1995) described the primary usefulness of the TTM to help counselor trainees identify the positive resources of clients through the positive and negative messages of the client's internal dialogue.

> The model unveiled negative thought both about counseling and the counselor. It allowed a student to work with the client's resistance and reframe the client's problem in a positive working direction. It aided in understanding the concept of payoffs, an important part of the problem that influences the patterns of a client's behavior. (p. 17)

Most of the supporting research on the TTM describes its value in giving the counselor trainees increased awareness of their own and their client's cultural context. The counselor's assumptions are constantly being tested by the anticounselor and procounselor through their immediate and continuous feedback. Biases and stereotypes by the trainee are quickly identified and made more visible during the simulated interview so that the counselor is better able to articulate the problem from the client's cultural perspective. Awareness of the culturally appropriate process or style of counseling as well as the content of the interview are likewise illuminated. By increasing the trainee's multicultural awareness, these structured experiences also encourage the development of ICE for counseling in multicultural contexts.

Hernandez and Kerr (1985) trained three groups of students using a didactic mode, a didactic plus role play with feedback mode, and a didactic plus TTM mode with the anticounselor but without a procounselor. On completion of training, the students were videotaped in a counseling session with a coached male Mexican American Chicano client. The videotaped segments were randomly distributed to six professional colleagues familiar with cross-cultural counseling. The videotapes were rated using the Global Rating Scale, the Counselor Rating Form—Short, and the Cross-Cultural Counseling Inventory. The control group had the lowest average on five of the six measures, and the TTM group scored the highest mean scores on four of the six measures. The role-play group earned the highest average on the Cross-

Cultural Counseling Inventory and the control group on the Global Rating Scale. The more experiential training produced counselors who were more culturally sensitive, expert, attractive, and trustworthy from the client's viewpoint. According to Hernandez and Kerr (1985),

> The findings supported experiential training of counselors in general and particularly the use of the triad training model for training. These findings support experiential training, and especially the continued use of Pedersen's triad model, which is geared towards sensitizing and preparing counselors to work more effectively and efficiently with clients from diverse ethnic backgrounds. (p. 14)

Neimeyer, Fukuyama, Bingham, Hall, and Mussenden (1986) compared the reactions of 20 counseling students using the TTM with an anticounselor version versus the reactions of students trained using a procounselor version. The two self-report measures used were the Self-Assessment Survey and the Analysis of Values Questionnaire. The Self-Assessment Survey contains 5 Likert-type items assessing participant feelings of control, competence, confusion, feelings of being understood, and the likelihood of returning for counseling. The Analysis of Values Questionnaire contains 13 seven-point Likert-type items measuring cultural values such as individuality versus groupness, control of nature versus harmony with nature, egalitarian social relationships versus hierarchical social relationships, and future time orientation versus present time orientation.

Objective ratings of counselor performance were measured by the Global Rating Scale and the Counselor Rating Form. Results from the Self-Assessment Survey and the Analysis of Values Questionnaire indicated that participants trained in the more confrontational anticounselor version felt more confused and less competent than did participants trained in the procounselor version. No differences were discovered from the scores on the Global Rating Scale and the Counselor Rating Form. The more confrontational anticounselor model, when used alone, was described as better suited to more advanced students who have already developed some confidence in their multicultural understanding, whereas the procounselor model might be better suited for beginning counselors to provide them with a more supportive multicultural training experience. According to Neimeyer et al. (1986), expert counselors were not rated as more effective by their clients in the anticounselor treatment although they were perceived as more effective in the procounselor treatment, suggesting a difference between perceived and actual counselor effectiveness when the person in a counseling role is under pressure.

Wade and Bernstein (1991) examined cultural sensitivity training using the TTM with Black female clients and found that Black female clients' perception of the counselors and of counseling was more positive about counselors who had been trained in the TTM than by same-race counselors not trained using the model. Counselors trained in the TTM received higher ratings by 80 low-income Black women on expertness, trustworthiness, attractiveness, unconditional positive regard, satisfaction, and empathy, and these women returned for more follow-up sessions than counselors who had not been trained with the TTM. Wade and Bernstein noted,

> Counselors assigned to the culture sensitivity training condition received 4 hours of training. The training included an overview of the issues and concerns culturally distinct individuals bring to counseling, a group discussion on self-awareness and the minority client, and a skills training component based on Pedersen's Triad Model of cross cultural counseling. (p. 10)

A major finding of this study was that Black female clients' perception of the counselors and the counseling process was influenced more by the training than by the race of the counselor.

> Clients assigned to experienced counselors who had received culture sensitivity training rated their counselor higher on credibility and relationship measures, returned for more follow-up sessions, and expressed greater satisfaction with counseling than did clients assigned to experienced counselors who had not received the additional training (control condition). Although same-race counseling dyads resulted in less client attrition, this factor did not influence client perceptions of counselors and the counseling process. (Wade & Bernstein, 1991, p. 9)

Irvin and Pedersen (1995) trained one group in the TTM using procounselor training first and anticounselor training second, and a second group of counselors using the anticounselor training first and the procounselor training second. In Irvin and Pedersen's research, 20 graduate counselors in training produced two 10-minute interviews with simultaneous feedback from an anticounselor and a procounselor in simulated interviews.

Ten trainees experienced the anticounselor before the procounselor, and 10 trainees experienced the procounselor before the anticounselor to determine the importance of sequencing. Three Kenyan undergraduate students were trained to role play the coached client, procounselor, and anticounselor team. Two self-report measures were used in this study. The Self-Assessment Survey with five Likert items assessed the participant's feelings of anxiety and competence, the participant's perceived clarity of role play, estimates of the client's feelings of being understood, and the likelihood of the client's continuing in counseling. The Analysis of Values Questionnaire assessed the counselor trainees' values and their assumptions about the client's values. Results indicated a decrease in the counselor trainees' values and their assumptions about the client's values.

Results indicated a decrease in the counselor trainees' sense of anxiety, apprehension, and defensiveness when the anticounselor was presented first. However, trainees reported a greater sense of control when the procounselor was presented first. Students experiencing the procounselor first were more likely to anticipate future contact with the client, seemed to understand the problem better, and were better able to absorb a confrontation with the anticounselor later. Students who experienced the anticounselor first felt less anxious and more comfortable, demonstrated more self-awareness, and demonstrated a lower level of confusion and less defensiveness. There appeared to be both advantages and disadvantages in experiencing either the anticounselor or the procounselor version of the TTM. First the TTM seems to prepare the counselor trainees to better comprehend the facts and information available to them about the client's cultural context. Merely making those facts available to trainees is not sufficient until and unless they can be made ready to comprehend the meaning of those facts, from the client's perspective. Feedback from the anticounselor or procounselor seems to increase the trainee's ability to more accurately process the information in a meaningful way. In conjunction with readings, lectures, and other training approaches, the TTM helps trainees attend both to the content and the process of gathering information useful to multicultural counseling.

Chambers (1992) combined the TTM with Ivey's microskills approach. This variation of the TTM was found to be effective for increasing the frequency of good verbal counseling responses and decreasing the frequency of poor verbal counseling responses in training and afterward. Chambers used a two-phase five-step process for teaching counseling skills to chemical dependency counselors. The first phase introduced counselors to the TTM using the anticounselor but not the procounselor version and addressed skills for listening and questioning. The second training phase addressed clarifying and reflecting skills.

> The use of Triad Training was found to be an effective method of (a) increasing the frequency of good verbal counseling responses overall (i.e., from training phase one through follow-up) and (b) decreasing the frequency of poor verbal counseling responses from baseline to training phase one and overall (i.e., from training phase one through follow-up). (Chambers, 1992, p. 2)

The most significant results occurred during training Phase 1 when counselors were introduced to the TTM. The counselor's verbal responses were reported to change as soon as the TTM was introduced, and positive effects were sustained throughout the course of the training. Feedback provided by the anticounselor seemed to be corrective and had the greatest effect on reducing poor counselor responses. Anecdotal reports indicated that learning generalized from the role-played situation to counseling sessions and actual interviews later.

In discussing these findings, Chambers (1992) indicated,

[T]he positive results seemed to be directly related to the pairing of the anticounselor's feedback to misapplied skills. The participants have told me that the anticounselor's reaction to skills not used or misapplied was permanently imprinted in their memory, hence it generalized to actual sessions. . . . This is why the anticounselor was more effective with the reduction of poor responses. I believe that the procounselor condition paired with positive applications of basic skills would be helpful, but I must admit I do not think the procounselor condition would increase good responses as significantly as the anticounselor condition reduces poor responses. (p. 1)

Chen, Chen, and Liao (1995) examined the different effects in counselor training using the TTM compared with using a microcounseling model with 26 students from the Taiwan Teacher's College, Taipei, Taiwan, Republic of China. All the training and testing were done in the Mandarin Chinese language. Participants were randomly divided into two groups and provided with 15 hours of basic counseling training over a 6-week period. At that point each group was trained for 10 hours over a 4-week period, using the two different training models. After training, all students were audiotaped working with culturally similar and dissimilar clients, and the audiotapes were scored using the Counselor Technique Evaluation Scale. All trainees also completed the Counseling Technique Self-Report Inventory. Findings showed that those trained with microcounseling skills were significantly more able than those trained with the TTM. Those trained in the TTM scored slightly less than those receiving microskills training in their counseling skills such as empathy, respect, specification, honesty, probing, and summarizing when counseling culturally similar clients, but differences were not statistically significant. However, when counseling clients from a different culture, those trained with the TTM scored relatively higher in their ability to demonstrate these same counseling skills, but again, with no statistical significance.

The study concluded that students should first be trained in microcounseling skills and that training with the TTM should come later in the training process. Suggestions for future research were (a) to increase the hours of training in each model, (b) to train students in the procounselor version before training them in the anticounselor version, (c) to select older clients with more life experiences when testing the trainee's skill level, and (d) to measure changes in the trainee's level of self-awareness as a result of training. Strous, Skuy, and Hickson (1993) used the TTM in training family counselors in South Africa. Multicultural training of counselors is particularly important in South Africa, where the ethnically diverse majority of 80% have been oppressed by a White minority under apartheid. This research attempted to design a culturally sensitive skill training design using the TTM.

The research involved a role-play presentation of a family counseling session using a procounselor and an anticounselor version, which was sent to family counseling trainers in South Africa, together with a 17-item evaluation questionnaire to measure the supervisor's perception of the potential relative efficacy for training family counselors, according to the conventional family counseling supervision, the anticounselor version of the TTM, or the procounselor version of the TTM. According to Strous et al. (1993),

> The role plays focused on the plight of a black domestic worker who lives with her husband on her white employers' premises. Their son lives in a segregated black township with his uncle who demands greater financial support from the boy's parents. This brings his parents/spouses into conflict and results in a warning from the mother/wife's employer that she will lose her job if her noisy altercations with her husband persist. (pp. 310–311)

Of the 16 university and 25 clinic-based trainers approached, 12 returned the questionnaire. Results reflected a significant and consistent preference for the procounselor over the anticounselor version and for the anticounselor version over conventional family counseling. These results encouraged Strous et al. (1993) to advocate more research using the TTM in South Africa. Strous et al. demonstrated how the TTM takes into account the sociopolitical context of culture and class for training counselors in South Africa. They found the TTM compatible to systemic family therapy training whereby the person and environmental context are seen as a whole. There was a high degree of consistency in the respondents' perceptions of the procounselor version as most effective (92%) and the anticounselor version as second most effective (83%) when compared with conventional counselor training designs.

Strous (2003), who also works in South Africa, modified the TTM into a proclient–anticlient training that focused more on the internal dialogue of the counselor than of the client.

> Both Triad Model training and Anticlient–Proclient training have benefits and may prove useful when sensitively applied. When combined, the two training techniques, incorporating anticounselor, anticlient, procounselor and proclient combinations may facilitate awareness of client self-talk as well as counselors' own biases. In psychodynamic terms, the Triad Model may improve counselor insight into transference issues in intergroup contexts. The Anticlient–Proclient Model may increase insight into countertransference issues. (p. 126)

The anticlient–proclient model tries to promote a greater degree of inclusion on the part of counselors in examining their ideological orientation. Subtle racism and other counseling-hindering attitudes are personified in the hope that a culturally inclusive perspective will help them to move away from any racist practices and exclusionary prejudices they may inadvertently hold (Strous, 2006).

Strous (2003, 2006) discovered that the anticlient disclosed the reasons for empathic failure just as the proclient encouraged a healthy empathic perspective.

> The empathic failure and therapy-hindering consequences of the anticlient position stand in opposition to the proclient promotion of such therapeutic relationships as the Working Alliance or the Real Relationship. Self-awareness, intimacy emotional joining, nondefensiveness and a nonpejorative approach were dominant values that therapists believed were facilitating of effective interracial therapy. (Strous, 2003, p. 112)

Youngs (1996) tested the effectiveness of the TTM, incorporating the anticounselor and procounselor simultaneously in training White school counselors to improve service delivery to African American clients. The TTM was compared with a contrast model and a control group using both quantitative and qualitative data from a random sample of African American clients in Grades 8 through 12 at a suburban, culturally diverse school district. The results

> demonstrated that clients rated White school counselors trained in the Triad Model higher in expertness than White counselors trained in the contrast method. Control clients, however, also rated their counselors higher in expertness than did contrast clients. Triad clients did not rate their counselors higher than contrast and control clients in the areas of attractiveness, trustworthiness and empathy. (Youngs, 1996, p. 133)

Additionally, clients in the TTM group "reported greater satisfaction with the school counseling program than contact clients did. Control group clients, however, also indicated greater satisfaction with the school counseling program than contrast clients did" (Youngs, 1996, p. 133). Even though the quantitative hypotheses were not supported, findings from the quantitative analysis pointed out the effectiveness of the TTM over the contrast method in the areas of expertness and client satisfaction with school counseling.

Analysis of the qualitative data offered support for the utility of the TTM. Youngs (1996) showed that the counseling techniques and strategies used by the counselors trained in the TTM differed from those trained in the contrast or control techniques, especially in the areas "of phone contacts to families, home visits, use of non-traditional interventions, addressing the issues of culture and race during counseling interviews, and showing sensitivity to the individual needs of clients" (p. 136).

Clients also reported that counselors trained in the TTM emphasized the personal quality of the relationship more, used the group process more, included more life skills instruction, and demonstrated higher expectations for their clients. Counselors trained in the TTM did not limit their counseling to educational and career goals but addressed personal and emotional needs, such as grief and loss, illness of family members, and relationship difficulties.

Youngs (1996) evidenced the effectiveness of the TTM as a multicultural training intervention for school counselors and identified or affirmed specific strategies that have significance for African American school children. The study demonstrated that the TTM fosters change in counseling technique and that high school age students can serve effectively as coached clients, procounselors, and anticounselors.

The TTM forces the counselor trainee to become more inclusive and examine her or his preferred style of counseling as it does or does not fit the needs of culturally different clients. Trainees are given the opportunity to develop credibility on the basis of their responses to the coached client, anticounselor, and procounselor team from the host culture. When the trainee has made a mistake, they learn recovery skills for getting out of trouble. Training with the TTM seems to influence the counselor's counseling style of counseling and increase the counselor's constructive use of nontraditional techniques or strategies in counseling.

The TTM is presented as one of many examples of structured experiences for developing ICE among counselors in an efficient and effective approach. As the counselor internalizes the voices of procounselors and anticounselors in her or his own internal dialogue, the range of opportunities and difficulties is likely to expand profoundly, giving the counselor a more inclusive perspective of the client's cultural context. The insights from this internalized anti and pro self-talk will help the counselor match the appropriate method and context of counseling to the client's changing perspective.

DEMONSTRATING THE TRIAD TRAINING MODEL IN ACTION

The following exercise allows the reader to try on the TTM in action to better understand how this approach to training might increase competence of ICE. Exhibit 9.1 is transcribed from an interview between a White male counselor and a Black female client discussing relationship problems the Black female client is having at the university.

Procedure

1. Review the brief transcript excerpts in Exhibit 9.1 and write in what you believe an anticounselor and a procounselor might say in the blanks provided.
2. You may choose to role play the scripted dialogue in a training session.

EXHIBIT 9.1
The Triad Training Model

Part 1

The first set of statements is transcribed from an interview between a White male counselor and a Black female client discussing relationship problems the Black female client is having at the university.

1. Identity

Client: OK, my problem is that I don't seem to be able to trust the White people here on campus. Being Black, I seem to have sort of a problem with this sort of thing and I don't know what to do about it and somebody recommended you. This person said that you were a good counselor, so I decided to come and get some help from you.

Counselor: Do you have any problems relating to the Black students on campus, Terry?

Client: No, not really. You know, there are people everywhere. Some you don't like, some you do like.

Anticounselor:

Procounselor:

2. Relationship

Counselor: How do you feel in terms of our relationship now? You came here and we have been talking for about 2 to 3 minutes. How do you feel about the way we've been talking?

Client: Well, you haven't helped me for one thing. I mean you just . . .

Anticounselor:

Procounselor:

3. Comfort Evaluation

Counselor: Do you feel uncomfortable with me?

Client: Um, not now, not yet.

Counselor: I um . . . I, ah, . . . (pause) I don't feel any discomfort with you at all.

Client: Oh, well, cuz I'm a friendly person I suppose. (laugh)

Anticounselor:

Procounselor:

4. Counselor's Culture

Counselor: Are you getting a little uncomfortable, Terry? . . . Perhaps because I'm White? In sharing some of these things with me?

Client: Um . . . Not really, and it's like I said, you know, I try to be pretty open-minded about what I'm talking about. But the thing I want to know is can you really understand where I'm coming from? What kind of things I'm really dealing with?

Anticounselor:

Procounselor:

Part 2

The second set of statements is transcribed from an interview between a White male counselor and a Latin American female client discussing relationship problems the Latin American female is having at the university.

1. Identity

Client: Yeah, they treat me like dirt, that's it, you know? And I feel divided inside. Like they don't care for me as a whole person.

Counselor: Ummm . . . You said divided. What is the division?

EXHIBIT 9.1
The Triad Training Model (*Continued*)

Client: The division is that they just want sex. They don't want to see me as a whole person.
Anticounselor:
Procounselor:

2. Relationship

Counselor: Could you tell me what you would rather have from them? How you would like a man to treat you when you go out with him?
Client: Well, it's just that, especially the first time . . . for some time . . .
Counselor: Um mmm . . .
Client: I like to get to know the person in a different way.
Anticounselor:
Procounselor:

3. Comfort Level

Counselor: OK, I better ask you another question then. How comfortable are you with me? Should . . . maybe I'm not the right person to work with you . . . because I'm an American man.
Client: So far you're OK because you are far enough . . .
Anticounselor:
Procounselor:

4. Counselor's Culture

Client: Yeah, you see this thing, these things for me are very intense for me right now because I just came. I've been here for only about a month.
Counselor: Would you feel better if I got back behind the desk and we sort of had that between us?
Client: No, then you remind me of my father.
Anticounselor:
Procounselor:

Note. From *110 Experiences for Multicultural Learning* (pp. 153–155), by P. B. Pedersen, 2004, Washington, DC: American Psychological Association. Copyright 2004 by Paul B. Pedersen. Adapted with permission.

3. When all the students have written in the responses of an anti-counselor and a procounselor for the scripted transcript segment, compare the different responses.

4. You may choose to have small groups of 3 to 4 students work together to figure out what a procounselor and anticounselor would say.

5. When the students have finished discussing their responses, move to the next scripted segment in Exhibit 9.1 and repeat the process.

6. When you have completed the transcript segments, organize the whole group into a general discussion.

Debriefing

Review the statements you made as a procounselor or as an anticounselor in dyads or small groups. Pay attention to how your response was similar to or different from the response of others in the group. Consider the following questions in your discussion:

1. Were the statements of the anticounselor and procounselor accurate? Why or why not?
2. How might the counselor respond on hearing the anticounselor or procounselor statements?
3. How might the client respond on hearing the anticounselor or procounselor statements?
4. How might it be useful for multicultural counselors to monitor the anticounselor and procounselor messages in a client's internal dialogue?
5. Can you listen to the procounselor, anticounselor, client, and your own internal dialogue at the same time?

The anticounselor and procounselor voices are helpful in demonstrating the full range of internal dialogue for both the counselor and the client. When the counselor is able to imagine or guess more accurately what a client is thinking but not saying, the counselor is at a great advantage.

CONCLUSION

In the last nine chapters we described how helping professionals of all kinds can develop ICE. The first stage is becoming aware of one's own and others' learned assumptions and networks of comemberships in different cultures. The second stage is increasing knowledge and comprehension of specific similarities and differences between oneself and the client(s) within each counseling relationship. The third stage is using concrete skills to help counselors and ultimately help clients draw on their own multicultural resources to overcome their problem or find balance.

The next two chapters show how ICE can extend beyond the helping relationship, from increasing client empowerment over the problem to acting on behalf of the client in advocacy work at the level of social policy. We also discuss our hopes that ICE can lead psychology and the human service professions through a paradigm shift, placing multiculturalism at the heart of every helping relationship.

10

EMPOWERMENT APPLICATIONS OF INCLUSIVE CULTURAL EMPATHY

The primary purpose of this chapter is to demonstrate the empowering impact of inclusive cultural empathy (ICE) for clients. The chapter shows how insights described in the earlier chapters build a strategy toward that empowerment to demonstrate the broad impact of inclusion. A broad and inclusive definition of counseling interventions includes both the educational and the medical model to accommodate the diversity of culturally different consumer populations. "Even our definitions of health and pathology can be culture-bound, especially in the area of mental health. Thus what constitutes healthy human development may also vary according to the sociocultural context" (Kagitcibasi, 1988, p. 25). The task of inclusion is to recognize the many different voices in each client's cultural context that influence the client's behavior. As the client and counselor become more aware of their many culture teachers, they become better able to understand one another. It is essential to recognize the importance of an inclusive perspective to accurately understand each cultural context.

The educational model lends itself to an inclusive interpretation of counseling and therapy. According to the educational model, the consumer is typically regarded as an essentially healthy, normal person wanting to learn new information. The provider's task is to teach the client new ways of learning new information and the consumer's task is to learn new strategies. Just as all counseling interventions are to some extent educative, so educational change also has a therapeutic dimension to it. The inclusive perspective provides a wider range of choices and alternative explanations to the counselor and the client.

The inclusive perspective recognizes and accommodates differences between Western and non-Western perspectives described in chapter 2. In many non-Western cultures the teacher is expected to guide people toward appropriate personal growth goals. Seeking help from a mental health specialist for a "mental" problem in these cultures carries a stigma and almost certainly reduces that person's status in the community. However, a teacher can provide the same functions of counseling guidance and learning in ways that will enhance one's status.

MULTICULTURALISM IS INCLUSIVE AND BROADLY DEFINED

ICE as defined in chapter 3 seeks to provide a conceptual framework that recognizes the complex diversity of a plural society while, at the same time, suggesting bridges of shared concern that bind culturally different people to one another. The ultimate outcome may be a generic multicultural theory, as Segall, Dasen, Berry, and Poortinga (1990) suggested.

> There may well come a time when we will no longer speak of cross cultural psychology as such. The basic premise of this field—that to understand human behavior, we must study it in its sociocultural context—may become so widely accepted that all psychology will be inherently cultural. (p. 352)

Multiculturalism has more often been regarded as a method than as a theory. If multiculturalism refers exclusively to narrowly defined culture-specific categories such as nationality or ethnicity, then multiculturalism might indeed best be considered merely as a method of analysis. The multicultural method can then be applied to the encounter of specific cultural groups with one another while emphasizing the culture-specific characteristics of each group. If, however, multiculturalism refers to inclusively defined social-system variables such as ethnography, demography, status, and affiliations, then multiculturalism might better be considered a theory. In that case, the underlying principle of multicultural theory would emphasize both the culture-specific characteristics that differentiate and the culture-general characteristics that unite in the explanation of human behavior. The accommodation of both within-group and between-groups differences is required for a comprehensive understanding of complicated cultures (Pedersen, 2000a).

By defining culture broadly, to include demographic variables (e.g., age, sex, place of residence), status variables (e.g., social, educational, economic), and affiliations (formal and informal), as well as ethnographic variables such as nationality, ethnicity, language, and religion, the construct *multicultural* becomes generic to all counseling relationships. The narrow definition of culture has limited multiculturalism to what might more appropriately be called "multiethnic" or "multinational" relationships between groups with a shared sociocultural heritage that includes similarities of religion, history, and common ancestry. Ethnicity and nationality are important to individual and familial identity as one subset of culture, but the construct of culture—inclusively defined—goes beyond national and ethnic boundaries. People from the same ethnic or nationality group may still experience cultural differences. Not all Blacks have the same experience, nor do all Asians, nor all American Indians, nor all Hispanics, nor all women, nor all old people, nor all people with a disability. No particular group is unimodal in its perspective. Therefore, the broad and inclusive definition of culture is particularly important in preparing counselors to deal with the complex differences among and between clients from every cultural group.

Just as differentiation and integration are complementary processes, so are the emic (culture specific) and etic (culture general) perspectives necessarily interrelated. The basic problem facing counselors is how to describe behavior in terms that are true to a particular culture while at the same time comparing those behaviors with a similar pattern in one or more other cultures (Pedersen, 1997). Combining the specific and general viewpoints provides a multicultural perspective. This larger perspective is an essential starting point for mental health professionals seeking to avoid cultural encapsulation by their own culture-specific assumptions and the empowerment of clients to avoid encapsulation by their own cultural biases and exploitation by the cultural biases of others.

Poortinga (1990) defined culture as shared constraints that limit the behavior repertoire available to members of a sociocultural group in a way that is different from individuals belonging to some other group. Segall et al. (1990) affirmed that ecological forces are the prime movers and shapers of cultural forms, which in turn shape behaviors. "Given these characteristics of culture, it becomes possible to define it simply as the totality of whatever all persons learn from all other persons" (Segall et al., 1990, p. 26). Culture is part of the environment, and all behavior is shaped by culture, so it is rare (perhaps even impossible) for any human being ever to act without responding to some aspect of culture.

Culture provides a unique perspective in which two people can disagree without one necessarily being right and the other being wrong, when their arguments are based on culturally different assumptions. It becomes possible for a counselor to identify common ground between two culturally different people whose expectations and ultimate goals are the same even though their behaviors may be very different. The same individual may even change her or his cultural referent group during the course of the interview—from emphasizing gender, to age, to socioeconomic status, to nationality or ethnicity, to one or another affiliation. Unless the counselor is skilled enough to understand that each changing salient culture requires a different understanding and interpretation of that person's behavior, the counselor is not likely to be accurate in assessing the person's changing behavior. The same culturally learned behavior may have very different meanings for different people and even for the same person across time and situations.

Multiculturalism needs to be understood in a perspective that does not replace or displace traditional theories by invalidating them. Multiculturalism should complement rather than compete with traditional theories of counseling. Taking the inclusive definition of culture, it is difficult for a counselor to be accurate and skilled according to any theory without in some way accounting for the ever-changing cultural salience in her or his client's perspective.

EMPOWERMENT THROUGH INCLUSIVE CULTURAL EMPATHY

Power is difficult to measure, but generally it refers to a person's ability to act independently from the influence or control of others. However, in a collective, less individualistic society, power might be demonstrated by the person's having chosen to be influenced by the group. ICE emphasizes a sensitivity to the balance of power in counseling. Competence requires that the counselor and client "manage" and regulate the distribution of power in the interview. The counselor must know how much power to exert in a multicultural interview to facilitate the client's empowerment. If the counselor exerts too much power the client will reject counseling as more of a hassle than the problem was in the first place; if the counselor exerts too little power the client will reject counseling as ineffective and useless (Pedersen, 2000b). Some theories of counseling define successful outcomes as *empowering* the client so that the client becomes less helpless and more powerful through the counseling relationship. Functionally, we might define ICE as the process of transferring power to the client in a safe context while preventing the problem from controlling the client.

In a collectivist culture the needs of the family may supersede the needs of individual members. The exercise of power that separated husband from wife or children from parents might have a destructive long-term effect in isolating one parent from the other or a child from the larger family. Empowerment would be developed much differently in this collectivist context than in a more individualistic society in which the rights and privileges of individuals are the primary vehicles of empowering clients.

If the task of counseling is to increase the power of the client and reduce the power of the problem over the client, then counseling can be described as a three-way distribution of power through a temporary means-oriented coalition between the client and the counselor against the problem. There are several methods for the effective multicultural training of counselors to manage power effectively from the client's cultural perspective.

First, counselors must be able to define power in each client's unique and different cultural context. Second, counselors must be able to appropriately adjust their own increase or decrease of power in the multicultural interview over time, as the salient balance of power changes. Third, counselors must have a wide repertoire of counseling styles to meet the culture-specific needs of each culturally different client as they change over time. Fourth, counselors must be able to develop and maintain rapport with culturally different clients in an enduring coalition of the counselor and client against the problem. Fifth, counselors must be able to work toward the client's ability to function in her or his cultural context without the counselor's assistance.

Figure 10.1 describes this triadic interaction between the counselor, client, and problem in which the client is initially dominated by the problem and the counselor intervenes to restore a balance of power for the client. Counseling then becomes a process whereby a client's contribution of power or influence increases and, as an inverse function of this process, the prob-

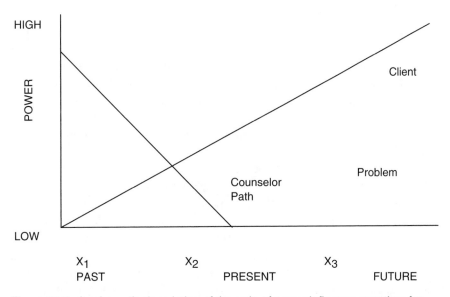

Figure 10.1. A schematic description of the ratio of power influence over time for counselor, counselee, and problem with three points (X_1, X_2, X_3) in the counseling process. From *The Triad Training Model,* by P. Pedersen, 1966, master's thesis, University of Minnesota, Minneapolis.

lem's capacity for power or influence decreases. The counselor intervenes to encourage the client's progress up the slope through a client–counselor coalition that balances the power influence of the problem.

As Figure 10.1 illustrates, at any point along the scale the power of the counselor plus the power of the client should be approximately equal to or greater than the power of the problem (Counselor + Client < Problem). The effective counselor needs to vary the power of intervention according to the client's changing needs.

The three situations (X_1, X_2, X_3) are indicated in Figure 10.1. In X_1, the client has little power and is dominated by the problem, requiring the counselor to exert more power than the client. In X_2, the client is able to exert enough power so that the counselor may back off and reduce power. Situation X_3 shows the client as being able to manage the problem almost independently and maintain a balance. The measures of high and low power influence are metaphors and not absolute entities to accommodate a relatively effective client facing a difficult problem or a relatively ineffective client facing a mild problem.

The counselor needs to coordinate the power of intervention according to the variable rate and direction of a client's movement to maintain a client–counselor coalition and balance of power in the interview. Counselors might exert more power through confrontation and interpretation and less power through reflection and nondirective accommodation. To the extent that a counselor and a client come from different cultures, it is particularly difficult to maintain the appropriate balance of power in a counseling interview. The research indicating that a positive relationship is the most important predictor of success in counseling, however, suggests that this balance of power must be maintained for counseling to be successful. Figure 10.1 provides a conceptual framework for demonstrating the counseling interaction and for defining the goal of training as increasing a counselor's skill in maintaining an effectively balanced relationship in counseling. ICE provides the strategy for maintaining a balance in counseling as the means of empowering clients.

Balance suggests a broad and inclusive frame of reference to the system or field surrounding each unit or identity. Although Western approaches acknowledge the importance of solutions, there is less understanding of how problems are also important in social services. In many non-Westernized systems there is less emphasis on separating the person or persons from a presenting problem or source of difficulty than there is in Westernized systems. There is also less of a tendency to locate the problem inside an isolated individual and more of an attempt to relate the individual's problem to other persons or even the cosmology. For example, if a person believes external forces in the cultural context shape the events around her or him, then that person's relationships to others and to the environment become particularly important. Balance in the context of counseling skill is a dynamic process within a context in which all elements, pain as well as pleasure, serve a useful and necessary function. This non-Western emphasis is typically more holistic in acknowledging the interaction of persons and environments in both their positive and negative aspects.

The restoration of balance through ICE provides an alternative goal to the more individualized goal of solving social problems. In the context of balance as a criterion of health, social change is perceived as a process of unresolved ambiguity, tension, and reciprocity of contrasting alternatives rather than the end goal of resolving differences in favor of one preferred alternative over the others. Balance is a process rather than a conclusive event. In a similar mode, the problems, pain, and otherwise negative aspects of social situations also provide necessary resources for creating a dynamic balance with pleasure and happiness, recognizing the importance of both negative and positive aspects.

Counseling occurs in a force field of push-and-pull factors in which the counselor seeks to be helpful, the client seeks to reconcile internalized ambiguity, and the problem—as a metaphorical third presence—seeks to continue controlling the client, all aspects of which are culturally mediated. In the mode of social power theory, counseling occurs in the context of an equilibrium between the counselor seeking coalition with the client against the resistance of a problem. Negotiating a coalition between the client and the counselor describes the task functions of counseling in operational terms.

Cultural variables can intervene in a counseling interview in at least three different ways. One way is through the cultures of the client, another is through the cultures of the counselor, and the third is through the cultures of the problems that define the context of a counseling interview and take on characteristics from contributing cultural aspects of the environment.

There are numerous implications for counseling and education in the accommodation of complexity and balance in our analysis. First of all, simple explanations are temptingly convenient but dangerous approaches to understanding the real world around us. The counselor is guilty of reductionism when assuming that all persons from a particular group or culture have *exactly* the same needs and behaviors, substituting symbiotic stereotypes for the real world of the unique individual before them. Reductionism ignores cultural variations among clients from the same culture. The measure of counseling competence is not merely identifying the many cultures, groups, or identities to which we each belong but being able to track which of those identities is salient at any given point in time from the client's viewpoint. The competent counselor will avoid reductionism through ICE.

Second, complexity is our friend and not our enemy in the search for the fuzzy, approximate, and indeterminate truths of reality. Every counselor is looking for easy answers and the magic bullet to cure all problems. Teachers usually help students simplify their understanding of problems and solutions. Sometimes that simplification results in distorting reality. If a teacher can accept the necessity and even the potential usefulness of helping a student accept and understand problems in more complicated—but perhaps more culturally authentic—terms, then the positive value of complicated thinking will become apparent.

Third, only those who are able to escape being caught up in the web of their own assumptions and maintain a balanced perspective will be able to demonstrate ICE. The dangers of cultural encapsulation and the dogma of increasingly technique-oriented definitions of the educational process have frequently been mentioned in the theories of professional counseling associations and criteria for accreditation of counselor educational programs. To escape from encapsulation, counselor educators need to challenge the cultural bias of their own untested assumptions. To leave our assumptions untested or, worse yet, to be unaware of our culturally learned assumptions is not consistent with the standards of good professional counseling (Pedersen, 2000a).

There are several implications of considering balance as a multicultural counseling skill. Each implication contributes toward a capability for understanding and facilitating a balanced perspective in multicultural social services. The following examples demonstrate how ICE promotes client empowerment through maintaining a balance of power.

1. Concepts of knowledge must be expanded to go beyond the boundaries of rational process. Knowledge in other cultures has many forms. There are many ways to gain knowledge, for example, intuition and other forms of knowledge accumulated through experience. Although reasoning is a valuable skill, it is presumed to get in the way of knowledge in many non-Western cultures and cut off sources of information. For that reason, what appears to be logical inconsistency and paradox become valuable approximations of truth in many societies. Logic is only one form of validation, dependent on a scientific, rational, and abstract principle to describe human behavior. The criteria of balance suggest other sources of validation as well.

2. The importance of relationships must be recognized when working in societies that do not emphasize individualism. In many societies, individual development is less important for a client's fulfillment. Appropriate spiritual alternatives describe the self as participating in a unity with all things and not limited by the changing illusions of self and nonself. In the non-Western perspective, an individual's unity with the universe goes beyond the self to cosmic unity. The individual is in a context of relationships between people in a cosmos.

3. Westernized perspectives, which have dominated the field of counseling, must not become the single criterion of "modernized" perspectives. Although non-Western cultures have had a profound impact on the West in recent years, many non-Western cultures seem more determined than ever to emulate the West as a social model. There is also evidence that the more modernized a society, the more their problems and solutions resemble those of a Westernized society. Whereas Western society is fearful of technological domination that might deteriorate social values and destroy the meaning of traditional culture, non-Western societies are frequently more concerned that the technology will not be available to them. The task is one of differentiating between modernized alternatives outside the Western model; otherwise we end up teaching Westernization in the name of modernization. We need indigenous, non-Western models of modernity to escape from our own reductionistic assumptions. Modernization does not necessarily require Westernization if the persons are empowered to modernize through their own indigenous ideologies.

4. Change is not inevitably a positive and good outcome of counseling. A balanced perspective between changing and unchanging values requires that we recognize that many cultures do not accept change and development as desirable. In Western cultures we say, "If you don't know what to do, at least do something!" There is a strong predisposition toward valuing change itself as intrinsically good, moving toward a solution, reconciling ambiguity, and promising better things for the future in Western cultures. A contrasting perspective suggests that change may be bad. To understand this change process, we need to identify those values that do not change but rather become the hinges on which the door of change swings. In a cosmic perspective, it is possible to deny the reality of change entirely, along with the cause–effect thinking, in favor of an external unchanging picture of ultimate reality. A balanced perspective allows the individual to see events as both positive and negative at the same time without oversimplifying events.

5. We do not control our environment, but neither does our environment control us. In the range of value orientations, there is a clear division among cultures that believe it is one's right and even responsibility to control the environment, other cultures that teach just as firmly that one is controlled by one's environment, and a third group that teaches that one interacts with the environment so that the question of control is irrelevant.

Whichever basic assumption is made will profoundly affect the criteria for intercultural training in any situation. An increased awareness of ecological balance has helped us understand the interaction with persons and environment as a complex and certainly not a simple phenomenon.

6. Ability to recover from mistakes is more important than perfection as a criterion for social service. Counselors working in an intercultural environment and not making mistakes may perhaps not be taking enough chances. The skilled professional will make as many errors as the novice. The difference is the skilled professional will be able to recover and the novice will not. In learning about intercultural criteria, it is important to break out of a success–failure dichotomy because ultimately the outcomes of social interaction are seldom defined clearly as a success or as a failure. The emphasis in identifying intercultural criteria needs to go beyond dichotomies to develop the potentially positive effects of each problem as an analogue or a range of possibilities.

7. Very few institutions offer specializations in cross-cultural mental health, although increasingly departments are offering isolated courses in cross-cultural communication. There is a need for a network across disciplines and institutions to coordinate the efforts of multicultural social services. Furthermore, there is a need to involve the "real world" of the community and reduce the artificiality of classroom training. Points 6 and 7 both demonstrate empowerment through exclusion of alternatives rather than excluding choices.

8. The literature on intercultural counseling is diffuse, varies a great deal in quality, and is published in journals of limited circulation. There is a need for a series of review publications that establish the threshold for quality control in previous as well as current publications. In the same regard, there is a need for more attention to multicultural issues in national meetings of professional associations, which presently invest too little time on cross-cultural papers. There is also a need for developing criteria from research on the range of non-Western alternatives to "talk therapy."

9. Finally, intercultural research has failed to develop grounded theory for multicultural social services. There are a number of reasons why this is true. First, the emphasis of multicultural research has been on abnormal rather than normal behavior across cultures. Second, only in the 1970s has research identified universal aspects across cultures, and then only for the more

serious categories of disturbance such as schizophrenia and affective psychoses. Third, the complexity of multicultural variables in research is difficult to quantify. Fourth, multicultural research that is available has lacked an applied emphasis and has remained largely theoretical or abstract. Fifth, there has not been sufficient interdisciplinary collaboration among mental health related disciplines on multicultural research. Sixth, the emphasis of multicultural research has been on the symptom rather than the interaction of person, profession, institution, or community.

THE DANGERS OF CULTURAL ENCAPSULATION AND EXCLUSION

It is possible to argue for inclusion from the moral and ethical perspective of social justice by linking exclusion and encapsulation to the values we espouse in counseling. ICE provides an alternative to the exclusion and encapsulation that can capture a counselor. The culturally encapsulated individual is just as able to evade reality through ethnocentrism ("mine is best") as through relativism ("to each her or his own"). Maintaining a cocoon is accomplished by evading reality and depending entirely on one's own internalized value assumptions about what is good for society. Isolation is accentuated by the inherent capacity of culture-bound and time-honored values to prevail against the tentativeness of present knowledge. It is therefore necessary for the culture-sensitive individual not only to learn new knowledge and skills but also to reorganize the old knowledge that no longer applies. The encapsulated individual is singularly unable to adapt to a constantly changing sociocultural context.

The most familiar illustration of powerlessness is cultural encapsulation. Encapsulation, as we discussed in chapter 5 of this volume, as a component of knowledge competence, is a result of several basic and familiar processes in our professional activity as a component of skill competence (Wrenn, 1985). Wrenn's five-point description of encapsulation demonstrates how counseling *as a profession* has protected itself against the complex inclusion of multiculturalism.

1. We define reality according to one set of cultural assumptions and stereotypes that becomes more important than the real world outside.
2. We become insensitive to cultural variations among individuals and assume that our view is the only real or legitimate one. It is not surprising that the assumption that "I know better than they do what is good for them" is offensive to the target audience.

3. Each person has unreasoned assumptions he or she accepts without proof. When these assumptions are threatened by another religion, political view, or culture, individuals can easily become fearful or defensive. When people of the host culture are perceived as threatening, they quickly become an "enemy" to be opposed and ultimately defeated in the name of self-preservation.

4. A technique-oriented job definition further contributes toward and perpetuates the process of encapsulation. The world is simplistically divided into a polarity of friends and enemies, us and them, with each relationship being evaluated according to whether or not it contributes to getting the job done.

5. When there is no evaluation of other viewpoints, individuals may experience encapsulation by absolving themselves of any responsibility to interpret the behavior of others as relevant and meaningful to their own life activity.

Some people have developed a dependency on one authority, one theory, one truth. These encapsulated people tend to be trapped in one way of thinking, believing that theirs is the universal way. They are trapped in an inflexible structure that resists adaptation to alternative ways of thinking. In contrast, a liberated mode of thinking represents an effort to establish empathy with other people different from ourselves. Empathy is a process of learning foreign beliefs, assumptions, or perspectives, feelings, and consequences in such a way that the outsider participates in the host culture. Through multicultural contact, people can be liberated to cope with constant change and to feel empathy with other alternatives available to them.

THE INTRAPERSONAL CULTURAL GRID

The starting point for education and training about ICE is to clarify how culture controls one's behavior with or without one's permission. Imagine that several hundred culture teachers, collected by you over your lifetime, are sitting with you discussing the decisions you are now making. These culture teachers include family, friends, fantasies, mentors, and any others who have made a significant impact on your life. This self-talk or internal dialogue shapes your decisions and behaviors from within (Pedersen, 2000b). Our students and clients, of course, bring their culture teachers with them also. To understand how these culture teachers control behavior, ask yourself three questions. First, what specific behavior are you trying to understand? Second, what did you expect to happen as a result of displaying that behavior? Third, who were the culture teachers who taught you to display that particular behavior at that particular time to get that positive expectation? This chain of questions was described earlier in chapter 5 (this volume) and displayed in the intrapersonal cultural grid in Figure 5.1.

The intrapersonal (inside-the-person) cultural grid incorporates broadly defined social system variables on one dimension and personal behavior–expectation–values on the other, in a personal–cultural orientation. Culture controls each specific behavior or identifiable action of each individual through that person's expectations. Expectations are the cognitive variables that include behavior–outcome and stimulus–outcome expectancies that guide the individual's choice of behavior. Expectations, in turn, are controlled by underlying values. Values are the belief systems that explain the importance and prioritize expectations. Social system variables are the sources in society from which values are learned. An accurate understanding of culture requires that we understand how an individual's behaviors in a particular context are controlled by learned expectations and values based on or taught by broadly defined social system variables.

Cultural teachers might come from family relationships such as relatives or from business associates, fellow countrypersons, ancestors, or those with shared beliefs. Power relationships based on social friendships, sponsors and mentors, subordinates, and supervisors or superiors may provide cultural teachers. Memberships shared with coworkers or in organizations, gender or age groups, and workplace colleagues may contribute cultural teachers. A wide range of nonfamily relationships, friendships, classmates, neighbors, or just people like yourself may also have contributed teachers.

THE INTERPERSONAL CULTURAL GRID

ICE recognizes that the same behaviors may have different meanings and that different behaviors may have the same meaning. By establishing the shared positive expectations between and among people, the accurate interpretation of behaviors becomes possible. The interpersonal (between-persons) cultural grid (see Figure 10.2) is useful in understanding how cultural differences influence the interaction of two or more individuals. It is important to interpret behaviors accurately in terms of the intended intentions, expectations, and values expressed by those behaviors. If two people are accurate in their interpretation of one another's expectation, they do not always need to display the same behavior. The two people may agree to disagree about which behavior is appropriate and continue to work together in harmony despite their different styles of behavior.

Exhibit 10.1 lists an exercise for applying the interpersonal cultural grid. According to the exercise, perhaps the shared expectation of *best friendship* that you and your friend share and in which you both trust provides a common

	BEHAVIOR OR ACTION	

	SAME	DIFFERENT
	POSITIVE	NEGATIVE
SAME **POSITIVE**	I	II
DIFFERENT **NEGATIVE**	III	IV

EXPECTATION OR INTENTION

Figure 10.2. The interpersonal cultural grid. From *A Handbook for Developing Multicultural Awareness, Third Edition* (p. 98), by P. B. Pedersen, 2000, Alexandria, VA: American Counseling Association. Copyright 2000 by the American Counseling Association. Reprinted with permission.

EXHIBIT 10.1
Applying the Interpersonal Cultural Grid

- Identify your best friend and write that individual's name here:
  _____.
- Now make a list of behaviors that your best friend does that are different from how you might behave in a similar situation.
- Now make a list of behaviors that you do that are different from how your friend might behave in a similar situation.
- What are some of the things that your best friend does to or with you that would not be acceptable if done to a stranger?
- What are some of the things that you do to or with your best friend that would not be acceptable if done by a stranger?

---

ground that is so powerful and important that your tolerance of different behaviors is much greater with regard to your friend than it would be for a stranger. This is an example of the interpersonal cultural grid in action.

Figure 10.2 divides the interaction between two individuals into four possible quadrants (Pedersen, 2000). In the first quadrant, two individuals have similar behaviors and similar positive expectations. There is a high level of accuracy in both individuals' interpretation of each other's behavior and expectation. This aspect of the relationship would be congruent and probably harmonious. We are focusing exclusively on positive expectations here. If the two individuals share the same negative expectations ("I hate you") and behavior ("I am beating you up!"), the relationship may be congruent but certainly not harmonious.

In the second quadrant, two individuals have different behaviors but share the same positive expectations. There is a high level of agreement that the two people both expect trust and friendliness, for example, but there is a low level of accuracy because each person perceives and interprets the other individual's behavior incorrectly. This relationship is characteristic of multicultural conflict in which each person is applying a self-reference criterion to interpret the other individual's behavior in terms of this person's own self-reference expectations and values. The conditions described in the second quadrant are very unstable and, unless the shared positive expectations are quickly made explicit, the relationship is likely to change toward the third quadrant.

In the third quadrant, two people have the same behaviors but differ greatly in their expectations. There is actually a low level of agreement in positive expectations between the two people even though similar or congruent behaviors give the appearance of harmony and agreement. One person may continue to expect trust and friendliness, whereas the other person is now negatively distrustful and unfriendly, for example. Both persons are, however, presenting the same smiling, glad-handing behaviors.

If these two people discover that the reason for their conflict is their differences of expectation, and if they are then able to return their relationship to an earlier stage when they did perhaps share the same positive expectations of trust and friendliness, for example, then their interaction may return to the second quadrant. This would require each person to adjust their interpretation of the other's different behavior to fit their shared positive expectation of friendship and trust. If, however, their expectations remain different, then even though their behaviors are similar and congruent, the conflict is likely to increase until their interaction moves to the fourth quadrant.

In the fourth quadrant the two people have different behaviors and also different or negative expectations. Not only do they disagree in their behaviors toward one another, but now they also disagree on their expectations of friendship and trust. This relationship is likely to result in hostile disengagement. If the two people can be coached to increase their accuracy in identifying one another's positive expectations, however, there may still be a chance for them to return to an earlier stage of their relationship in which their positive expectations were similar even though their behaviors might have been very different, as in the second quadrant.

Take smiling, for instance. Smiling is an ambiguous behavior. It may or may not imply trust and friendliness. The smile may or may not be interpreted accurately. Outside of its culturally learned context the smile has no fixed meaning. Two people with similar expectations of friendliness may not both be smiling. However, one person may expect friendliness and the other may want to sell a used car, even though both of them are smiling. In a similar mode, two people may have the same expectation of trust, respect, happiness, or success, even though the culturally learned behaviors attached to that expectation may be very different for each of the two persons.

Let us take, for example, a counselor working with a client from a different culture. The counselor is very formal in counseling relationships and sometimes even professionally cool toward clients, keeping them at a distance. The client seems almost the opposite in style, preferring to be friendly and informal toward everyone. Now let us consider how this relationship might progress using the four quadrants of the interpersonal cultural grid.

Before the counselor and client got together, they had heard good things about each other, about how the other person was friendly, trusting, respectful, and competent, so both were looking forward to working together. This might describe the conditions of Quadrant I in Figure 10.2. The positive expectations and behaviors were congruent and similar.

During the first week the counselor and client behaved quite differently, with the client being informal and the counselor being very formal in their interactions. Each person interpreted the other's behavior negatively and contrary to the original expectation. They failed to recognize that they really shared the same expectation. Because their behaviors were so different from one another, neither one realized that they both had the same positive expectation for trust, respect, and harmony. These are the conditions of Quadrant II. This quadrant defines an example of cross-cultural conflict when the two persons misinterpret the other's behaviors and impose their own culturally learned interpretation on the other person's behaviors.

In the second week the differences in behavior between the counselor and client have continued and are now a source of irritation and conflict between them as the interaction moves to Quadrant III. The counselor has now demanded that the client become more formal and less informal, and the client has reluctantly agreed. At this point the client no longer expects trust, respect, and harmony, as had been the case in Quadrant I and II, but both counselor and client are displaying the same congruent behaviors to give the appearance of harmony. Their similar behaviors might lead them and others to assume that they had the same expectations, but ultimately both counselor and client would discover the differences in expectation and probably feel betrayed by the other person.

In the third week the client is feeling very hostile at having to behave in such an unnaturally formal way, and the conflict between the counselor and client becomes more pronounced as indicated in Quadrant IV. The client gives up and leaves counseling to preserve self-esteem and dignity, and the counselor willingly gives up the client to preserve self-esteem and dignity. Both counselor and client will be very confused by the other person and what happened between them. The confusion is likely to result in open hostility and alienation between the counselor and client.

The hostile disengagement of culturally different counselors and clients is not, however, inevitable. If we look at a second scenario of this hypothetical relationship, we can identify an alternative outcome. Here again, the same counselor favors formality working with the same client who favors informality. Before getting together, each has heard good things about the other and shared the positive expectations and behaviors described in Quadrant I.

During the first week both the counselor and the client notice that they are behaving differently. In discussing these very different behaviors, they discover that they have the same expectations for trust, respect, and harmony, as indicated in Quadrant I and II, but that their behaviors for expressing those expectations are very different, as in Quadrant II. By calling attention to the differences in behavior and the similarity of expectations, several options are now available to the counselor and client. One, they might agree to disagree about what kind of behavior is appropriate, and each person may continue with the formal or informal behavior, but now the other person is better able to interpret that incongruent behavior accurately as an expression of trust and respect. Two, they might both try to bend their behavior toward the other person's preference, making an exception for that particular instance because it is important that the shared expectation for trust and respect be communicated to the other person. Three, by focusing on the shared common-ground expectation and not being distracted by the incongruent or different behaviors, the counselor and client have now established a basis for their continuing relationship without either person having to sacrifice cultural integrity by compromising values.

During the third week the counselor and client may well be bothered by the differences in behavior although they are now able to interpret each other's behavior accurately and appropriately. They decide to concentrate on their similar positive expectations rather than their different behaviors, and they each adjust their behavior accordingly. Their interaction is not without conflict, but the positive shared expectations provide a common ground for them to work out differences in behavior and accommodate one another as in Quadrant II. The relationship does not move to the interpersonal conflict of Quadrants III and IV.

In the fourth week, the client and counselor discover some advantages of working with a person whose behaviors are so different as long as they can be certain of their shared positive expectations for trust, respect, and harmony as in Quadrant II. In the fifth week, the counselor and client find that they have both modified their behaviors at least with regard to one another and now they quite often share the same behaviors as well as the same positive expectations, as in Quadrant I and II. In the sixth week, both counselor and client have learned to accurately assess each other's behavior, and the shared positive expectation for trust, harmony, and respect has been strengthened as in Quadrant I and II, contributing to the success of the counseling.

In this way the interpersonal cultural grid provides a conceptual road map for ICE to interpret another person's behavior accurately in the context of that person's culturally learned expectations. It is not necessary for the counselor and client to share the same behaviors as long as they share the same positive expectations.

The interpersonal cultural grid can be a useful tool for analyzing the ways that culture influences behavior both within the person and between persons. It provides practical assistance in managing the complexity of culturally learned behaviors, expectations, and values. This combining of personal with cultural suggests a way out of a dilemma for cross-cultural research. On the one hand, there are data suggesting that cultural differences exist and must be accounted for in cross-cultural contact. On the other hand, attempts to describe cultural aspects through labels have tended to result in stereotyping. Consequently, attempts to discriminate according to cultural differences have been disguised in ways that would protect an organization or person against being accused of racism.

Although the cultural label may be predictive in aggregate data about large groups from the same culture, it is less helpful in dealing with a particular individual from that culture as in a counseling situation. It is apparent that an accurate perception of another person's complex cultural perspective is an important skill for counselors in any and all situations.

Unless the cross-cultural misunderstanding or conflict is identified and distinguished from the elements of personal conflict, the following *negative* chain of events may occur.

1. The different behaviors will suggest that expectations may also be different.
2. As different behaviors persist, the two persons may conclude that they do not share the same positive expectations and intentions.
3. One of the two persons may choose to modify behaviors to match the other person, perhaps caused by the power constraints of the more powerful partner. However, the sense of shared positive expectations will become more and more questionable.

4. Both partners may ultimately resort to total conflict in which both expectations and behaviors are different and war is declared.
5. Both partners will conclude that there is a low level of agreement between them.
6. Neither partner will be aware that there is also a low level of accuracy in their communication.

If the multicultural context of the situation is identified and distinguished as separate from personal hostility, the following *positive* chain of events is likely to occur.

1. The different behaviors will be understood as expressions of shared positive expectations.
2. The two or more persons will conclude that they do share the same positive expectations in spite of their different behaviors.
3. One or both of the two persons may choose to modify their behavior to match the other person so that both the positive expectations and the behaviors will be similar.
4. Both partners may ultimately move toward a more harmonious situation in which both the positive expectations and the behaviors are similar.
5. Both partners may conclude there is a high level of agreement between them.
6. Both partners will be aware that there is a high level of accuracy in their communication.

There is good reason to believe that counseling fulfills a need for both the counselor and the client beyond gathering information. The interpersonal cultural grid provides structure to the culture-centered counseling interview process, suggesting criteria for evaluating both the individual performance and interaction. Culturally learned values and expectations are essential data for culture-centered counseling. The interpersonal cultural grid is a heuristic framework to help culture-centered counselors differentiate cultural from personal aspects of the interview.

A young teaching assistant goes to meet his foreign-born professor for the first time and finds the professor to be loud and overly friendly. In the young teaching assistant's culture, he has learned not to trust people who are so forward in their manner. The young man could see that his own contrasting quiet and submissive style was not respected by the professor, although he wanted and needed to work in harmony with his professor. During this initial meeting, the young man decides to become boisterous, loud, and overly friendly to reflect his professor's manner so that they would get along with one another. Nevertheless, his first impressions of the professor are negative, and he begins to resent having to change his own ways to accommodate the professor's preferred style.

1. Describe both the young man and the professor as you see them in your mind's eye. Use at least 10 adjectives and categorize each adjective as a demographic, ethnographic, status, or affiliation variable.
2. How do you think the professor and the young man are feeling as the young man enters the room?
3. What are some positive and negative thoughts in each of their minds?
4. What might each conclude at the end of the first meeting?
5. What cultural assumptions have influenced *your own* perceptions of these two people?

As an example of how the interpersonal cultural grid might be used to analyze this complex cultural situation, let us examine three different behaviors from this brief case study. We work in two different directions in our analysis of these behaviors. On the one hand, we want to consider possible alternative meanings behind the behavior and decide which meaning is more likely. On the other hand, we want to consider the range of social system variables inferred about the person performing the behavior and decide which social system variable is the most salient in this situation.

The three behaviors are as follows: (a) The professor greets the teaching assistant in a loud and overly friendly way; (b) The teaching assistant responds to the professor in a quiet and submissive style; and (c) The teaching assistant decides to become loud and boisterous toward his professor.

First, the loud and friendly greeting by the professor might express the positive expectation for friendliness grounded in the value of international harmony and learned from social systems such as his family and his previous contacts with other international students. There is the possibility of course that the professor really does not expect friendliness and is showing his superior status or is being patronizing toward foreign-born persons. Even in the midst of many negative expectations and mixed motives, it may still be possible to identify some small area of shared positive expectation. This area of common ground, however small it may be, provides the platform on which a counselor can begin to construct a meaningful and lasting relationship.

Second, the quiet and submissive greeting by the teaching assistant might express friendliness and respect grounded in the value of status and learned from social systems such as his family, religion, social status group, and other sources. There is the possibility here also that the student is actually being unfriendly, apathetic, or disinterested. Here again, however, the task is to discover some small area of shared positive expectation so that the similar values can be allowed to bring the two persons closer together.

Third, the loud and boisterous adaptation by the teaching assistant might express a willingness to change his behavior in deference to the preferences of the professor as an expression of friendliness and respect grounded in values learned from social system groups back home. The task is to go beyond the behaviors being displayed to the expectations and values behind those behaviors so that the behaviors can be interpreted accurately and appropriately.

There are several specific ways in which the interpersonal cultural grid can be used as a practical tool for counselors.

1. The interpersonal cultural grid provides a framework for analyzing how culturally different behaviors might derive from culturally similar expectations and values.
2. Personal–cultural orientations can be compared across time or people to demonstrate how the same behavior can be explained by different expectations or values in different cultural settings.
3. The dynamic and changing priorities of social system variables can be matched with personal cognitive variables for each time and place and person to prevent stereotyping.
4. A comprehensive description of culture emerges from the framework that includes demographic, status, affiliation, and ethnographic variables in a broad and comprehensive range of cultural resources for each individual.
5. The close relationship between culturally learned behaviors and culturally different expectations or values behind similar behaviors combines the culturally specific emic with the culturally general etic aspects of a multicultural situation by separating areas of similarity from areas of difference.

Let us consider several examples in which the interpersonal cultural grid might facilitate ICE. In each example, the same series of steps for applying the interpersonal cultural grid would follow. These guidelines are offered as sources of working hypotheses or best-guess interpretations that would be checked out with actual clients in actual counseling situations.

Step 1. Identify the relevant behaviors being displayed or presented by the person or persons.
Step 2. Identify the positive expectations that would or might be attached to the behavior. "If I do this, then that will happen."
Step 3. Identify the value variable that is most likely to be salient for the person or persons being considered at the time the behavior was displayed.

Step 4. Identify the social systems that may have taught the person the value on which the expectation and ultimately the behavior are based.

Step 5. Develop rival hypotheses that put both positive and negative interpretations on the client's behavior and consider the range of alternatives for counseling goals.

Step 6. Identify those positive expectations that you think might be shared by both the persons in the brief case examples as the basis of common ground in working with both persons.

Example 1: Your client grew up as an immigrant in a fairly rough section of New York City, but his wife grew up in a quiet rural small town. They have adopted an Indochinese refugee child to live with them in New York City. They argue constantly about the child. The husband encourages the child to spend time in the streets getting to know other children in the neighborhood and learning to fit in. The wife wants the child to avoid contact with other children in the neighborhood because of the dangers the child might encounter. The husband wants the child to learn the rules of the street because it is an unsafe neighborhood to live in if you don't know the rules. The wife wants to discourage the child from spending time in the neighborhood and on the streets because it is unsafe to be there.

Common ground: Both husband and wife have the same expectation for *safety of the child* although their behaviors are very different.

Example 2: Your client is a minority person with a physical disability who does not work as hard as the other employees, even though the disability should not interfere with the person's work. How are you going to determine whether the resulting disagreements between the employee and coworkers are caused by the cultural differences between them or whether that person is manipulating the system by using cultural differences as an excuse? You would need to look beyond the behavior itself to get at the employee's expectations and values. Whether the employee does more or less work is perhaps less important than the reason why the employee is working. Once you have established through contacts with the employee and other coworkers what the employee's expectations are, it should be easier to assess whether the employee is using cultural differences to manipulate the system.

Common ground: Look for *shared values* behind the expectations and work style to find values that both the employee and the coworkers share.

Example 3: You have been asked to consult with the mental health clinic of a large university by the International Student Association. The student association complained that all foreign students who go to the mental health clinic are diagnosed as crazy because of their different and unusual behaviors compared with American students. You work with the therapists at the mental health clinic and get across the idea that people from different cultures have appropriately different behaviors and are not necessarily crazy. A month later the International Student Association again asks you to consult with the mental health clinic because now foreign students who urgently require therapy have been turned away even though their behavior clearly indicated a need for psychological assistance. The therapists say that the behavior of foreign students is naturally and appropriately bizarre, and therapy is not required. Your task is to work with the therapists to match appropriately and accurately the range of behaviors and expectations with social system variables.

Common ground: Behavior is not data until and unless it is interpreted within the context of *culturally learned expectations*.

Example 4: Two people have come to you for help in mediating their disagreement before resorting to legal action. They had grown up across the street from each other and have known each other all their lives. Their backgrounds are very similar, although one person has become increasingly more conservative and the other person increasingly more liberal in their lifestyles. Because they appear to one another as culturally similar, they assume that they begin with the same assumptions and any disagreement requires one of them to be wrong.

Common ground: Cultural differences may divide people who perceive themselves as belonging to the same culture even if they grew up across the street or in the same family if you *define culture broadly* as these two people do.

The practical advantage of the interpersonal cultural grid is to increase a person's ICE and accurate assessment of another person's behavior in the context of that person's culture. Without reference to these culturally learned expectations and values, we are unable to interpret accurately any behavior outside its cultural context. The matching of cultural with personal data provides a framework for understanding how culture is related to behavior and suggests specific procedures for culture-centered counseling

If culture is indeed within the person, then constructing a multicultural identity becomes an essential part of each person's development. The practical advantages of the interpersonal cultural grid are that it increases a person's accurate assessment of another person's behavior in the context of that person's culture. Without reference to these expectations and values, we are unable to accurately interpret any behavior outside its cultural context. The matching of cultural with personal data provides a framework for understanding how culture works both in the aggregate and in the individual instance. Culture-centered counselors need to go beyond the obvious labels used to describe individual and collective cultural identities. Culture-centered counselors need to recognize multicultural identity as including the synthesis of many cultures in our lives through complex and dynamic but not chaotic ways. This understanding of culture will be an important foundation for developing culture-centered counseling skills in subsequent chapters.

CONCLUSION

ICE is not an abstraction but rather a practical application of everything we know about counseling relationships. ICE applies to all counseling and human service theories and defines both the cultural context and the counseling methods in broad and inclusive perspectives. ICE applies to all clients and all counseling relationships, and in this chapter we discuss some of the practical applications of ICE for counselors and counselor educators.

First, it is necessary to define culture and multiculturalism broadly rather than narrowly, recognizing that each individual belongs to many different cultures at the same time and that different cultural identities will be more salient at different times and in different places. This idea has been presented as the imagined collectivity of a thousand culture teachers gathered over a lifetime for each individual and who influence and even control her or his decisions. Multicultural awareness requires people to be articulate about those culture teachers they carry in their imaginations.

Second, this chapter examined the process of empowerment through ICE. By monitoring the client's relationships with others in that client's multicultural context, it becomes possible to increase the client's power over time while reducing the client's dependence on the counselor. The counselor adjusts the amount of power influence figuratively so that the power of the client plus the power of the counselor is always equal to or slightly greater than the power of the problem. By following this "counselor path" over time and adjusting the counselor's influence on the client's multicultural context, the counseling relationship provides a safe place for the client to take risks and grow in a positive direction.

Third, whereas conventional counseling has focused on a formal setting and formal method, ICE takes a more inclusive perspective. In many multicultural contexts, counseling is more appropriately provided through informal methods and in less formal contexts, according to each situation. By confining counseling to formal methods and settings exclusively, the counselor is more likely to experience cultural encapsulation.

Fourth, the interpersonal cultural grid is provided as a framework to separate expectations from behavior in a conflict situation. Cross-cultural conflict is defined as a situation in which two people or groups display different behaviors even though they share the same common-ground expectations.

11

CONCLUSION: DEVELOPING MULTICULTURAL AWARENESS, KNOWLEDGE, AND SKILL

The construct of empathy typically assumes an individualistic outlook, as demonstrated in the assumptions behind professional conduct, ethical guidelines, and ethics code. By revising empathy into inclusive cultural empathy (ICE), we acknowledge the important influence of our culture teachers on all psychological services. ICE is one aspect of a revolution in the field of counseling in which multiculturalism is emerging as a generic perspective of all counseling relationships.

Multiculturalism is emerging as a fourth dimension or *fourth force* in the delivery of psychological services complementary to humanism, behaviorism, and psychodynamic perspectives. As service providers become more aware of cultural similarities and differences, those providers will take a more inclusive perspective of the client's multicultural context. Increased multicultural awareness, knowledge, and skill is one of the most significant movements in the field of counseling during this decade and promises to bring about many changes. Multiculturalism is not competing with humanism, behaviorism, or psychodynamic perspectives but rather demonstrates the importance of making the cultural context central to whichever psychological theory is being applied. Because all behaviors are learned and displayed in a cultural context, accurate assessment, meaningful understanding, and appropriate intervention require the counselor to make the cultural context central to the counseling process. This final chapter restates the core ideas of all previous chapters to demonstrate how they contribute to a comprehensive perspective of ICE.

MULTICULTURALISM AS A FOURTH FORCE

ICE provides a perspective for counselors to constantly adjust and adapt counseling to the complex, dynamic, and ever-changing context of culturally different clients. We are only beginning to understand the ways that psychology has been changed in this decade (Mahoney & Patterson, 1992) in what has come to be called a paradigm shift. The underlying assumptions about psychology are moving from a monocultural to a multicultural basis with profound consequences for counseling. The old rules of psychology focused on dissonance reduction. The new rules focus on the tolerance of ambiguity.

Smith, Harré, and Van Langenhove (1995) contrasted the new with the old paradigms. The new paradigms emphasize (a) understanding and description of a context more than just measuring variables, (b) predicting consequences more than causation, (c) social significance more than statistical significance, (d) language and discourse more than numerical reductionism, (e) holistic perspectives more than atomistic trivia, (f) complex interacting particulars more than simplistic universals, and (g) subjectively derived meaning more than objectively imposed meanings.

The idea of a "fourth force" is not new. Transpersonal psychology (Tart, 1975) was the first branch of psychology to claim fourth-force status based on the spiritual revolution in modern society. Since that time, many of the principles of transpersonal psychology have been subsumed into the larger and more diffuse multicultural movement. Mahoney and Patterson (1992) described the new paradigm as a cognitive revolution with an interdisciplinary perspective in which human behavior is described as reciprocal and interactive rather than linear and unidirectional. Wrightsman (1992) described the new paradigm as beginning with George Kelly's personal construct theory based on collectivistic and non-Western indigenous psychologies. Smith et al. (1995) described the new perspective of psychology as advocating tolerance of ambiguity rather than dissonance reduction, multidimensional reality rather than unidimensionalism, the validity of subjective as well as objective proof, and the recognition of cultural bias by the dominant culture in the applications of psychology.

The newly popular methods of chaos theory and complexity theory in the hard sciences and more recently in the soft sciences have been providing alternatives to the "linear, reductionistic thinking that has dominated science since the time of Newton—and that has now gone about as far as it can go in addressing the problems of our modern world" (Waldrop, 1992, p. 13). Butz

(1992) borrowed from chaos theory to explain how the self organizes complex experiences into coherent thought. Self is viewed as the coherence or integrity of each individual's complex experiences. Culture provides us with transitory models of our self-identity, part of which is always changing and part of which remains the same. The self is dynamic like other self-organizing, nonlinear states in which stability becomes a stage of the system's developmental process. Culture becomes the perfect metaphor for understanding this new complex concept of self and its modern applications to psychology.

There are several trends that give rise to optimism. First, Rosensweig (1992) pointed out that psychology and psychological publications are growing much more rapidly outside than within the United States. Second, all fields are becoming more global in their focus as a result of new technologies. Third, there is a multicultural movement in the social sciences that has increased attention to cultural issues. Fourth, the topic of cultural and multicultural issues has become more widely accepted in psychological meetings and publications. Fifth, the American Psychological Association journals have included articles on a regular basis in which there is a reexamination of cultural bias in psychological services. The topic of cultural theory is becoming more popular than before.

Thompson, Ellis, and Wildavsky (1990) described cultural theory as providing the basis of a new perspective, dimension, or force in psychology and counseling.

> Social science is steeped in dualism: culture and structure, change and stability, dynamics and statics, methodological individualism and collectivism, voluntarism and determinism, nature and nurture, macro and micro, materialism and idealism, facts and values, objectivity and subjectivity, rationality and irrationality, and so forth. Although sometimes useful as analytic distinctions, these dualisms often have the unfortunate result of obscuring extensive interdependencies between phenomena. Too often social scientists create needless controversies by seizing upon one side of a dualism and proclaiming it the most important. Cultural theory shows that there is no need to choose between, for instance, collectivism, values, and social relations or change and stability. Indeed, we argue there is a need not to. (p. 21)

Pedersen (1998) examined some of the issues involved in declaring multiculturalism as a fourth force in psychology.

- First, we know that society is experiencing rapid social change, even though there is disagreement about the nature of those changes.

- Second, we know that multiculturalism is becoming an important global and domestic concept.

- Third, we know that multiculturalism has sometimes been used to rationalize oppression, such as in South Africa, and as a consequence has a bad reputation in those countries.
- Fourth, we know that it may be premature to describe multiculturalism as a fourth force, although in the more applied areas of psychology—such as counseling—it has had a powerful impact.
- Fifth, we know that the U.S. version of multiculturalism is grounded in the individualistic values of that cultural context more than in a non-Western collectivistic perspective.
- Sixth, we know that within-group differences of ethnocultural groups such as demographic, status, and affiliation function like cultures in issues of age, disability, gender, and other special interests.
- Seventh, we know that cultural similarities—among youth-age strata, for example—probably exceed similarities across generations in each separate ethnocultural group.
- Eighth, we know that multiculturalism will not only change the content of our thinking but the very process of thinking itself.
- Ninth, we know that making culture central enhances the meaningful usefulness of traditional psychological theories in ways that might lead us to call this new perspective a fourth *dimension* (like time is a fourth dimension to help one understand three-dimensional space) rather than a fourth force.

The generic application of multicultural competence in counseling leads to understanding the importance of multiculturalism as a fourth force or dimension to supplement but not displace the psychological dimensions of psychodynamism, humanism, and behaviorism (Pedersen, 1998; D. W. Sue, Bingham, Porche-Burke, & Vasquez, 1999). The multicultural movement is flourishing around the world as minority and indigenous groups exert their influence on the dominant majority in their cultural context. The importance of multiculturalism is particularly evident in psychological counseling. It may be premature to declare multiculturalism as a fourth force, but its importance is evident. Significant bottom-up changes are happening in psychology even though there is disagreement about the exact nature of those changes. Multiculturalism has become a powerful domestic force in the United States and in many other developed cultures. In South Africa and elsewhere, multiculturalism has been used to rationalize oppression and has earned a bad reputation among minorities. Culture is defined broadly so that ethnographic, demographic, status, and affiliations may each become most salient and that each person belongs to many different cultures at the same time. The attacks on multiculturalism have increased, indicating its growing power. It is not only the content of our thinking but the process itself that is being challenged. The tolerance of ambiguity has replaced dissonance reduction in psychology. The often misunderstood goal of multiculturalism is to strengthen rather than weaken psychological theories of counseling.

S. Sue (1998) identified sources of resistance to the phrase "multiculturalism as a fourth force." First, some view multiculturalism as competing with already established theories of psychological explanation in ways that threaten the professions of counseling and psychology. Second, the terms *multiculturalism* and *diversity* are loosely associated with affirmative action, quotas, civil rights, discrimination, reverse discrimination, racism, sexism, political correctness, and other highly emotional terms. Third, to the extent that multiculturalism is connected with postmodernism, the arguments against postmodernism as a valid theory are also applied to multiculturalism. Fourth, those favoring a universalist perspective contend that the same practices of counseling and therapy apply equally to all populations without regard to cultural differences. Fifth, others contend that there are no accepted standards for describing multiculturalism as a theory in practice and that it is too loosely defined to be taken seriously. Sixth, there are no measurable competencies for multicultural applications of counseling or adequate standards of practice. Seventh, multiculturalism is too complicated and it would be unrealistic to expect counselors to attend to such a range of factors simultaneously. Eighth, more research is needed on multicultural competencies, standards, methods, and approaches. Ninth, multicultural standards cannot be incorporated into the counseling profession until all groups have been included. Tenth, multiculturalism represents reverse racism and quotas and is anti-White. In discussing these sources of resistance, S. Sue (1998) pointed out the tendency to misrepresent or misunderstand the notion of multiculturalism and the dangers of that misunderstanding. Nevertheless, psychology is changing.

Kuhn (1970) expressed the belief that a major paradigm shift will occur when scientific theories cannot adequately account for ideas, concepts, or data and when some new competing perspective better accommodates these data. Elements of analytical reductionism in psychology and counseling seem to be moving toward a more holistic, culturally inclusive, and integrative approach that recognizes how people from all populations are both similar and different at the same time. In that regard the dual emphasis on both the universal and the particular becomes complementary and necessarily joined in a combined explanation.

Advocacy is becoming more popular. According to Shore (1996),

> Cultural models are empirical analogues of culture understood as knowledge. As we shall see, they are not analogues in any simple sense, since public models are not exactly the same thing as mental models. But approaching culture as a collection of models has the advantage of showing that making sense of culture as an aspect of mind requires that we both distinguish and relate these two notions of model. (p. 44)

CULTURE-CENTERED ADVOCACY COMPETENCIES

In 2002, a task force was appointed by Jane Goodman, president of the American Counseling Association (ACA), to construct a set of advocacy competencies (Toporek, Gerstein, Fouad, Roysircar, & Israel, 2005). The task force members, Judy Lewis, Mary Arnold, Reese House, and Rebecca Toporek, completed the ACA advocacy competencies in 2003. It was approved by the ACA Governing Council shortly thereafter.

Advocacy competence is the understanding, knowledge, and capability to carry out advocacy ethically and effectively. In order for counselors to develop advocacy competence, counselors must come to recognize and understand the impact of social, political, economic, and cultural factors on human development. The development of advocacy competence requires that counseling professionals become aware of their own beliefs, attitudes, and biases revolving around social issues and their impact on marginalized populations. Therapists must also develop the scope of their knowledge and skill at intervening within the different domains of advocacy (Toporek et al., 2005).

The ACA Advocacy Task Force developed the advocacy competencies along two dimensions: client involvement and level of intervention. Thus, the advocacy competencies clarify counseling interventions into "acting with" or "acting on behalf" of clients and their systems at three different dimensions of interaction (client–student, school–community, and public arena), ultimately resulting in six different domains of counseling advocacy: client–student empowerment, client–student advocacy, community collaboration, systems advocacy, public information, and social–political advocacy (see Figure 11.1).

Client–Student Dimension

Counseling advocacy in the client–student dimension includes actions focused on the individual client or student and the specific issue brought forth by the client or student. Work in this dimension may be focused on working with the client or student (*empowerment*) or on behalf of the client or student (*client advocacy*). In the *client–student empowerment* domain, efforts of the counselor are focused on facilitating the identification of external barriers and the development of client self-advocacy skills, strategies, and resources. This is accomplished through helping the client recognize and understand systemic, sociopolitical, and environmental factors that affect her or his well-being and to identify developmentally appropriate strategies for responding to these factors. In the *client–student advocacy* domain, the counselor assesses the need for direct intervention within the client's system on behalf of the client. Client–student advocacy is especially relevant when the counselor is

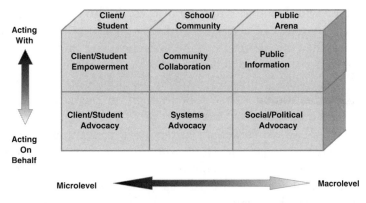

Figure 11.1. Advocacy competency domains. From "Promoting Systematic Change Through the Advocacy Competencies," by R. L. Toporek, J. A. Lewis, and H. Crethar, in press. *Journal of Counseling & Development.*

in a position of relative privilege and thus has better access to resources than does the client. In this domain, advocacy competence requires that the counselors be skilled at developing an action strategy, developing diverse and multidisciplinary allies, and carrying out a plan of advocacy.

School–Community Dimension

The school–community dimension of counseling advocacy includes actions focused on community needs as they are associated with the presenting issues of the student or client and others who might be in similar positions because of systemic and institutionalized conditions. The *community collaboration* domain includes collaborative actions that the counselor takes with various members of the community, through alerting them regarding a specific issue, supporting efforts of groups working toward systemic change, or functioning as an ally to groups focused on addressing institutionalized and systemic issues. The *systems advocacy* domain entails the counselor acting at a systems level apart and on behalf of the affected group. In this domain, the counselor identifies systemic challenges, developing insight and understanding from those who are most affected and then advocating on their behalf. Similar to the client–student advocacy domain, counselors who are in positions of relative privilege and access to power have the responsibility to use their privilege in the benefit of those less privileged.

Public Arena Dimension

The third dimension of the advocacy competencies is the public arena dimension. As in the previous two dimensions, the public arena dimension is divided into two domains. The first of these is the *public information* domain. In this domain, the counselor works in a collaborative fashion with the client and the community to create awareness and understanding of institutional and systemic problems at a broader, societal level. This form of counseling advocacy commonly involves developing strategies for dis-seminating information on a large scale through the media and pertinent associations and organizations. This variety of advocacy is often necessary to raise the types of awareness and understanding that eventually bring cul-tural and structural changes necessary to prevent the types of problems addressed in the client–student dimension as well as the school–community dimension. The final domain of the advocacy competencies is that of *social and political advocacy*. This class of counseling advocacy calls for counselors to recognize when the challenges facing clients and their related systems could effectively be addressed at a legislative or public policy level. This often occurs after the counselor makes note of a pattern of systemic oppres-sion or injustice associated with problems that consistently arise with clients or students. An assertion of this domain is that, although it is prefer-able, relevant, and appropriate for counselors to empower their clients to advocate for their needs, professional counselors are in a unique position to advocate on their behalf. Both ACA and the American School Counselor Association offer legislative advocacy training oriented toward the profes-sion and the needs of their clients. Counselors' ongoing contact with the visages of privilege and oppression is a call for counselors to step up on behalf of clients at the societal level through carefully targeted legislative and public policy advocacy.

Each of the six domains of the advocacy competencies represents coun-seling advocacy at varying levels of client interaction and involvement. The advocacy competencies are also based on assumptions of systemic and struc-tural oppression, both intentional and unintentional, as well as the assump-tion of responsibility of those who have relative privilege to serve those with less privilege for the greater good.

THE AWARENESS–KNOWLEDGE–SKILL MODEL

ICE is about accurate assessment, meaningful knowledge, and appropri-ate skill. Each behavior is learned and displayed in a specific cultural context. Therefore, accurate assessment, meaningful understanding, and appropriate intervention—the foundations of generic competence—require an awareness of each multicultural context for counseling. The basic multicultural compe-tencies have been best described in D. W. Sue et al. (1998). Sue described 34 basic multicultural competencies in three dimensions, on the basis of the original three-stage developmental sequence of awareness, knowledge, and skill. These competencies demonstrate generic abilities that are always important in good counseling (Ponterotto, Casas, Suzuki, & Alexander, 2001; D. W. Sue & Sue, 1999).

Dimension 1 is focused on the counselors' awareness of their own assumptions, values, and biases. Competent counselors (a) are aware of their cultural heritage and comfortable with differences but aware of their limitations; (b) know about oppression, racism, and discrimination; and (c) are skilled in self-improvement toward a nonracist identity.

Dimension 2 involves knowing about and comprehending the worldview of culturally different clients. Competent counselors (a) are aware of their emotional reactions toward other racial and ethnic groups; (b) know the culture of their client populations and its influence on counseling and society in general; and (c) are skilled in mental health issues of other cultures through active involvement with ethnic minority groups.

Dimension 3 involves developing appropriate intervention strategies and techniques. Competent counselors (a) are aware of religious–spiritual indigenous mental health resources; (b) know how counseling fits with other cultures, institutions, and assessments; and (c) are skilled in culturally appropriate counseling of indigenous people.

This book on ICE has focused on how these sometimes abstract competencies can be applied in the generic practice of counseling. Attending to the cultural context is central to competent counseling (S. Sue, 1998). A 2-hour videotape (Pedersen, 2003a) provides specific discussion and illustration of culture-centered counseling competence and the practice of ICE mobilizing those multicultural competencies.

Indicators of multicultural competence include familiarity with cultural and language differences, interest in other cultures, awareness of stereotypes, concern for the welfare of culturally different clients, awareness of one's own culture, appreciation for cultural orientation, awareness of relationships between cultures, knowing how culture shapes psychology, knowing their limits, and feeling comfortable in a multicultural context. Indicators of multicultural incompetence are even more easily identified than cultural competence (S. Sue, 1999).

The consequences of multicultural incompetence can be measured in financial and emotional costs that are real and concrete. Incompetence will result in biased evaluation, derogation, disparagement and denigration, dehumanizing others, fear of contamination through contact with others, viewing all outsiders as enemies, approval of destructive behavior, blaming the victim, self-righteousness, and a tendency to desecrate others. Incompetence results in cultural exclusion, which depends on deindividuation and "group-think" abstractions, psychological distancing, dependence on quick and easy answers, double standards, acceptance of harm-doing, displacing responsibility, glorifying violence, and a short-term perspective.

THE BENEFITS OF MULTICULTURAL AWARENESS

Making the cultural context central rather than marginal to ICE offers uniquely valuable social benefits that are recognized as having generic value across cultures.

1. Attending to the cultural context enhances accuracy in our assessments because all behaviors occur in a cultural context. Multiculturalism is not advocating for any special interest group but a pursuit of accuracy in counseling.
2. Finding common ground across cultures enhances the effectiveness of conflict management. Identifying both cultural similarities and differences inclusively acknowledges the conflict while also demonstrating shared interests.
3. Learning about our culture teachers helps us articulate our own complex identity. All behaviors are learned and displayed in a cultural context shaped by our culture teachers.
4. The diversity of sociocultural identity, like biodiversity, is essential to cultivating a healthy environment. The alternative of imposed monoculturalism is dangerous to all of us.
5. Encapsulation by our own self-reference criteria can only be prevented through understanding the importance of cultural diversity. Searching for easy answers to complex questions is also an oversimplification and dangerous to the delivery of appropriate services.
6. Preparing for a future beyond our imagination requires familiarity with and facility for working with different cultures. Instead of hanging out with people like ourselves, we can learn much by seeking the company of those who are different from ourselves.
7. Each culture that has been dominated by a majority culture has sacrificed social justice toward minorities. History is the story of how dominant groups overpower minorities resulting in the long-term destruction of both minorities and majority members.
8. Not just the content of our thoughts but the linear–nonlinear thinking process itself is culturally learned. The majority of the world's societies prefer a nonlinear thinking process that might seem irrational to linear thinkers.

9. Learning the spiritual beliefs of other cultures enhances our understanding of our own spirituality. The ultimate questions of meaning and purpose are only partially articulated by any one social perspective.

10. Cultural pluralism offers the only alternative to the unacceptable alternatives of absolutism or relativism. The democratic values for shared power and equal rights presume the architecture of a plural society.

11. The goal of multiculturalism is not to win a competition between different special interests but the search for accuracy in all multicultural contexts. The dangers of multicultural incompetence threaten all people and societies alike.

For these many reasons, multicultural awareness increases our generic competence through the practice of ICE. ICE is not an easy answer to the complexity of multicultural counseling. Culture is necessarily complex and not simple. Simple solutions to the complex problems of society are dangerous, and for that reason, complexity is our friend. It is also important to recognize that behaviors have no meaning until those behaviors are connected to the cultural context in which the behavior was learned and is displayed. This is demonstrated in an intrapersonal cultural grid and an interpersonal cultural grid (Pedersen, 2000a, 2000b).

The cultural grid provides a framework for connecting our culturally learned behaviors with the cultural expectations and those culture teachers who taught us what to expect. When we or someone else displays a behavior that we do not like, our first question to ourselves should be "Why did you do that?" Only when we understand the culturally learned expectations behind a person's behavior from that person's perspective can we truly understand the meaning of that behavior. Our second question should be "Who taught you?" Only when we have identified the culture teachers in the person's life can we determine whether that behavior can or should be changed or replaced by a more effective behavior for getting the person what he or she needs and wants.

THE GENERIC IMPORTANCE OF MULTICULTURAL KNOWLEDGE

Indicators of multicultural understanding or comprehension are specific knowledge about the client's target culture and the adjustment process in those cultures, an articulate understanding of one's own cultural experiences and the ability to teach others about culture, understanding the importance of socioeconomic pressures across the range of cultural values, understanding multiple possible interpretations of the same behavior across the customs and language of different cultures, valuing and respecting other cultural traditions as meaningful resources, understanding how cultures relate to one another, and knowing how to train others in this knowledge (Ponterotto et al., 2001).

Cultural differences relate to the way of life that people make. One's skin color at birth had nothing to do with culture and was an "individual difference" among many other individual differences that make one unique. However, over time and experience, skin color and other uniquely individual characteristics take on cultural meaning. Culture learning is transmitted to other generations or to others within the group as "rules" to follow and are learned through socialization, childhood experiences, and internalized values. These cultural patterns are consistent and clear as conveyed by the culture teachers in one's life. Although there is occasional variation in cultural patterns, there is great resistance to permanent change of cultural assumptions. Examples of cultural assumptions by the dominant culture in the European American context would include the following assumptions leading to multicultural incompetency:

1. There is a unimodal definition of what is "normal" that can be applied broadly across cultures.
2. Individualism is the preferred perspective in describing how society works and is changed.
3. Professional boundaries need to be narrowly defined to discourage contamination by others working to solve the same problems.
4. A low-context perspective is preferred to a high-context perspective, to avoid subjectivity and encourage objectivity.
5. Dependency in individuals is not healthy and should be changed to help individuals become more independent.
6. The individual needs to be separated from the "support systems" surrounding the individual before treatment.
7. Rational thinking is always linear and nonlinear thinking is inferior.
8. We need to change the client and not attempt to change the system, even when we know the system is wrong.
9. The historical background of an individual's past is of minimal value and the emphasis should be on the "here and now."
10. We have already successfully identified our own culturally learned assumptions.

D. W. Sue et al. (1996) examined counseling theories to explore how to avoid cultural encapsulation and identified six important insights toward that end: (a) Western and non-Western theories are different; (b) counseling must focus on complex relationships without simplification; (c) the cultural identities of the counselor and the client influence the counseling process; (d) the ultimate goal of a culture-centered approach is an expanded repertoire; (e) conventional models of Western counseling are rejected in many non-Western cultures; and (f) an expanded consciousness of the cultural context is primary to competent counseling. These insights apply to the counseling process as a generic whole, not only to counseling special interest groups.

One of the most dangerous examples of cultural encapsulation is evident in the ethical guidelines by professional counseling and human service associations that guide counselors. Some examples of these encapsulated assumptions follow.

1. An individualistic perspective is good.
2. Dependency is bad.
3. Freedom of choice is not ever destructive.
4. Differences should be overlooked.
5. Counselors already have self-awareness.
6. Dual relationships are bad.
7. Counselors should withdraw from conflict.
8. Services should be paid for with money.
9. Privacy is universally valued.
10. There are universal guidelines for competence.
11. Counseling as a profession is defined narrowly.
12. Quantitative data are better than qualitative data.
13. Measures do not always require validation.
14. Teachers do not learn from students.
15. There is no need to make any allowance for responsible disobedience.

The generic applications of multicultural knowledge demonstrate how completely encapsulated we counselors are by a relatively narrow "exclusionary" system of culturally learned assumptions from the dominant cultures. The consequences of encapsulation are to inhibit the understanding or comprehension of reality as a whole.

THE GENERIC APPLICATION OF MULTICULTURAL SKILL

Indicators of generic multicultural skill for ICE include knowing the appropriate teaching or service techniques for different situations, recognizing different learning styles, developing empathic rapport across relationships, being able to give and receive feedback, being able to evaluate accurately, discovering new and original methods, assessing accurately, understanding the consequences of skill usage, being appropriate, and having the ability for self-assessment. These generic indicators suggest that competent counselors need to manage complexity effectively rather than relying on oversimplifications.

A competent counselor accepts conflicting viewpoints between and within individuals and is accurate in assessing the perspectives of others in an organized manner that identifies feelings, topics, support systems, and other relevant information. A competent counselor sees positive aspects of negative experiences and negative aspects of positive experiences in the search for meaning, avoids taking sides, and is sensitive to collective forces that disrupt a harmonious balance. A competent counselor is sensitive to changes of persons, topics, roles, and power.

Rather than limit counseling to a formal process taking place in a formal or prearranged context, it is useful to demonstrate ICE through formal, less-formal, and informal methods and contexts in which counseling occurs (Pedersen, 1997). Figure 1.1 describes nine different examples of counseling in a variety of different cultural contexts.

1. The formal method/formal context describes an office interview, which is the more conventional or typical example of counseling.
2. The formal method/less-formal context might include a setting of community service in which counseling is taught.
3. The formal method/informal context might include simple advice-giving.
4. The less-formal method/formal context might include training groups.
5. The less-formal method/less-formal context might include support groups.
6. The less-formal method/informal context might include self-help.
7. The informal method/formal context might include inspirational presentations to a group.
8. The informal method/less-formal context might include help from family and friends.
9. The informal method/informal context might include our daily encounters with things that help us to feel good.

A broad definition of appropriate counseling methods and contexts suggests generic alternatives to how counseling might be best provided to a needy client.

It is difficult to manage the culturally complex variables of a counseling relationship, but rather than oversimplify the cultural context and to manage the cultural complexity, it is useful to separate a client's behaviors from expectations to identify common ground. Figure 10.2 in chapter 10 demonstrates that process for managing conflict between two individuals. The interpersonal cultural grid presented in chapter 10 provides a framework for managing ICE in managing conflicts.

There are four quadrants in Figure 10.2 indicating different combinations between expectations and behaviors. Although every relationship will include examples from all four combinations, the salience is likely to shift from one to another combination of variables as the conflict between the two individuals evolves. Examples of similar expectations or intentions might include trust, love, fairness, respect, and success. Examples of different behaviors might include loud–soft, direct–indirect, open–closed, and confrontational–nonconfrontational. In the first quadrant both persons have the same positive expectation or intention and display the same behaviors as well. This describes a pleasant relationship in which both persons are relaxed but little new learning occurs. The second quadrant is where both persons have the same positive expectation or intention but express themselves by very different behaviors that are easily misunderstood. This second "cross-cultural" quadrant is where profound learning can occur because both persons share the same expectations or intentions, regardless of their different behaviors. This most valuable quadrant is fragile and tends to evolve into the third quadrant, in which the stronger member imposes the rules of desired behavior on the other, at the cost of losing the shared positive expectations and intentions. Ultimately, the conflict will evolve to the last quadrant, in which both persons declare war, no longer pretending to like each other and allowing their perspective to be guided by hostile expectations, intentions, and behaviors (Pedersen, 2004).

ICE offers us the opportunity to work with intrapersonal and interpersonal conflict between or within people who may expect and intend the same positive values even though their culturally learned behaviors are different. Family conflict between a parent and child, for example, might not initially be seen as an example of multicultural conflict. However, by reframing the two sides into cultural categories, it becomes possible for both persons to disagree without either one being necessarily wrong. By reframing conflict between people into examples of cross-cultural conflict, it becomes possible to build a platform of common-ground expectations and intentions shared by both parties. When that platform becomes strong enough for both persons to stand on it, then—and only then—can the two persons begin to discuss which culturally learned behaviors might be the most useful. Reframing conflict into a multicultural perspective provides a clear example of the generic application of multicultural competence to generic competencies. Exhibit 11.1 lists an inventory of questions for self-assessment of one's multicultural awareness, knowledge, and skills.

EXHIBIT 11.1
A Self-Assessment of Awareness, Knowledge, and Skill

This inventory of questions allows the reader to self-assess the extent to which multi-cultural awareness, knowledge, and skill have been achieved. Some participants will overestimate their degree of competence and others will underestimate their competence. This list of questions resembles a test in which readers will grade their own answers if and when they were to take the time required to answer the questions. Each reader will assign her- or himself a grade based on her or his own self-assessment.

Read the following items and indicate how well you think you would be able to answer the item (using your own criteria) if you were to write out an answer. If you think you would provide an excellent answer, give yourself an "A"; if you think your answer would be generally good, give yourself a "B"; if you think your answer would be acceptable but not as good as you would like, give yourself a "C"; and if you feel unable to answer the question, give yourself an "F."

At the end of this self-assessment you will be encouraged to compute your "grade point average" (GPA) with an A counting for 3 points, a B for 2 points, a C for 1 point, and an F for 0 points. Divide the number of points you awarded yourself by the number of items to get your GPA. When you have finished, think about the following questions.

1. Is it possible to earn an "A" grade in the multicultural awareness, knowledge, and skill competencies?
2. Did you underestimate your level of competence before taking this test?
3. Did you overestimate your level of competence before taking this test?
4. What are the consequences of not having multicultural competence?
5. How do you plan to increase your level of multicultural competence?

A. Awareness questions
 1. Can you construct a genogram of your family for the last three generations on your mother's and father's side?
 2. What is your "cultural heritage"?
 3. How well do you value, respect, and model cultural differences in your life?
 4. Who are the significant people in your life who have influenced your attitudes, values, and biases?
 5. Who are the culture teachers you least understand and why?
 6. What do you do to recruit clients who are different from you in race, ethnicity, culture, and beliefs?
 7. What culturally learned assumptions do you have that are different from those of other counselors?
 8. In what ways do issues of oppression, racism, discrimination, and stereotyping influence how you do counseling?
 9. To what extent would you consider yourself as having "racist attitudes, beliefs, and feelings"?
10. Have you had any social impact in your career as a counselor?
11. Can you do counseling in a variety of different communication styles?
12. Do you know how your culturally different clients feel about your natural communication style?
13. In what specific ways have you trained yourself to work with culturally different clients?
14. In what specific ways do you evaluate your counseling work with culturally different clients?
15. When do you refer your culturally different clients to others better trained to work with them?
16. When have you sought consultation from more qualified resource persons when working with culturally different clients?
17. How well do you understand yourself and your own cultural identity?

EXHIBIT 11.1

A Self-Assessment of Awareness, Knowledge, and Skill (*Continued*)

18. How well are you able to present a nonracist identity as a counselor to culturally different clients?
19. Do you have a plan for increasing your multicultural awareness in the future?
20. Do you consider yourself to have achieved multicultural awareness?

B. Knowledge
 1. Can you describe the social, political, and economic history of negative emotional reactions toward specific racial and ethnic groups?
 2. How well can you do counseling with clients whose beliefs and attitudes are profoundly different from your own?
 3. Can you be nonjudgmental toward clients whose beliefs are profoundly different from your own?
 4. Are you aware of stereotypes and preconceived notions in your counseling practice?
 5. Do you provide counseling to clients without knowing about their cultural attitudes, values, and backgrounds?
 6. Are you aware of the life experiences, cultural heritages, and historical backgrounds of your culturally different clients?
 7. Are you aware of the similarities and differences between yourself and your clients?
 8. Are you able to explain how your client's cultural background affects personality formation?
 9. . . . vocational choices?
 10. . . . manifestation of psychological disorders?
 11. . . . help-seeking behavior?
 12. . . . appropriate counseling approaches?
 13. Can you intelligently discuss sociopolitical issues that influence the quality of life of your clients?
 14. Can you discuss immigration issues that influence the quality of life of your clients?
 15. . . . poverty?
 16. . . . racism?
 17. . . . stereotyping?
 18. . . . powerlessness?
 19. In the last month, have you read books and/or articles regarding culture and mental health issues of clients within your client population?
 20. In the last month, have you participated in training to increase your knowledge and understanding of cultural contexts where counseling occurs?
 21. In the last month, have you been actively involved with cultural minority groups outside your role as a counselor?
 22. . . . community events?
 23. . . . social functions?
 24. . . . political functions?
 25. . . . celebrations?
 26. . . . friendships?
 27. . . . neighborhood gatherings?

C. Skills
 1. Do you refer in counseling to your client's religious and/or spiritual beliefs and values?
 2. . . . attributions?
 3. . . . taboos?
 4. . . . worldviews?
 5. Do you understand how these beliefs and attitudes affect psychosocial functioning and expressions of distress?

(continued)

EXHIBIT 11.1
A Self-Assessment of Awareness, Knowledge, and Skill (*Continued*)

6. Can you talk with your clients about their indigenous helping practices and respect indigenous help-giving networks?
7. Are you able to defend the positive value of bilingualism or multilingualism?
8. Do you understand the generic characteristics of counseling and therapy?
9. . . . culture-bound features?
10. . . . class-bound features?
11. . . . linguistic features?
12. Can you explain why clients from a minority group might be reluctant to seek out counseling?
13. Can you identify ways that your own cultural background might cause conflict with your minority clients from a different background?
14. Do you compensate for the cultural bias in tests developed in and for one cultural context when those tests are used with a culturally different population?
15. Do you interpret your assessment data differently to culturally different clients who come from significantly different backgrounds?
16. Do you incorporate information about your client's indigenous family structure into your counseling interviews?
17. . . . hierarchies?
18. . . . values?
19. . . . beliefs?
20. . . . community resources?
21. Are you able to change relevant discriminatory practices in the community that affect the psychological welfare of your clients?
22. Do you have a large repertory of verbal and nonverbal skills to match with the cultural contexts of your different clients?
23. Is the verbal message your client receives the same as the message sent and intended?
24. Is the nonverbal message your client receives the same as the message sent and intended?
25. Are you skilled in a variety of different helping roles, methods, or approaches?
26. When your helping style is limited or inappropriate, will you know enough to change?
27. Are you able to intervene with and change the social institutions in your client's cultural context?
28. Are you able to tell when a client's problem relates to cultural bias by others from when the problem might be personal to the client?
29. Do you consult with traditional healers from your client's cultural context?
30. . . . religious leaders?
31. . . . spiritual leaders?
32. . . . other practitioners?
33. Are you fluent in the first language of your clients?
34. Do you use a translator when working with clients whose language you do not understand?
35. Do you incorporate traditional assessment and testing instruments from your clients' cultural context into your counseling with them?
36. Do you always have the necessary technical skills in the tests or measures you use with your culturally different clients?
37. Do you work actively to eliminate biases, prejudices, and discriminatory practices in your community?
38. Do you take responsibility for educating your clients about your own culturally learned orientation to psychological intervention, outcome goals, expectations, and legal rights?

Note. From *110 Experiences for Multicultural Learning* (pp. 101–104), by P. B. Pedersen, 2004, Washington, DC: American Psychological Association. Copyright 2004 by Paul B. Pedersen. Adapted with permission.

CONCLUSION

In the generic application of multicultural awareness, knowledge, and skill through ICE, we take an orthogonal perspective, recognizing that each person belongs to many different cultures at the same time. We define culture broadly to include ethnographic, demographic, and affiliation variables. We recognize the inevitable multicultural dimensions of every counseling relationship. We recognize that culture controls our lives, with or without our permission.

Those who would oppose ICE, we believe, are avoiding the inevitable. They can pretend or ignore the broadly defined cultural perspectives around us and ignore the potentially positive effects of ICE but the unrelenting inclusive influences of the client's cultural context are themselves inevitable.

APPENDIX A

GUIDELINES FOR THE FOUR SYNTHETIC CULTURES

ALPHA CULTURE (HIGH POWER DISTANCE)

Power distance indicates the extent to which a culture accepts that power is unequally distributed in institutions and organizations.

1. Language
    1.1. Alphas will use the following words with a *positive* meaning: respect, father (as a title), master, servant, older brother, younger brother, wisdom, favor, protect, obey, orders, and pleasing.
    1.2. Alphas will use the following words with a *negative* meaning: rights, complain, negotiate, fairness, task, necessity codetermination, objectives, question, and criticize.

2. The Cultural Grid
    The following behaviors by Alphas will indicate the following expectations:

Behavior	Expectation
Soft-spoken, polite, listening	Friendly
Quiet, polite, and not listening	Unfriendly
Ask for help and direction	Trust
Do not ask for help and direction	Distrust
Positive and animated, but no eye contact	Interest
Expressionless, unanimated, but with eye contact	Boredom

3. Barriers
    3.1. Language: Alphas are very verbal but usually soft spoken and polite.
    3.2. Nonverbals: Alphas are usually restrained and formal.
    3.3. Stereotypes: Alphas are hierarchical and seek to please.
    3.4. Evaluation: Alphas tend to blame themselves for any problems that come up.
    3.5. Stress: Alphas internalize stress and express stress indirectly.

4. Gender Roles
    4.1. Role of gender: Leadership roles may be held by either male or female. If the society is matriarchal, the visible power of

women in decision making is likely to be more obvious than in patriarchal societies where the visible power of males would be more obvious.

4.2. Role of women: In home and family affairs, women are likely to be very powerful even though that power might be less visible than the more visible male roles. While women may seem subservient, that may not in fact be true.

4.3. Role of men: Males in leadership roles are often held accountable for the consequences of their decisions. If they lose the support of the women, new leaders will emerge. While males may be the visible traditional leaders, the men may be much more subservient in less visible and more private social roles in a balance of power.

BETA CULTURE (STRONG UNCERTAINTY AVOIDANCE)

Uncertainty avoidance indicates the lack of tolerance in a culture for uncertainty and ambiguity.

1. Language
   1.1 Betas will use the following words with a *positive* meaning: structure, duty, truth, law, order, certain, clear, clean, secure, safe, predictable, and tight.
   1.2 Betas will use the following words with a *negative* meaning: maybe, creative conflict, tolerant, experiment, spontaneous, relativity, insight, unstructured, loose, and flexible.

2. The Cultural Grid
   The following behaviors by Betas will indicate the following expectations:

Behavior	Expectation
Detailed responses, formal and unambiguous, specific	Friendly
Generalized, ambiguous responses and anxious to end the interview	Unfriendly
Polarized structures in response separate right from wrong unambiguously	Trust
Openly critical and challenging the other person's credentials	Distrust
Verbal and active questioning with direct eye contact, task oriented	Interest
Passive and quiet with no direct eye contact	Boredom

3. Barriers
   3.1 Language: Betas are very verbal and well organized, some-what loud.
   3.2 Nonverbal: Betas are animated in using hands but with little or no physical contact.
   3.3 Stereotypes: Betas have rigid beliefs that don't change easily.
   3.4 Evaluation: Betas quickly evaluate a situation to establish right and wrong, sometimes prematurely.
   3.5 Stress: Betas externalize stress and usually make the other person feel the stress rather than her- or himself.

4. Gender Roles
   4.1 Role of gender: The right and appropriate roles of men and women are rigidly defined without ambiguity. The dress, behavior, and functions of men and women are defined by rules, traditions, and carefully guarded boundaries.
   4.2 Role of women: Women tend to be in charge of home, fam-ily, children, and religious or traditional spiritual rituals as guardians of society through the romantic and idealized role of who the woman should be. Society can be very unforgiv-ing to women who rebel or violate those rules, although elderly women may take on traditional power roles other-wise reserved for males.
   4.3 Role of men: Men are expected to take care of women and protect the home and family by providing for material need and demonstrating strength in their public posture. Men are expected to be more visible in their public roles than women, and women—especially younger women—might have difficulty sharing power with men in public or work roles.

GAMMA CULTURE (HIGH INDIVIDUALISM)

Individualism indicates the extent to which a culture believes that people are supposed to take care of themselves and remain emotionally independent from groups, organizations, and other collectivities.

1. Language
   1.1. Gammas will use the following words with a *positive* mean-ing: self, friendship, do-your-own-thing, contract, litiga-tion, self-respect, self-interest, self-actualizing, individual, dignity, I/me, pleasure, adventurous, and guilt.

1.2. Gammas will use the following words with a *negative* meaning: harmony, face, we, obligation, sacrifice, family, tradition, decency, honor, duty, loyalty, and shame.

2. The Cultural Grid

The following behaviors by Gammas will indicate the following expectations:

Behavior	Expectation
Verbal and self-disclosing	Friendly
Criticize the other person behind their back, sabotage enemies	Unfriendly
Aggressively debate issues and control the interview actively	Trust
Noncommittal on issues and more passive, ambiguous, or defensive	Distrust
Loudly verbal with lots of questions, touching, and close physical contact	Interest
Maintain physical distance with no questions or eye contact	Boredom

3. Barriers

3.1. Language: Gammas are verbal and self-centered, using "I" and "me" a lot.

3.2. Nonverbal: Gammas touch a lot and are somewhat seductive.

3.3. Stereotypes: Gammas are defensive and tend to be loners who see others as potential enemies.

3.4. Evaluation: Gammas use other people and measure the importance of others in terms of how useful they are.

3.5. Stress: Gammas like to take risks and like the challenge of danger to continually test their own ability.

4. Gender Roles

4.1 Role of gender: Power might as easily be held by males as by females, especially in urban and modernized areas. Gender roles are less rigidly defined with each gender taking on the roles of the other—to serve her or his self-interests—in public and/or private activities.

4.2 Role of women: Women are free as long as they have the power to protect themselves. Attractive women can gain power by being manipulative and taking advantage of their beauty. Less assertive—and particularly older—women are likely to become victims of exploitation by both younger men and women.

4.3 Role of men: Men excel in areas requiring physical strength. Younger, taller, and physically attractive men can be expected to be aggressive in asserting their power over others. Men who are uncomfortable being competitive—especially older men—are likely to be ridiculed as weak and losers.

DELTA CULTURE (HIGH MASCULINITY)

Masculinity indicates the extent to which traditional masculine values of assertiveness, money, and things prevail in a culture as contrasted to traditional feminine values of nurturance, quality of life, and people.

1. Language
    1.1 Deltas will use the following words with a *positive* meaning: career, competition, fight, aggressive, assertive, success, winner, deserve, merit, balls, excel, force, big, hard, fast, and quantity.
    1.2 Deltas will use the following words with a *negative* meaning: quality, caring, solidarity, modesty, compromise, help, love, grow, small, soft, slow, and tender.

2. The Cultural Grid
   The following behaviors by Deltas will indicate the following expectations:

Behavior	Expectation
Physical contact, seductive, and loud	Friendliness
Physical distance, sarcastic, and sadistic	Unfriendly
Tend to dominate discussion and be competitive	Trust
Openly critical, disparaging, and attempts to end the discussion	Distrust
Sports oriented and eager to debate every issue from all points of view	Interest
No eye contact, discourteous, and drowsy	Boredom

3. Barriers
    3.1. Language: Deltas are loud and verbal with a tendency to criticize and argue with others.
    3.2. Nonverbal: Deltas like physical contact, direct eye contact, and animated gestures.
    3.3. Stereotypes: Deltas are macho, hero and status oriented, and like winners.

3.4. Evaluation: Deltas are hard to please, tend to be over-achievers, defensive, and blame others for their mistakes.

3.5. Stress: Deltas are Type A personalities, generating stress through fast-paced lifestyles.

4. Gender Roles

4.1. Role of gender: Men and more masculine women are typically more powerful and are highly favored in leadership roles. Passive and facilitating behaviors are tolerated for women but not for men. Men are stereotyped as strong and women as weak.

4.2. Role of women: Women tend to be either masculine in their personal style as "one of the guys" or completely subservient and docile, with few women in between. Young and attractive women can use their beauty to win but without romantic illusions. Older or less attractive women are at a great disadvantage.

4.3. Role of men: Young, strong, tall, and attractive men are idealized as heroes and are admired or envied by others. Men see life as a game played by men with women as cheerleaders.

APPENDIX B

PRACTICING INCLUSIVE CULTURAL EMPATHY WITH SYNTHETIC CULTURES

In the following presenting problem statements by four clients—one an Alpha, one a Beta, one a Gamma, and one a Delta—indicate when you would use an encourager by writing on the transcript. Indicate what sort of paraphrase you would do by filling in the brief spaces provided. At the end of the presenting problem, outline how you would summarize what the client has told you.

THE ALPHA CLIENT

I am very sorry to trouble you but my family thought that I should make an appointment with you because of your reputation as a wise and experienced counselor. I hope you understand how hard it is for me to come and talk with you about personal problems. If I hesitate or am unclear, I apologize. I want very much to be a good client for you and to please you.

(Paraphrase)_____

_____

My problem is that persons I work with often take advantage of me. I like to protect the people working under me, to be helpful to my coworkers, and to obey my supervisors, but I think they interpret my pleasing them as a sign of weakness rather than as a sign of respect. They often complain to me about one another and force me to become involved in their negotiations for changing things. If I show any reluctance, they criticize me and say that I am only pretending to be their friend.

(Paraphrase)_____

_____

They are also angry because I am reluctant to ask them for help. They say that my always wanting to give help but never wanting to receive help is not right. But I can't ask them for help if I don't trust them. They say that I act sneaky, never looking at them straight in the eye, and they say that they can't trust that kind of behavior and it makes me so frustrated! I feel like a tree uprooted by the flood and being washed downstream. I really don't know what I can do or where to start. Can you help me?

(Summarize)_____

_____

_____

_____

Answer the following questions or discuss them with your partner about your interview with the Alpha client:

1. Where did you write in encouragers and why?
2. Check your paraphrases against the rules for Alpha culture to see whether you were sensitive to Alpha culture rules.
3. Check your summary against the rules for Alpha culture to see whether you were sensitive to Alpha culture rules.

THE BETA CLIENT

I called the Psychological Association and they gave me your name as a competent service provider in this district. I notice that, according to the certificates on your wall, you have a degree in counseling and that you are experienced. That is good. I need your advice. When I walk out of here, I want a list of things to do that will improve my ability to get my staff to work with me better.

(Paraphrase)_____

_____

My staff do not follow the rules as well as I would like, so that there are no clearly defined principles that we can all count on to be followed. They tend to criticize me for being right, but since I know I am right, why shouldn't I stay with what I believe to be true?

(Paraphrase)_____

_____

It is very frustrating to see my staff not taking things as seriously as they should. It is very frustrating when sometimes I find orders are not obeyed and carried out as I had expected. It is very frustrating to have them complain about me being the leader, even though I am their boss! I feel sorry for them sometimes because they are destroying their own security.

(Paraphrase)_____

_____

I am not able to talk with them anymore and avoid the topic of efficiency or effectiveness as much as I can. When they push me, however, I tell them just what I think, and then they really get angry. They can give criticism but they can't take it. So I usually just withdraw into my own routine and let them wallow in the chaos. To hell with them! That's what I say. What do you say?

(Summarize)_____

_____

_____

_____

Answer the following questions or discuss them with your partner about your interview with the Beta client:

1. Where did you write in your encouragers and why?
2. Check your paraphrases against the rules for Beta culture to see whether you were sensitive to Beta culture rules.
3. Check your summary against the rules for Beta culture to see whether you were sensitive to Beta culture rules.

THE GAMMA CLIENT

I am here on my own. Nobody knows that I have come here, and I will require you to keep this visit confidential. I presume that anything I say here will be kept private, between just you and I. That is our contract, and if you can't keep it let me know now so I can leave.

(Paraphrase)_____

_____

My problem involves the people who work for and with me. They seem to have a hard time getting along with me and I can't understand why. I certainly do my best to get along with them! They don't show me the respect they used to so I don't respect them anymore either. It gets pretty tense around the place where we work and that makes me uncomfortable.

(Paraphrase)_____

_____

They insist on all these rules and regulations, which are sometimes okay but generally just get in the way. I like to do my own thing and be left alone. That way I work best and have the highest production record of anybody. They can take all this other stuff and stick it you know where! Anyway, I don't like getting angry and it's getting in the way of how I do my job, which is why I'm here talking with you.

(Paraphrase)_____

_____

I might be wrong, you know. I might even be part of the problem, but if so, I need to know so I can fix things. I keep wanting them to argue things out but they run away from me when I do that. I'm tired of trying to help them run the place. There's nothing in it for me anymore. See, feel how tense I am right here in my shoulders because of all this stress!

(Summarize)_____

_____

_____

_____

Answer the following questions or discuss them with your partner about your interview with the Gamma client.

1. Where did you mark your encouragers and why?
2. Check your paraphrases against the rules for Gamma culture to see whether you were sensitive to Gamma culture rules.
3. Check your summary against the rules for Gamma culture to see whether you were sensitive to Gamma culture rules.

THE DELTA CLIENT

Hi there! It's really great to see you! I've really been looking forward to spending some time with you here . . . if you know what I mean. . . . It's a dog-eat-dog world out there and I'm tired of eating dog all the time. I just want to get ahead with my career, you know? I want to make it and time's a-wasting! You ever think about how short life is? Anyway, I'm working with a couple of screw-ups who are making my life hell.

(Paraphrase)_____

_____

I know what I want and I want you to help me get it. I've got the ball and now I want to shoot and score! I deserve it. I've been doing most of the work around the place while these goof-offs have been sitting on the bench. Don't get me wrong. I don't mind working hard. I like to make things work. Hey! I'm a team player whatever they say. I'm no spoilsport. All I want is to kick a little ass or do whatever it takes to get these guys to do their part.

(Paraphrase)_____

_____

I think the big problem is that I'm surrounded by a bunch of wusses. If I tell them what I think is wrong they run like hell. How can you work with somebody if you can't disagree with them once in awhile? Bunch of chickens. I think they're afraid of me now because I got kind of loud the other day. They told the boss on me, and he's the one who sent me to see you. He says he "cares" but I think he's just as chicken shit as they are.

(Paraphrase)_____

_____

So, . . . what should I do now? All the guys have their backs up against me. My boss thinks I'm a troublemaker. If I lose this job, I'm back out on the street, which is just not cool right now. I need a partner to win this game. That's clear. Hey! I'm ready to change if you can prove to me that I'm wrong. I've got no problem with that. Lay it on me!

(Summarize)_____

_____

_____

_____

Answer the following questions or discuss them with your partner about your interview with the Delta client.

1. Where did you mark in your encouragers and why?
2. Check your paraphrases against the rules for Delta culture to see whether you were sensitive to Delta culture rules.
3. Check your summary against the rules for Delta culture to see whether you were sensitive to Delta culture rules.

As you read over the four different presenting problems by the Alpha, Beta, Gamma, and Delta client, which cultures would you have done best with and which ones would you have done worst? What parts of each culture did you see as similar to yourself? What parts of each culture did you see as different from yourself? Did you use the paraphrasing, summarizing, and encouraging skills differently with each culture? Look beyond the skill itself to the function that skill provides in each different cultural setting so that you can use each skill appropriately. It is important to recognize that these skills build on the feedback-giving and attending skills of the chapters.

REFERENCES

Adams, H. E., Wright, L. W., & Lohr, B. A. (1996). Is homophobia associated with homosexual arousal? *Journal of Abnormal Psychology, 105,* 440–445.

Adams, M., Bell, L. A., & Griffin, P. (1997). *Teaching for diversity and social justice: A sourcebook.* New York: Routledge.

Aguero, J. L., Bloch, L., & Byrne, D. (1984). The relationships among sexual beliefs, attitudes, experience, and homophobia. *Journal of Homosexuality, 10,* 95–107.

Airhihenbuwa, C. O. (1995). *Health and culture: Beyond the Western paradigm.* Thousand Oaks, CA: Sage.

American Psychiatric Association. (2000). *Diagnostic and statistical manual of mental disorders* (4th ed., text revision). Washington, DC: Author.

Anderson, H., & Goolishian, H. A. (1998). Human systems as linguistic systems: Preliminary and evolving ideas about the implications for clinical theory. *Family Process, 27,* 371–393.

Archer, S. L., & Waterman, A. S. (1993). Appendix C: Identity Status Interview: Adult Form. In J. E. Marcia, A. S. Waterman, D. R. Matteson, S. L. Archer, & J. L. Orlofsky (Eds.), *Ego identity: A handbook for psychosocial research* (pp. 318–333). New York: Springer-Verlag.

Argyle, M. (1996). Rules for social relationships in four cultures. *Australian Journal of Psychology, 38,* 309–318.

Atkinson, D. R., Morten, G., & Sue, D. W. (Eds.). (1998). *Counseling American minorities* (5th ed.). Boston: McGraw-Hill.

Baker, J. M. (2002). *How homophobia hurts children: Nurturing diversity at home, at school, and in the community.* New York: Harrington Park Press.

Bank, B. J., & Hall, P. M. (1997). *Gender, equity, and schooling: Policy and practice.* New York: Garland.

Barrett-Lennard, G. T. (1962). Dimensions of therapist response as causal factors in therapeutic change. *Psychological Monographs: General and Applied, 76*(43, Whole No. 562).

Basic Behavioral Science Task Force, National Advisory Mental Health Council. (1996). Basic behavioral science research for mental health: Sociocultural and environmental processes. *American Psychologist, 51,* 722–731.

Beck, A. T. (1996). Beyond belief: A theory of modes, personality and psychopathology. In P. M. Salkovskis (Ed.), *Frontiers of cognitive therapy* (pp. 1–25). New York: Guilford Press.

Belgrave, L. L. (1993). Discrimination against older women in health care. In D. J. Garner & A. A. Young (Eds.), *Women and healthy aging: Living productively in spite of it all* (pp. 181–199). New York: Harrington Park Press/Haworth.

Bell, P. D., Micke, M. M., & Kasa, R. M. (1998). Equity in the diagnosis and treatment of chest pain: Gender, age, comorbidity. *American Journal of Health Behavior, 22,* 443–450.

Bem, S. L. (1974). The measurement of psychological androgyny. *Journal of Consulting and Clinical Psychology, 42,* 155–162.

Bemak, F., Chung, R., & Pedersen, P. (2003). *Counseling refugees: A psychosocial approach to innovative multicultural interventions.* Westport, CT: Greenwood Press.

Bergin, A. E. (1980). Psychotherapy and humanistic values. *Journal of Consulting and Clinical Psychology, 48,* 95–105.

Berry, J. W. (1980). Ecological analysis for cross-cultural psychology. In N. Warren (Ed.), *Studies in cross-cultural psychology* (pp. 157–189). New York: Academic Press.

Berry, J. W., Poortinga, Y. H., Segall, M. H., & Dasen, P. R. (1992). *Cross-cultural psychology: Research and applications.* New York: Cambridge University Press.

Blackless, M., Charuvastra, A., Derryck, A., Fausto-Sterling, A., Lauzanne, K., & Lee, E. (2000). How sexually dimorphic are we? Review and synthesis. *American Journal of Human Biology, 12,* 151–166.

Blazina, C., & Watkins, C. E. (2000). Separation/individuation, parental attachment, and male gender role conflict: Attitudes toward the feminine and the fragile masculine self. *Psychology of Men and Masculinity, 1,* 126–132.

Bohart, A., & Greenberg, L. S. (1997). *Empathy reconsidered: New directions in psychotherapy.* Washington, DC: American Psychological Association.

Bolman, W. (1968). Cross-cultural psychotherapy. *American Journal of Psychiatry, 124,* 1237–1244.

Bound, J., & Freeman, R. (1992). What went wrong? The 1980's erosion of the economic well-being of Black men. *Quarterly Journal of Economics, 107,* 201–232.

Bowling, A. (1999). Ageism in cardiology. *British Medical Journal, 319,* 1353–1355.

Bozarth, J. (1997). Empathy from the framework of client-centered theory and the Rogerian hypothesis. In A. Bohart & L. Greenberg (Eds.), *Empathy reconsidered: New directions in psychotherapy* (pp. 81–102). Washington, DC: American Psychological Association.

Braithwaite, V. A. (1986). Old age stereotypes: Reconciling contradictions. *Journal of Gerontology, 41,* 353–360.

Brammer, L. (1988). *The helping relationship: Process and skills* (4th ed.). Englewood Cliffs, NJ: Prentice-Hall.

Brew, F. P., & Cairns, D. R. (2004). Do culture or situational constraints determine choice of direct or indirect styles in intercultural workplace conflicts? *International Journal of Intercultural Relations, 28,* 331–352.

Brief, A. P., Dietz, J., Cohen, R. R., Pugh, S. D., & Vaslow, J. B. (2000). Just doing business: Modern racism and obedience to authority as explanations for employment discrimination. *Organizational Behavior and Human Decision Processes, 81,* 72–97.

Britton, D. (1990). Homophobia and homosexuality: An analysis of boundary maintenance. *Sociological Quarterly, 31,* 423–439.

Brooks, N. A., & Matson, R. R. (1982). Social-psychological adjustment to multiple sclerosis. *Social Science and Medicine, 16,* 2129–2135.

Broverman, I. K., Vogel, S. R., Broverman, D. M., Clarkson, E. E., & Rosenkrantz, P. S. (1972). Sex-role stereotypes: A current appraisal. *Journal of Social Issues, 28,* 59–78.

Brown, M. T., Fukunaga, C., Umemoto, D., & Wicker, L. (1996). Annual review, 1990–1996: Social class, work, and retirement behavior. *Journal of Vocational Behavior, 49,* 159–189.

Bruce, K., Schrumm, J., Trefethen, C., & Slovik, L. (1990). Students' attitudes about AIDS, homosexuality, and condoms. *AIDS Education and Prevention, 2,* 220–234.

Buie, D. H. (1981). Empathy: Its nature and limitations. *Journal of the American Psychoanalytic Association, 29,* 281–307.

Busse, I. W. (1968). Viewpoint: Prejudice and gerontology. *The Gerontologist, 8,* 66.

Butler, R. N. (1969). Age-ism: Another form of bigotry. *The Gerontologist, 9,* 243–246.

Butler, R. N. (1995). Ageism. In G. Maddox (Ed.), *The encyclopedia of aging* (2nd ed., pp. 38–39). New York: Springer.

Butz, M. R. (1992). Chaos: An omen of transcendence in the psychotherapeutic process. *Psychological Reports, 71,* 827–843.

Carlson, T. D., Kirkpatrick, D., Hecker, L., & Killmer, M. (2002). Religion, spirituality, and marriage and family therapy: A study of family therapists' beliefs about the appropriateness of addressing religious and spiritual issues in therapy. *American Journal of Family Therapy, 30,* 157–171.

Carson, V. B., & Green, H. (1992). Spiritual well-being: A predictor of hardiness in patients with acquired immunodeficiency syndrome. *Journal of Professional Nursing, 8,* 209–220.

Carter, R. T. (1991). Cultural values: A review of empirical research and implications for counseling. *Journal of Counseling and Development, 70,* 164–173.

Cass, V. C. (1979). Homosexual identity formation: Testing a theoretical model. *Journal of Homosexuality, 4,* 219–235.

Cassidy, J. (1998). Who killed the middle class? In P. A. Rothenberg (Ed.), *Race, class, and gender in the United States: An integrated study* (4th ed., pp. 215–220). New York: St. Martin's Press.

Center for Universal Design. (1997). *The principles of universal design.* Raleigh: North Carolina State University, College of Design. Retrieved from http://www.design.ncsu.edu/cud/about_ud/udprinciples.htm

Chambers, J. C. (1992). *Triad-training: A method for teaching basic counseling skills to chemical dependency counselors.* Unpublished doctoral dissertation, University of South Dakota, Rapid City.

Chen, Y. H., Chen, B. H., & Liao, F. C. (1995). A comparative study on the effects of counselor training by using the triad training model and the microcounseling model. *Journal of Teaching and Counseling, 1,* 265–277.

Chiu, L.-H. (1972). A cross-cultural comparison of cognitive styles in Chinese and American children. *International Journal of Psychology, 7,* 235–242.

Chung, R. C.-Y., & Bemak, F. (2002). The relationship of culture and empathy in cross cultural counseling. *Journal of Counseling and Development, 80,* 154–159.

Clark, A. J. (2007). *Empathy in counseling and psychotherapy.* Mahwah, NJ: Erlbaum.

College Entrance Examination Board and Educational Testing Service. (1996). *1996 college-bound seniors: A profile of state test takers.* Princeton, NJ: Educational Testing Service.

Constantine, M. G. (2002). Predictors of satisfaction with counseling: Racial and ethnic minority clients' attitudes toward counseling and ratings of their counselors' general and multicultural competence. *Journal of Counseling Psychology, 49,* 255–263.

Constantine, M. G., Juby, H. L., & Liang, J. J.-C. (2001). Examining multicultural counseling competence and race-related attitudes among White marital and family therapists. *Journal of Marital and Family Therapy, 27,* 353–362.

Corey, G. (2004). *Theory and practice of group counseling* (6th ed.). Pacific Grove, CA: Brooks/Cole.

Corey, G., Corey, M. S., & Callanan, P. (2003). *Issues and ethics in the helping professions* (6th ed.). Pacific Grove, CA: Brooks/Cole.

Cormier, W. H., & Cormier, L. S. (1991). *Interviewing strategies for helpers.* Pacific Grove, CA: Brooks/Cole.

Cornell, S., & Hartmann, D. (1998). *Ethnicity and race: Making identities in a changing world.* Thousand Oaks, CA: Pine Forge Press.

Corning, A. F. (2002). Self-esteem as a moderator between perceived discrimination and psychological distress among women. *Journal of Counseling Psychology, 49,* 117–126.

Council on American Islamic Relations. (2001). *Civil rights report.* Washington, DC: Author. Retrieved August 15, 2005, from http://www.CAIR-net.org/civilrights

Council on American Islamic Relations. (2002). *The status of Muslim civil rights in the United States.* Washington, DC: Author. Retrieved August 15, 2005, from http://www.CAIR-net.org/civilrights

Crabb, W. T., Moracco, J. C., & Bender, R. C. (1983). A comparative study of empathy training with programmed instruction for lay helpers. *Journal of Counseling Psychology, 30,* 221–226.

Crigger, N. J. (1996). Testing an uncertainty model for women with multiple sclerosis. *Advances in Nursing Science, 18,* 37–47.

Cross, W. E. (1991). *Shades of Black: Diversity in African American identity.* Philadelphia: Temple University Press.

Cross, W. E. (1995). The psychology of nigrescence: Revising the Cross model. In J. G. Ponterotto, J. M. Casas, L. A. Suzuki, & C. M. Alexander (Eds.), *Handbook of multicultural counseling* (pp. 93–122). Thousand Oaks, CA: Sage.

D'Andrea, M., & Daniels, J. (2000). Expanding our thinking about white racism: Facing the challenge of multicultural counseling in the 21st century. In J. G. Ponterotto, J. M. Casas, L. A. Suzuki, & C. M. Alexander (Eds.), *Handbook of multicultural counseling* (2nd ed., pp. 289–310). Thousand Oaks, CA: Sage.

De Lone, R. (1978). *Small futures*. New York: Harcourt Brace Jovanovich.

Deaux, K., & Lewis, L. L. (1983). Components of gender stereotypes. *Psychological Documents, 13*, 25. (Ms. No. 2583)

Decety, J., & Jackson, P. L. (2004). The functional architecture of human empathy. *Behavioral and Cognitive Neuroscience Reviews, 3*, 71–100.

Dermer, S. B., Smith, S. D., & Barto, K. K. (in press). Identifying and correctly labeling sexual prejudice, discrimination, and oppression. *Journal of Counseling and Development*.

Dinkmeyer, D., & Sperry, L. (2000). *Counseling and psychotherapy: An integrated, individual psychology approach*. Upper Saddle River, NJ: Prentice Hall.

Doi, L. (1969). Japanese psychology, dependency need, and mental health. In W. Caudill & T. Lin (Eds.), *Mental health research in Asia and the Pacific* (pp. 335–342). Honolulu, HI: East West Center Press.

Dreger, A. D. (1998). *Hermaphrodites and the medical invention of sex*. Cambridge, MA: Harvard University Press.

Duncan, G. J., & Brooks-Gunn, J. (2000). Family poverty, welfare reform, and child development. *Child Development, 71*, 188–196.

Egan, G. (1986). *The skilled helper*. Monterey, CA: Brooks/Cole.

Egan, G. (1994). *The skilled helper: A problem management approach*. Pacific Grove, CA: Brooks/Cole.

Egan, G. (2002). *The skilled helper: A problem-management and opportunity-development approach to helping*. Pacific Grove, CA: Brooks/Cole.

Ellis, A. (1962). *Reason and emotion in psychotherapy*. New York: Lyle Stuart.

Ellis, A. (1987). The evolution of rational-emotive therapy (RET) and cognitive behavior therapy (CBT). In J. K. Zeig (Ed.), *The evolution of psychotherapy* (pp. 107–132). New York: Brunner/Mazel.

Erera, P. I. (1997). Empathy training for helping professionals: Model and evaluation. *Journal of Social Work Education, 33*, 245–260.

Ernulf, K. E., & Innala, S. M. (1987). The relationship between affective and cognitive components of homophobic reaction. *Archives of Sexual Behavior, 16*, 501–509.

Faiver, C., Ingersoll, R. E., O'Brienn, E., & McNally, C. (2001). *Explorations in counseling and spirituality: Philosophical, practical, and personal reflections*. Pacific Grove, CA: Brooks/Cole.

Falicov, C. J. (1996). *Latino families in therapy: A guide to multicultural practice*. New York: Guilford Press.

Fassinger, R. E. (1991). The hidden minority: Issues and challenges in working with lesbian women and gay men. *The Counseling Psychologist, 19*, 157–176.

Feshback, N. D. (1975). Empathy in children: Some theoretical and empirical considerations. *Counseling Psychologist, 5*, 25–30.

Feshback, N. D. (1978). Studies of empathic behavior in children. In B. Maher (Ed.), *Progress in experimental psychology research* (pp. 1–47). New York: Academic Press.

Fischel, J. R. (2005). The new anti-Semitism. *Virginia Quarterly Review, 81*, 225–235.

Fischer, A. R., & Moradi, B. (2001). Racial and ethnic identity: Recent developments and needed directions. In J. G. Ponterotto, J. M. Casas, L. A. Suzuki, & C. M. Alexander (Eds.), *Handbook of multicultural counseling* (2nd ed., pp. 341–370). Thousand Oaks, CA: Sage.

Fitzgerald, L. F., & Betz, N. E. (1994). Career development in a cultural context: The role of gender, race, class, and sexual orientation. In M. L. Savikas & R. W. Lent (Eds.), *Convergence in career development theories* (pp. 103–117). Palo Alto, CA: Consulting Psychologists Press.

Fouad, N. A., & Brown, M. T. (2001). Role of race and social class in development: Implications for counseling psychology. In S. D. Brown & R. W. Lent (Eds.), *Handbook of counseling psychology* (pp. 379–408). New York: Wiley.

Frable, D. E. S. (1997). Gender, racial, ethnic, sexual, and class identities. *Annual Review of Psychology, 48*, 139–162.

Fraboni, M., Saltstone, R., & Hughes, S. (1990). The Fraboni Scale of Ageism (FSA): An attempt at a more precise measure of ageism. *Canadian Journal on Aging, 9*, 56–66.

Frankl, V. (1963). *Man's search for meaning.* Boston: Beacon Press.

Franklin, K. (2000). Antigay behaviors among young adults: Prevalence, patterns and motivators in a noncriminal population. *Journal of Interpersonal Violence, 15*, 339–362.

Friedman, M. L., Friedlander, M. L., & Blustein, D. L. (2005). Toward an understanding of Jewish identity: A phenomenological study. *Journal of Counseling Psychology, 52*, 77–83.

Furnham, A., & Forey, J. (1994). The attitudes, behaviors and beliefs of patients of conventional vs. complementary (alternative) medicine. *Journal of Clinical Psychology, 53*, 458–469.

Gaertner, S. L., & Dovidio, J. F. (1977). The subtlety of White racism arousal and helping behavior. *Journal of Personality and Social Psychology, 35*, 691–707.

Garstka, T. A., Schmitt, M. T., Branscombe, N. R., & Hummert, M. L. (2004). How young and older adults differ in their responses to perceived age discrimination. *Psychology and Aging, 19*, 326–335.

Gatz, M., & Smyer, M. A. (1992). The mental health system and older adults in the 1990s. *American Psychologist, 47*, 741–751.

Geertz, C. (1975). On the nature of anthropological understanding. *American Scientist, 63*, 47–53.

Gekoski, W. L., & Knox, V. J. (1990). Ageism or healthism? Perceptions based on age and health status. *Journal of Aging and Health, 2*, 15–27.

Gelatt, H. B. (1962). Decision-making: A conceptual frame of reference for counseling. *Journal of Counseling Psychology, 9*, 240–245.

Gelatt, H. B. (1989). Positive uncertainty: A new decision-making framework for counseling. *Journal of Counseling Psychology, 36*, 252–256.

Gelatt, H. B. (1991). *Creative decision making using positive uncertainty.* Los Altos, CA: Crisp.

Goldstein, A. P., & Michaels, G. Y. (1985). *Empathy: Development training and consequences*. Hillsdale, NJ: Erlbaum.

Goleman, D. (2003). *Destructive emotions: A scientific dialogue with the Dalai Lama*. New York: Bantam.

Gordon, R. A., & Arvey, R. D. (2004). Age bias in laboratory and field settings: A meta-analytic investigation. *Journal of Applied Social Psychology, 34,* 468–492.

Greenlinger, V. (1985). Authoritarianism as a predictor of response to heterosexual and homosexual erotica. *High School Journal, 68,* 183–186.

Griffith, R., & Brian, A. (1999). Families and spirituality: Therapists as facilitators. *The Family Journal, 7,* 161–165.

Gudykunst, W., & Ting-Toomey, S. (1988). *Culture and interpersonal communication*. Newbury Park, CA: Sage.

Gurin, P. (2006). Informing theory from practice and applied research. *Journal of Social Issues, 62,* 621–628.

Haaga, D. (1991). Homophobia? *Journal of Social Behavior and Personality, 6,* 171–174.

Haddock, G., & Zanna, M. (1998). Authoritarianism, values, and the favorability and structure of antigay attitudes. In G. M. Herek (Ed.), *Stigma and sexual orientation: Understanding prejudice against lesbians, gay men, and bisexuals* (pp. 82–107). Newbury Park, CA: Sage.

Hall, E. T. (1976). *Beyond culture*. Garden City, NY: Anchor Press.

Hansen, M. (1998). Suing bosses over beliefs. *ABA Journal, 84,* 30–32.

Harper, F. D. (2003). Background: Concepts and history. In F. D. Harper & J. McFadden (Eds.), *Culture and counseling: New approaches* (pp. 1–19). Boston: Allyn & Bacon.

Hassell, B. L., & Perrewe, P. L. (1993). An examination of the relationship between older workers' perceptions of age discrimination and employee psychological states. *Journal of Managerial Issues, 5,* 109–120.

Hayward, R. (2005). Historical keywords: Empathy. *The Lancet, 366,* 1071.

Healey, J. F. (1997). *Race, ethnicity, and gender in the United States: Inequality, group conflict, and power*. Thousand Oaks, CA: Pine Forge Press.

Heider, F. (1958). *The psychology of interpersonal relations*. New York: Wiley.

Helgesen, S. (2005). *The web of inclusion: A new architecture for building great organizations*. Washington, DC: Beard Books.

Helms, J. E. (1984). Toward a theoretical explanation of the effects of race on counseling: A Black and White model. *The Counseling Psychologist, 12,* 163–165.

Henley, N. M., Meng, K., O'Brien, D., McCarthy, W. J., & Sockloskie, R. J. (1998). Developing a scale to measure the diversity of feminist attitudes. *Psychology of Women Quarterly, 22,* 317–348.

Hepworth, D. W., & Larsen, J. A. (1993). *Direct social work practice: Theory and skills* (4th ed.). Pacific Grove, CA: Brooks/Cole.

Herek, G. M. (1984). Beyond homophobia: A social psychological perspective on attitudes toward lesbians and gay men. *Journal of Homosexuality, 10,* 1–18.

Herek, G. M. (1986). On heterosexual masculinity: Some psychical consequences of the social construction of gender and masculinity. *American Behavioral Scientist, 29,* 563–577.

Herek, G. M. (1987). Can functions be measured? A new perspective on the functional approach to attitudes. *Social Psychology Quarterly, 50,* 285–303.

Herek, G. M. (1990). The context of anti-gay violence: Notes on cultural and heterosexualism. *Journal of Interpersonal Violence, 5,* 313–363.

Herek, G. M. (2000). The psychology of sexual prejudice. *Current Directions in Psychological Science, 9,* 19–22.

Herek, G. M. (2004). Beyond "homophobia": Thinking about sexual prejudice and stigma in the twenty-first century. *Sexuality Research and Social Policy, 1,* 6–24.

Herek, G. M., & Glunt, E. (1993). Interpersonal contact and heterosexuals' attitudes toward gay men. *Journal of Sex Research, 30,* 239–244.

Hernandez, A. G., & Kerr, B. A. (1985, August). *Evaluating the triad model and traditional cross-cultural counselor training.* Paper presented at the 93rd Annual Convention of the American Psychological Association, Los Angeles, CA.

Hickson, J., & Kriegler, S. (1996). *Multicultural counseling in a divided and traumatized society.* Westport, CT: Greenwood.

Highlen, P. S. (1994). Racial/ethnic diversity in doctoral programs of psychology: Challenges for the twenty-first century. *Applied and Preventive Psychology, 3,* 91–108.

Hillerbrand, E., & Shaw, D. (1990). Age bias in a general hospital: Is there ageism in psychiatric consultation? *Clinical Gerontologist, 2,* 3–13.

Hodges, S. D., & Wegner, D. M. (1997). Automatic and controlled empathy. In W. Ickes (Ed.), *Empathic accuracy* (pp. 311–339). New York: Guilford Press.

Hoffman, M. L. (1982). Development of prosocial motivation: Empathy and guilt. In N. Eisenberg (Ed.), *The development of prosocial behavior* (pp. 281–313). New York: Academic Press.

Hofstede, G. (1991). *Cultures and organizations: Software of the mind.* London: McGraw Hill.

Hofstede, G. (2001). *Culture's consequences: Software of the mind* (2nd ed.). Thousand Oaks, CA: Sage.

Hofstede, G. J., Pedersen, P. B., & Hofstede, G. (2002). *Exploring culture: Exercises, stories and synthetic cultures.* Yarmouth, ME: Intercultural Press.

Hunter, D. (2005, June 6). *Unpacking the invisible knapsack: II. Sexual orientation.* Retrieved from http://www.cs.earlham.edu/~hyrax/personal/files/student_res/straightprivilege.htm

Hurst, M. D. (2004, April 7). Justice Dept. intervenes in school headscarf case. *Education Week, 23,* 4.

Huston, A. C., & Alvarez, M. M. (1990). The socialization context of gender role development in early adolescence. In R. Montemayor, G. R. Adams, & T. P.

Gullotta (Eds.), *Advances in adolescent development: Vol. 2. From childhood to adolescence: A transitional period?* (pp. 156–182). Newbury Park, CA: Sage.

Iannotti, R. J. (1975). The nature and measurement of empathy in children. *The Counseling Psychologist, 5*(2), 21–25.

Ickes, W. (1997). *Empathic accuracy.* New York: Guilford Press.

Irvin, R., & Pedersen, P. (1995). The internal dialogue of culturally different clients: An application of the triad training model. *Journal of Multicultural Counseling and Development, 23,* 4–11.

Ivey, A. E. (1986). *Developmental therapy.* San Francisco: Jossey-Bass.

Ivey, A. E. (1988). *Intentional interviewing and counseling: Facilitating client development.* Pacific Grove, CA: Brooks/Cole.

Ivey, A. E. (1994). *Intentional interviewing and counseling: Facilitating client development in a multicultural society* (3rd ed.). Pacific Grove, CA: Brooks/Cole.

Ivey, A. E., & Ivey, M. B. (2001). Developmental counseling and therapy and multicultural counseling and therapy: Metatheory, contextual consciousness, and action. In D. C. Locke, J. E. Myers, & E. L. Herr (Eds.), *The handbook of counseling* (pp. 219–236). Thousand Oaks, CA: Sage.

Ivey, A. E., & Ivey, M. B. (2007). *Intentional interviewing and counseling: Facilitating client development in a multicultural society* (6th ed.). Pacific Grove, CA: Brooks/Cole.

Ivey, A. E., Ivey, M. B., & Simek-Morgan, L. (1993). *Counseling and psychotherapy: A multicultural perspective.* Boston: Allyn & Bacon.

Jackson, R. L. (1999). White space, White privilege: Mapping the discursive inquiry into the self. *Quarterly Journal of Speech, 85,* 38–54.

Jahoda, G. (2005). Theodor Lipps and the shift from "sympathy" to "empathy." *Journal of the History of the Behavioral Sciences, 41,* 151.

James, J. W., & Haley, W. E. (1995). Age and health bias in practicing clinical psychologists. *Psychology and Aging, 10,* 610–616.

Jandt, F. E., & Pedersen, P. B. (1996). *Constructive conflict management: Asia-Pacific cases.* Thousand Oaks, CA: Sage.

Jones, J. M. (1997). *Prejudice and racism* (2nd ed.). New York: McGraw-Hill.

Jung, C. G. (1933). *Modern man in search of a soul* (W. S. Dell & C. F. Baynes, Trans.). New York: Harcourt, Brace.

Kafer, A. (2003). Compulsory bodies: Reflections on heterosexuality and able-bodiedness. *Journal of Women's History, 15*(3), 77–89.

Kagitcibasi, C. (1988). Diversity of socialization and social change. In P. Dasen, J. Berry, & N. Sartorius (Eds.), *Health and cross-cultural psychology: Towards applications* (pp. 23–47). Newbury Park, CA: Sage.

Kagitcibasi, C. (1996). *Family and human development across cultures: A view from the other side.* Mahwah, NJ: Erlbaum.

Kalavar, J. M. (2001). Examining ageism: Do male and female college students differ? *Educational Gerontology, 27,* 507–513.

Kanfer, F. H., & Goldstein, A. P. (1986). *Helping people change: A textbook of methods*. New York: Pergamon.

Kastenbaum, I. (1963). The reluctant therapist. *Geriatrics, 19,* 296–301.

Kaufman, D. R. (1995). Professional women: How real are the recent gains? In J. Freeman (Ed.), *Women: A feminist perspective* (5th ed., pp. 287–305). Mountain View, CA: Mayfield.

Keefe, T. (1976). Empathy: The critical skill. *Social Work, 21,* 10–14.

Kelly, G. (1955). *The psychology of personal constructs* (2 vols.). New York: Norton.

Kelly, T. A. (1990). The role of values in psychotherapy: A critical review of process and outcome effects. *Clinical Psychology Review, 10,* 171–186.

Kerns, J., & Fine, M. (1994). The relations between gender and negative attitudes toward gay men and lesbians: Do gender role attitudes mediate this relationship? *Sex Roles, 31,* 297–307.

Keysar, B. (1994). The illusory transparency of intention: Linguistic perspective taking in text. *Cognitive Psychology, 26,* 165–208.

Kilianski, S. E. (2003). Explaining heterosexual men's attitudes toward women and gay men: The theory of exclusively masculine identity. *Psychology of Men and Masculinity, 4,* 37–56.

Kilpatrick, S. D., & McCullough, M. E. (1999). Religion and spirituality in rehabilitation psychology. *Rehabilitation Psychology, 14,* 388–402.

Kim, U., Triandis, H. C., Kagitçibasi, C., Choi, S. C., & Yoon, G. (1994). *Individualism and collectivism*. Thousand Oaks, CA: Sage.

Kim, U., Yang, K. S., & Hwang, K. K. (2006). *Indigenous and cultural psychology: Understanding people in context*. New York: Springer.

King, M. C. (1992). Occupational segregation by race and sex, 1940–1988. *Monthly Labor Review, 115,* 30–37.

Kiselica, M. S. (2003). Anti-Semitism and insensitivity toward Jews by the counseling profession: A Gentile's view on the problem and his hope for reconciliation— A response to Weinrach (2002). *Journal of Counseling and Development, 81,* 426–440.

Kitchener, K. S., & Brenner, H. G. (1990). Wisdom and reflective judgment: Knowing in the face of uncertainty. In R. J. Sternberg (Ed.), *Wisdom: Its nature, origins, and development* (pp. 212–229). New York: Cambridge University Press.

Kite, M. E., & Johnson, B. T. (1988). Attitudes toward older and younger adults: A meta-analysis. *Psychology and Aging, 3,* 233–244.

Kite, M. E., Stockdale, G. D., Whitley, B. E., & Johnson, B. T. (2005). Attitudes toward younger and older adults: An updated meta-analytic review. *Journal of Social Issues, 61,* 241–266.

Klonoff, E. A., & Landrine, H. (1999). Cross-validation of the Schedule of Racist Events. *Journal of Black Psychology, 25,* 231–254.

Klonoff, E. A., Landrine, H., & Ullman, J. B. (1999). Racial discrimination and psychiatric symptoms among Blacks. *Cultural Diversity and Ethnic Minority Psychology, 5,* 329–339.

Kottler, J., Carlson, J., & Keeney, B. (2005). *American shaman*. New York: Routledge.

Kruse, D. L. (1998). Persons with disabilities: Demographic, income, and health care characteristics. *Monthly Labor Review, 121*(9), 13–22.

Kuhn, T. S. (1970). *The structure of scientific revolutions* (2nd ed.). Chicago: University of Chicago Press.

Labouvie-Vief, G. (1990). Wisdom as integrated thought: historical and developmental perspectives. In R. J. Sternberg (Ed.), *Wisdom: Its nature, origins, and development* (pp. 52–83). New York: Cambridge University Press.

Lamison-White, L. (1997). Poverty in the United States: 1996. In *Current population reports* (pp. 60–198). Washington, DC: U.S. Census Bureau.

Landrine, H., & Klonoff, E. A. (1996). The Schedule of Racist Events: A measure of racial discrimination and a study of its negative physical and mental health consequences. *Journal of Black Psychology, 22*, 144–168.

Landrine, H., & Klonoff, E. A. (1997). *Discrimination against women: Prevalence, consequences, remedies*. Thousand Oaks, CA: Sage.

Landrine, H., Klonoff, E. A., Gibbs, J., Manning, V., & Lund, M. (1995). Physical and psychiatric correlates of gender discrimination: An application of the Schedule of Sexist Events. *Psychology of Women Quarterly, 19*, 473–492.

Langer, S. L., & Wurf, E. (1997, August). *The effects of channel-consistent and channel-inconsistent interpersonal feedback on the formation of metaperceptions*. Paper presented at the 105th Annual Convention of the American Psychological Association, Chicago, IL.

Langman, P. F. (1999). *Jewish issues in multiculturalism: A handbook for educators and clinicians*. Northvale, NJ: Jason Aronson.

Lebowitz, B. D., & Niederehe, G. (1992). Concepts and issues in mental health and aging. In J. E. Birren, R. B. Sloane, & G. D. Cohen (Eds.), *Handbook of mental health and aging* (2nd ed., pp. 3–26). San Diego, CA: Academic Press.

Levine, D. N. (1985). *The flight from ambiguity: Essays in social and cultural theory*. Chicago: University of Chicago Press.

LeVine, R., & Padilla, A. (1980). *Crossing cultures in therapy: Pluralistic counseling for the Hispanic*. Monterey, CA: Brooks/Cole.

Levy, B. R., & Banaji, M. R. (2002). Implicit ageism. In T. D. Nelson (Ed.), *Ageism: Stereotypes and prejudice against older persons* (pp. 49–75). Cambridge, MA: MIT Press.

Liester, M. B. (1996). Inner voices: Distinguishing transcendent and pathological characteristics. *Journal of Transpersonal Psychology, 28*, 1–30.

Lifton, R. J. (1993). *The protean self*. New York: Basic Books.

Lin, T. Y., & Lin, M. C. (1978). Service delivery issues in Asian-North American communities. *American Journal of Psychiatry, 135*, 454–456.

Linver, M. R., Brooks-Gunn, J., & Kohen, D. E. (2002). Family processes as pathways from income to young children's development. *Developmental Psychology, 38*, 719–734.

Liu, J. H., & Liu, S. H. (1999). Interconnectedness and Asian social psychology. In T. Sugiman, M. Karasawa, J. H. Liu, & C. Ward (Eds.), *Progress in Asian social psychology: Vol. III. Theoretical and empirical contributions* (pp. 9–31). Seoul, South Korea: Kyoyook-Kwahak-Sa.

Liu, W. M., Ali, S. R., Soleck, G., Hopps, J., Dunston, K., & Pickett, T., Jr. (2004). Using social class in counseling psychology research. *Journal of Counseling Psychology, 51*, 3–18.

Locke, D. C. (1998). *Increasing multicultural understanding: A comprehensive model.* Thousand Oaks, CA: Sage.

Lowenthal, T. (2000). *The road to Census 2000: A chronology of key issues* (Report on Census 2000: KIDS COUNT and Population Reference Bureau). Washington, DC: U.S. Census Bureau.

Luzzo, D. A. (1992). Ethnic group and social class differences in college students' career development. *Career Development Quarterly, 41*, 161–173.

Maass, A., Castelli, L., & Arcuri, L. (2000). Measuring prejudice: Implicit versus explicit techniques. In D. Capozza & R. Brown (Eds.), *Social identity processes: Trends in theory and research* (pp. 96–116). London: Sage.

Mahoney, M. J., & Patterson, K. M. (1992). Changing theories of change: Recent developments in counseling. In S. D. Brown & R. W. Lent (Eds.), *Handbook of counseling and psychology* (2nd ed., pp. 665–689). New York: Wiley.

Mantsios, G. (1998). Class in America: Myths and realities. In P. A. Rothenberg (Ed.), *Race, class, and gender in the United States: An integrated study* (4th ed., pp. 202–214). New York: St. Martin's Press.

Maran, R. (2002). A report from the United Nations world conference against racism, racial discrimination, xenophobia, and related intolerance, Durban, South Africa, 2001. *Social Justice, 29*(1/2), 177–185.

Marshall, C. S., & Reinhartz, J. (1997). Gender issues in the classroom. *The Clearing House, 70*, 333–337.

Marsigilio, A. (1993). Attitudes towards homosexual activity and gays as friends: A national survey of heterosexual fifteen- to nineteen-year-old males. *Journal of Sex Research, 30*, 12–17.

McCarn, S. R., & Fassinger, R. E. (1996). Revisioning sexual minority identity formation: A new model of lesbian identity and its implications for counseling and research. *The Counseling Psychologist, 24*, 508–534.

McIntosh, P. (1992). White privilege and male privilege: A personal account of coming to see correspondences through work in women's studies. In M. L. Andersen & P. Hill Collins (Eds.), *Race, class, and gender: An anthology* (pp. 70–81). Belmont, CA: Wadsworth.

McLennan, N. A. (1999). Applying the cognitive information processing approach to career problem solving and decision making to women's career development. *Journal of Employment Counseling, 36*, 82–97.

McLoyd, V. C. (1998). Socioeconomic disadvantage and child development. *American Psychologist, 53*, 185–204.

McMullin, J. A., & Marshall, V. W. (2001). Ageism, age relations, and garment industry work in Montreal. *Gerontologist, 41*, 111–122.

McNeil, J. M. (2001). *Americans with disabilities: Household economic studies*. Washington, DC: U.S. Government Printing Office, U.S. Bureau of the Census, Current Population Reports.

McWhirter, E. H., Torres, D., & Rasheed, S. (1998). Assessing barriers to women's career adjustment. *Journal of Career Assessment, 6*, 449–479.

Meacham, J. (1990). The loss of wisdom. In R. J. Sternberg (Ed.), *Wisdom: Its nature, origins, and development* (pp. 181–211). New York: Cambridge University Press.

Meharbian, A., & Epstein, N. (1972). A measure of emotional empathy. *Journal of Personality, 40*, 525–543.

Meichenbaum, D. (1977). *Cognitive behavior modification: An integrative approach*. New York: Plenum.

Meichenbaum, D. (1986). Cognitive behavior modification. In F. H. Kanfer & A. P. Goldstein (Eds.), *Helping people change* (pp. 346–381). New York: Pergamon.

Miller, D. T. (1999). The norm of self-interest. *American Psychologist, 54*, 1053–1060.

Miller, L. (2005, August 29). In search of the spiritual. *Newsweek*, 46–65.

Mintz, R. D., & Mahalik, J. R. (1996). Gender role orientation and conflict as predictors of family roles for men. *Sex Roles, 34*, 805–821.

Moghaddam, F., & Taylor, D. M. (1986) What constitutes an "appropriate psychology" for the developing world? *International Journal of Psychology, 21*, 253–267.

Moradi, B., & Subich, L. M. (2002). Perceived sexist events and feminist identity development attitudes: Link to women's psychological distress. *The Counseling Psychologist, 30*, 44–65.

Moradi, B., & Subich, L. M. (2003). A concomitant examination of the relations of perceived racist and sexist events to psychological distress for African American women. *The Counseling Psychologist, 31*, 451–469.

Morin, A. (1993). Self talk and self awareness: On the nature of the relation. *Journal of Mind and Behavior, 14*, 223–234.

Morin, A. (1995). Characteristics of an effective internal dialogue in the acquisition of self information. *Imagination, Cognition and Personality, 15*(1), 45–48.

Morrow, S. L. (2000). First do no harm: Therapist issues in psychotherapy with lesbian, gay, and bisexual clients. In R. M. Perez, K. A. DeBord, & K. J. Bieschke (Eds.), *Handbook of counseling and psychotherapy with lesbian, gay, and bisexual clients* (pp. 137–156). Washington, DC: American Psychological Association.

Mosher, D. L., & Sirkin, M. (1984). Measuring a macho personality constellation. *Journal of Research in Personality, 18*, 150–163.

Murgatroyd, W. (1995). *Application of the triad model in teaching counseling skills and providing immediate supervision*. Unpublished manuscript, University of New Orleans.

Murphy, G., & Murphy, L. (1968). *Asian psychology*. New York: Basic Books.

Nagda, B. R. A. (2006). Breaking barriers, crossing borders, building bridges: Communication process in intergroup dialogues. *Journal of Social Issues, 62*, 553–576.

National Gay and Lesbian Task Force. (1990). *Antigay violence, victimization, and defamation in 1989*. Washington, DC: Author.

Neimeyer, G. J., Fukuyama, M. A., Bingham, R. P., Hall, L. E., & Mussenden, M. E. (1986). Training cross-cultural counselors: A comparison of the pro and anti-counselor triad models. *Journal of Counseling and Development, 64*, 437–439.

Newcomb, T. M. (1953). An approach to the study of communicative acts. *Psychological Review, 60*, 393–404.

Nicks, T. L. (1985). Inequalities in the delivery and financing of mental health services for ethnic minority Americans. *Psychotherapy, 22*, 469–476.

Nuessel, F. H. (1982). The language of ageism. *The Gerontologist, 22*, 273–276.

Oetting, E. R., & Beauvais, F. (1991). Orthogonal cultural identification theory: The cultural identification of minority adolescents. *International Journal of the Addictions, 25*, 655–685.

O'Neil, J. M., Helms, B. J., Gable, R. K., David, L., & Wrightsman, L. S. (1986). Gender Role Conflict Scale: College men's fear of femininity. *Sex Roles, 14*, 335–350.

Opotow, W. (1990). Moral exclusion and injustice: An introduction. *Journal of Social Issues, 46*, 1–20.

Opotow, W., & Weiss, L. (2000). Denial and the process of moral exclusion in environmental conflict. *Journal of Social Issues, 56*, 475–490.

Orpen, C. (1995). The effects of perceived age discrimination on employee job satisfaction, organizational commitment, and job involvement. *Psychology: A Journal of Human Behavior, 32*, 55–56.

Palma, T. V., & Stanley, J. L. (2002). Effective counseling with lesbian, gay, and bisexual clients. *Journal of College Counseling, 5*, 74–89.

Palmore, E. B. (2001). The ageism survey: First findings. *Gerontologist, 41*, 572–575.

Palombi, B. J., & Mundt, A. M. (2005). Achieving social justice for college women with disabilities: A model for inclusion. In R. L. Toporek, L. H. Gerstein, N. A. Fouad, G. Roysircar, & T. Israel (Eds.), *Handbook for social justice in counseling psychology: Leadership, vision, and action* (pp. 170–184). Thousand Oaks, CA: Sage.

Parrott, D. J., Adams, H. E., & Zeichner, A. (2002). Homophobia: Personality and attitudinal correlates. *Personality and Individual Differences, 32*, 1269–1278.

Pedersen, P. (1966). *The triad training model*. Unpublished master's thesis, University of Minnesota.

Pedersen, P. (1991). Multiculturalism as a fourth force in counseling. *Journal of Counseling and Development, 70*, 5–25.

Pedersen, P. (1997). *Culture-centered counseling interventions: Striving for accuracy*. Thousand Oaks, CA: Sage.

Pedersen, P. (1998). *Multiculturalism as a fourth force*. Philadelphia: Brunner/Mazel.

Pedersen, P. B. (1999). *Hidden messages in culture-centered counseling: A triad training model*. Thousand Oaks, CA: Sage.

Pedersen, P. (2000a). *A handbook for developing multicultural awareness* (3rd ed.). Alexandria, VA: American Counseling Association.

Pedersen, P. (2000b). *Hidden messages in culture-centered counseling: A triad training model*. Thousand Oaks, CA: Sage.

Pedersen, P. (2003a). *Culture-centered counseling* (APA Psychotherapy Videotape Series II). Washington, DC: American Psychological Association.

Pedersen, P. (2003b). *Pedersen: A videotape demonstrating the triad training model: Hearing the pro and anti-counselor in multicultural counseling*. Amherst, MA: Microtraining Associates.

Pedersen, P. (2004). *110 experiences for multicultural learning*. Washington, DC: American Psychological Association.

Pedersen, P., & Brooks-Harris, J. (2005). *Pedersen's triad training model: Five vignettes of culturally different counselors interviewing a single client* (Videotape and manual). Framingham, MA: Microtraining and Multicultural Development Press.

Pedersen, P., Draguns, J., Lonner, W., & Trimble, J. (Eds.). (2008). *Counseling across cultures* (6th ed.). Thousand Oaks, CA: Sage.

Pedersen, P. B., & Ivey, A. E. (1993). *Culture-centered counseling and interviewing skills*. Westport, CT: Praeger/Greenwood Press.

Peitchinis, J. (1990). The historical roots of empathy in the helping professions. In R. C. MacKay, J. R. Hughes, & E. J. Carver (Eds.), *Empathy in the helping relationship* (pp. 28–46). New York: Springer.

Pike, R. (1966). *Language in relation to a united theory of the structure of human behavior*. The Hague, the Netherlands: Mouton.

Plante, T. G. (1999). A collaborative relationship between professional psychology and the Roman Catholic Church: A case example and suggested principles for success. *Professional Psychology: Research and Practice, 30*, 541–546.

Podolsky, D., & Silberner, J. (1993, January 18). How medicine mistreats the elderly. *U.S. News and World Report*, 72–76, 78–79.

Polimeni, A., Hardie, E., & Buzwell, S. (2000). Homophobia among Australian heterosexuals: The role of sex, gender role ideology, and gender role traits. *Current Research in Social Psychology, 5*, 47–62.

Pollard, K., & O'Hare, W. (1999, September). America's racial and ethnic minorities. *Population Bulletin, 42*(3).

Ponterotto, J. G. (1988). Racial consciousness development among White counselor trainees. *Journal of Counseling and Development, 16*, 146–156.

Ponterotto, J. G., Casas, J. M., Suzuki, L. A., & Alexander, C. M. (2001). *Handbook of multicultural counseling* (2nd ed.). Thousand Oaks, CA: Sage.

Poortinga, Y. H. (1992). Towards a conceptualization of culture for psychology. In S. Iwawaki, Y. Kashima, & K. Leung (Eds.), *Innovations in cross-cultural psychology* (pp. 3–17). Amsterdam: Swets & Zeitlinger.

Pope-Davis, D. B., & Coleman, H. L. K. (Eds.). (2001). *The intersection of race, class, and gender in multicultural counseling*. Thousand Oaks, CA: Sage.

Pope-Davis, D. B., Coleman, H. L. K., Liu, W. M., & Toporek, R. L. (Eds.). (2003). *Handbook of multicultural competencies in counseling and psychology*. Thousand Oaks, CA: Sage.

Poston, W. S. C. (1990). The biracial identity development model: A needed addition. *Journal of Counseling and Development, 69*, 152–155.

Rauscher, L., & McClintock, J. (1996). Ableism curriculum design. In M. Adams, L. A. Bell, & P. Griffen (Eds.), *Teaching for diversity and social justice* (pp. 198–231). New York: Routledge.

Reasons, C. E., Conley, D. J., & Debro, J. (2002). *Race, class, gender and justice in the United States*. Boston: Allyn & Bacon.

Rich, A. (1986). Compulsory heterosexuality and lesbian existence. In *Blood, bread, and poetry: Selected prose 1979–1985* (pp. 23–75). New York: Norton.

Richards P. S., & Bergin, A. E. (1997). *A spiritual strategy for counseling and psychotherapy*. Washington, DC: American Psychological Association.

Richards, P. S., Rector, J. M., & Tjeltveit, A. C. (1999). Values, spirituality and psychotherapy. In W. R. Miller (Ed.), *Integrating spirituality into treatment: Resources for practitioners* (pp. 133–160). Washington, DC: American Psychological Association.

Ridley, C. R. (1989). Racism in counseling as an aversive behavioral process. In P. Pedersen, J. Draguns, W. Lonner, & J. Trimble (Eds.), *Counseling across cultures* (3rd ed., pp. 55–77). Thousand Oaks, CA: Sage.

Ridley, C. R. (1995). *Overcoming unintentional racism in counseling and therapy: A practitioner's guide to intentional intervention*. Thousand Oaks, CA: Sage.

Ridley, C. R., Ethington, L., & Heppner, P. P. (2008). Cultural confrontation: A skill of advanced cultural empathy. In P. Pedersen, J. Draguns, W. Lonner, & J. Trimble (Eds.), *Counseling across cultures* (6th ed., pp. 377–395). Thousand Oaks, CA: Sage.

Ridley, C., & Lingle, D. W. (1996). Cultural empathy in multicultural counseling: A multidimensional process model. In P. Pedersen, J. Draguns, W. Lonner, & J. Trimble. *Counseling across cultures* (4th ed., pp. 21–46). Thousand Oaks, CA: Sage.

Ridley, C. R., Mendoza, D. W., Kanitz, B. E., Angermeier, L., & Zenk, R. (1994). Cultural sensitivity in multicultural counseling: A perceptual schema model. *Journal of Counseling Psychology, 41*, 125–136.

Ridley, C., & Udipi, S. (2002). Putting cultural empathy into practice. In P. Pedersen, J. Draguns, W. Lonner, & J. Trimble (Eds.), *Counseling across cultures* (5th ed., pp. 317–334). Thousand Oaks, CA: Sage.

Robertson, J. M., & Fitzgerald, L. F. (1990). The (mis)treatment of men: Effects of client gender role and life-style on diagnosis and attribution of pathology. *Journal of Counseling Psychology, 37*, 3–9.

Robinson, D. T., & Schwartz, J. P. (2004). Relationship between gender role conflict and attitudes toward women and African Americans. *Psychology of Men and Masculinity, 5*(1), 65–71.

Robinson, T. L. (1999). The intersections of dominant discourses across race, gender, and other identities. *Journal of Counseling and Development, 77*, 73–79.

Robinson, T. L., & Howard-Hamilton, M. F. (2000). *The convergence of race, ethnicity, and gender: Multiple identities in counseling.* Upper Saddle River, NJ: Merrill.

Rochlin, M. (1982). Heterosexual questionnaire. *M: Gentle Men for Gender Justice, 8,* 9.

Rodriguez, J. (2004). Mestiza spirituality: Community, ritual, and justice. *Theological Studies, 65,* 317–339.

Rogers, C. R. (1959). A theory of therapy, personality, and interpersonal relationships, as developed in the client-centered framework. In S. Koch (Ed.), *Psychology: A study of science. Vol. 3: Formulations of the person and the social context* (pp. 184–256). New York: McGraw-Hill.

Rogers, C. R. (1961). *On becoming a person: A therapist's view of psychotherapy.* Boston: Houghton Mifflin.

Rogers, C. R. (1975). Empathic: An unappreciated way of being. *The Counseling Psychologist, 5,* 2–10.

Rogers, C. R. (1986). Reflection of feelings. *Person-Centered Review, 1,* 375–377.

Rosen, E. J., & Weltman, S. F. (1996). Jewish families: An overview. In M. McGoldrick, J. K. Pearce, & J. Giordano (Eds.), *Ethnicity and family therapy* (2nd ed., pp. 611–630). New York: Guilford Press.

Rosenberg, N. A., Pritchard, J. K., Weber, J. L., Cann, H. M., Kidd, K. K., Zhivotovsky, L. A., & Feldman, M. W. (2002, December 20). Genetic structure of human populations. *Science, 298,* 2381–2385.

Rosenkrantz, P., Vogel, S., Bee, H., Broverman, I., & Broverman, D. M. (1968). Sex-role stereotypes and self-concepts in college students. *Journal of Consulting and Clinical Psychology, 32,* 287–295.

Rosensweig, M. R. (1992). Psychological science around the world. *American Psychologist, 39,* 877–884.

Rowe, W., Bennett, S. K., & Atkinson, D. R. (1994). White racial identity models: A critique and alternative proposal. *The Counseling Psychologist, 22,* 129–146.

Rubinstein, D. (1993). Capitalism, social mobility, and distributive justice. *Social Theory and Practice, 19,* 183–194.

Ruiz, P. (1990). Ethnic identity: Crisis and resolution. *Journal of Multicultural Counseling and Development, 18,* 29–40.

Rupp, D. E., Vodanovich, S. J., & Credé, M. (2005). The multidimensional nature of ageism: Construct validity and group differences. *Journal of Social Psychology, 145,* 335–362.

Sadker, D. (2000). Gender equity: Still knocking at the classroom door. *Equity and Excellence in Education, 33*(1), 80–83.

Sadker, M., & Sadker, D. (1994). *Failing at fairness: How our schools cheat girls.* New York: Scribner's.

Satir, V. (1964). *Conjoint family therapy.* Palo Alto, CA: Science and Behavior Books.

Saxton, M. (1998). Disability rights and selective abortion. In R. Solinger (Ed.), *Abortion wars: A half-century struggle* (pp. 374–393). Berkeley: University of California Press.

Schor, J. B. (1992). *The overworked American: The unexpected decline of leisure*. New York: Basic Books.

Scogin, F. Y., & McElreath, L. (1994). Efficacy of psychosocial treatments for geriatric depression: A quantitative review. *Journal of Consulting and Clinical Psychology, 62*, 69–74.

Segall, M. H., Dasen, P. R., Berry, J. W., & Poortinga, Y. H. (1990). *Human behavior in global perspective: An introduction to cross-cultural psychology*. New York: Pergamon.

Segall, M. H., Dasen, P. R., Berry, J. W., & Poortinga, Y. H. (1999). *Human behavior in global perspective: An introduction to cross-cultural psychology* (2nd ed.). New York: Pergamon.

Seltzer, R. (1992). The social location of those holding antihomosexual attitudes. *Sex Roles, 26*, 391–398.

Seto, A., Young, S., Becker, K. W., & Kiselica, M. S. (2006). Application of the triad training model in a multicultural counseling course. *Counselor Education and Supervision, 45*, 304–318.

Sewell, W. H. (1971). Inequality of opportunity for higher education. *American Sociological Review, 36*, 793–809.

Sheikh, A., & Sheikh, K. S. (1989). *Eastern and Western approaches to healing: Ancient wisdom and modern knowledge*. New York: Wiley.

Shore, B. (1996). *Culture in mind: Cognition, culture and the problem of meaning*. New York: Oxford University Press.

Shweder, R. A. (1990). Cultural psychology: What is it? In J. W. Stigler, R. A. Shweder, & G. Herdt (Eds.), *Cultural psychology: Essays on comparative human development* (pp. 1–45). New York: Cambridge University Press.

Slack, C. W., & Slack, E. N. (1976, February). It takes three to break a habit. *Psychology Today*, 46–50.

Smith, J. A., Harré, R., & Van Langenhove, L. (1995). *Rethinking psychology*. London: Sage.

Solomon, R. (1971). *Mao's revolution and the Chinese political culture*. Berkeley: University of California Press.

Spence, J. T., & Helmreich, R. L. (1978). *Masculinity and femininity: Their psychological dimensions, correlates, and antecedents*. Austin: University of Texas Press.

Stanard, R. P., Sandhu, D. S., & Painter, L. C. (2000). Assessment of spirituality in counseling. *Journal of Counseling and Development, 78*, 204–210.

Stark, L. (1991). Traditional gender role beliefs and individual outcomes: An exploratory analysis. *Sex Roles, 24*, 639–650.

Stevens, M. J., & Wedding, D. (2004). *Handbook of international psychology*. New York: Brunner-Routledge.

Stewart, E. C. (1981). Cultural sensitivities in counseling. In P. B. Pedersen, J. G. Draguns, W. J. Lonner, & J. E. Trimble (Eds.), *Counseling across cultures* (pp. 61–86). Honolulu: University of Hawaii Press.

Stone, J. H. (Ed.). (2005). *Culture and disability*. Thousand Oaks, CA: Sage.

Stromquist, N. P. (1997). *Literacy for citizenship: Gender and grassroots dynamics in Brazil*. Albany: State University of New York Press.

Strong, S. (1978). Social psychological foundations of psychotherapy and behavior change. In S. Garfield & A. Bergin (Eds.), *Handbook of psychotherapy and behavior change: An empirical analysis* (pp. 101–136). New York: Wiley.

Strous, M. (2003). *Racial sensitivity and multicultural training*. Westport, CT: Praeger.

Strous, M. (2006). Facilitating reflexivity in interracial and multicultural psychotherapy. *International Journal for the Advancement of Counseling, 28*, 41–55.

Strous, M., Skuy, M., & Hickson, J. (1993). Perceptions of the Triad Model's efficacy in training family counsellors for diverse South African groups. *International Journal for the Advancement of Counseling, 16*, 307–318.

Sue, D. W. (1980). [Evaluation report from NIMH training project for Developing Interculturally Skilled Counselors, DISC: 1978–1979]. Unpublished document. Honolulu: East West Center.

Sue, D. W. (1991). A diversity perspective on contextualism. *Journal of Counseling and Development, 70*, 300–301.

Sue, D. W. (1995). Multicultural organizational development: Implications for the counseling profession. In J. G. Ponterotto, J. M. Casas, L. A. Suzuki, & C. M. Alexander (Eds.), *Handbook of multicultural counseling* (pp. 474–492). Newbury Park, CA: Sage.

Sue, D. W., Bingham, R. P., Porche-Burke, L., & Vasquez, M. (1999). The diversification of psychology: A multicultural revolution. *American Psychologist, 54*, 1061–1069.

Sue, D. W., Carter, R. T., Casas, J. M., Fouad, N. A., Ivey, A. E., Jensen, M., et al. (1998). *Multicultural counseling competencies: Individual and organizational development*. Thousand Oaks, CA: Sage.

Sue, D. W., Ivey, A. E., & Pedersen, P. B. (1996). *A theory of multicultural counseling and therapy*. Pacific Grove, CA: Brooks/Cole.

Sue, D. W., & Sue, D. (1999). *Counseling the culturally different: Theory and practice* (3rd ed.). New York: Wiley.

Sue, D. W., & Sue, D. (2003). *Counseling the culturally diverse: Theory and practice* (4th ed.). New York: Wiley.

Sue, S. (1998). In search of cultural competencies in psychology and counseling. *American Psychologist, 53*, 440–448.

Sue, S. (1999). Science, ethnicity, and bias: Where have we gone wrong? *American Psychologist, 54*, 1070–1077.

Szalita, A. B. (1976). Some thoughts on empathy. *Psychiatry, 39*, 142–152.

Szapocznik, J., & Kurtines, W. M. (1993). Family psychology and cultural diversity: Opportunities for theory, research, and application. *American Psychologist, 48*, 400–407.

Tart, C. T. (1975). Some assumptions of orthodox, Western psychology. In C. T. Tart (Ed.), *Transpersonal psychologies* (pp. 59–112). New York: Harper & Row.

Thompson, M., Ellis, R., & Wildavsky, A. (1990). *Cultural theory*. San Francisco: Westview Press.

Tix, A. P., & Frazier, P. A. (1998). The use of religious coping during stressful life events: Main effects, moderation, and mediation. *Journal of Consulting and Clinical Psychology, 66*, 411–422.

Toporek, R. L., Gerstein, L., Fouad, N. A., Roysircar, G., & Israel, T. (Eds.). (2005). *Handbook for social justice in counseling psychology: Leadership, vision and action*. Thousand Oaks, CA: Sage.

Triandis, H. C. (1977). *Interpersonal behavior*. Monterey, CA: Brooks/Cole.

Trimble, J. (1981). Value differentials and their importance in counseling American Indians. In P. Pedersen, J. Draguns, W. Lonner, & J. Trimble (Eds.), *Counseling across cultures* (2nd ed., pp. 203–226). Honolulu: University of Hawaii Press.

Troiden, R. R. (1989). The formation of homosexual identities. *Journal of Homosexuality, 17*, 43–73.

Truax, C. B., & Carkhuff, R. R. (1967). *Toward effective counseling and psychotherapy: Training and practice*. Chicago: Aldine.

Tseng, W.-S., & Hsu, J. (1972). The Chinese attitude toward parental authority as expressed in Chinese children's stories. *Archives of General Psychiatry, 26*, 28–34.

Tseng, W.-S., & Hsu, J. (1980). Minor psychological disturbances of everyday life. In H. Triandis & J. Draguns (Eds.), *Handbook of cross-cultural psychology: Vol. 6. Psychopathology* (pp. 61–98). Boston: Allyn & Bacon.

Turtle, A. M. (1987). A silk road for psychology. In G. H. Blowers & A. M. Turtle (Eds.), *Psychology moving East: The status of Western psychology in Asia and Oceanic* (pp. 1–23). London: Westview Press.

U.S. Census Bureau. (1995). *Poverty 1995*. Washington, DC: U.S. Government Printing Office.

U.S. Census Bureau. (1996). *1993 panel of the survey of income and program participation, October 1995–January 1996*. Washington, DC: U.S. Government Printing Office.

U.S. Census Bureau. (2000). *The population profile of the United States*. Washington, DC: Author. Retrieved June 19, 2005, from http://www.census.gov/population/www/pop-profile/profile2000.html

U.S. Census Bureau. (2001a). *A glossary of census terms: Report on Census 2000 Washington, DC: KIDS COUNT and Population Reference Bureau*. Washington, DC: Author.

U.S. Census Bureau. (2001b). *Population profile of the United States: America at the close of the 20th century*. Washington, DC: U.S. Government Printing Office.

U.S. Department of Justice. (2002). *FBI uniform crime reports*. Washington, DC: Author. Retrieved March 14, 2005, from http://www.fbi.gov/ucr/01hate.pdf

Utsey, S. O., & Ponterotto, J. G. (1996). Development and validation of the Index of Race-Related Stress (IRRS). *Journal of Counseling Psychology, 43*, 490–501.

Van de Ven, P., Bornholt, L., & Bailey, M. (1996). Measuring cognitive, affective, and behavioral components of homophobic reaction. *Archives of Sexual Behavior, 25*, 155–179.

VandenBos, G. R., Stapp, J., & Kilburg, R. R. (1981). Health service providers in psychology: Results of the 1982 APA Human Resources Survey. *American Psychologist, 38,* 1330–1352.

VanderStoep, S., & Green, C. (1988). Religiosity and homonegativism: A path analytic study. *Basic and Applied Social Psychology, 9,* 135–147.

Vygotsky, L. S. (1987). *The collected works of L. S. Vygotsky: Vol. 1. Problems of general psychology* (R. W. Rieber & A. S. Carton, Trans. & Eds.). New York: Plenum.

Wade, P., & Bernstein, B. L. (1991). Culture sensitivity training and counselor's race: Effects on Black female clients' perceptions and attrition. *Journal of Counseling Psychology, 38,* 9–15.

Waldrop, M. M. (1992). *Complexity: The emerging science at the edge of order and chaos.* New York: Touchstone.

Walsh, R. (1989). Toward a synthesis of Eastern and Western psychologies. In A. A. Sheikh & K. S. Sheikh (Eds.), *Eastern and Western approaches to healing* (pp. 542–555). New York: Wiley.

Watson, J. C., Goldman, R., & Vanaerschot, G. (1998). Empathic: A postmodern way of being? In L. S. Greenberg, J. C. Watson, & G. Lietaer (Eds.), *Handbook of experiential psychotherapy* (pp. 61–81). New York: Guilford Press.

Watts, R. J. (1992). Elements of a psychology of human diversity. *Journal of Community Psychology, 20,* 116–131.

Wei-Ming, T. (2000). Multiple modernities: A preliminary inquiry into the implications of East Asian modernity. In L. E. Harrison & S. P. Huntington (Eds.), *Culture matters: How values shape human progress* (pp. 256–266). New York: Basic Books.

Weidman, H. H. (1975). Concepts as strategies for change. *Psychiatric Annals, 5,* 312–313.

Weinberg, G. (1972). *Society and the healthy homosexual.* New York: St. Martin's Press.

Weinrach, S. G. (2002). The counseling profession's relationship to Jews and the issues that concern them: More than a case of selective awareness. *Journal of Counseling and Development, 80,* 300–314.

West, C. (1993). *Race matters.* Boston: Beacon Press.

West, C. (1999). *The Cornel West reader.* New York: Basic Civitas Books.

Wilson, W. J. (1987). *The truly disadvantaged.* Chicago: University of Chicago Press.

Wisch, A. F., & Mahalik, J. R. (1999). Male therapists' clinical bias: Influence of client gender roles and therapist gender role conflict. *Journal of Counseling Psychology, 46,* 51–60.

Wolf, C. T., & Stevens, P. (2001). Integrating religion and spirituality into marriage and family counseling. *Counseling & Values, 46,* 66–72.

Wong, P. T. P., & Wong, L. C. J. (2006). *Handbook of multicultural perspectives on stress and coping.* New York: Springer.

Wood, J. E. (2004). Religious human rights and a democratic state. *Journal of Church and State, 46,* 739–765.

World Health Organization. (2003). *World report on violence and health*. Geneva, Switzerland: Author.

Wrenn, G. (1962). The culturally encapsulated counselor. *Harvard Educational Review, 32*, 444–449.

Wrenn, G. (1985). Afterword: The culturally encapsulated counselor revisited. In P. Pedersen (Ed.), *Handbook of cross-cultural counseling and therapy* (pp. 323–329). Westport, CT: Greenwood.

Wrightsman, L. S. (1992). *Assumptions about human nature: Implications for researchers and practitioners*. Newbury Park, CA: Sage.

Yang, K. S., Hwang, K. K., Pedersen, P. B., & Daibo, I. (2003). *Progress in Asian social psychology: Conceptual and empirical contributions*. Westport, CT: Praeger.

Youngs, D. J. (1996). *Effects of the multicultural triad training model on African American students' perceptions of school counselors*. Unpublished doctoral dissertation, Seton Hall University, South Orange, NJ.

Yunger, J. L., Carver, P. R., & Perry, D. G. (2004). Does gender identity influence children's psychological well-being? *Developmental Psychology, 40*, 572–582.

Zinnbauer, B. J., & Pargament, K. I. (2000). Working with the sacred: Four approaches to religious and spiritual issues in counseling. *Journal of Counseling and Development, 78*, 162–171.

AUTHOR INDEX

McCarn, S. R., 73
McCarthy, W. J., 126
McClintock, J., 144
McCullough, M. E., 105
McElreath, L., 141
McIntosh, P., 82, 84
McLennan, N. A., 127
McLoyd, V. C., 149
McMullen, J. A., 141
McNally, C., 106
McNeill, J. M., 144
McWhirter, E. H., 127
Meacham, J., 109
Meharbian, A., 9
Meichenbaum, D., 157, 176
Mendoza, D. W., 72
Meng, K., 126
Michaels, G. Y., 9, 10, 11, 156
Micke, M. M., 141
Miller, D. T., 12, 24
Miller, L., 104
Mintz, R. D., 126
Moghaddam, F., 15
Moracco, J. C., 11
Moradi, B., 120, 127, 132
Morion, A., 160
Morrow, S. L., 129
Morten, G., 73
Mosher, D. L., 137
Mundt, A. M., 58
Murgatroyd, W., 187, 188
Murphy, G., 30
Murphy, L., 30
Mussenden, M. E., 189

Nagda, B. R. A., 24
National Gay and Lesbian Task Force, 136
Neimeyer, G. J., 189
Newcomb, T. M., 50
Nicks, T. L., 148
Niederehe, G., 141
Nuessel, F. H., 139

O'Brien, D., 126
O'Brienn, E., 106

Oetting, E. R., 70, 71
O'Hare, W., 123n
O'Neil, J. M., 127
Opotow, W., 57, 58
Orpen, C., 141

Padilla, A., 51
Painter, L. C., 105
Palma, T. V., 137
Palmore, E. B., 139
Palombi, B. J., 58
Pargament, K. I., 106, 107, 108
Parrott, D. J., 137
Patterson, K. M., 224
Pedersen, P. B., 3, 6, 7, 14, 16, 17, 20, 26, 29n, 30n, 32, 36, 36n, 46, 52, 53, 54, 64, 70n, 71, 75n, 93, 95n, 96, 101, 103, 143n, 155, 156, 157, 160–161, 166n, 167, 168, 172, 172n, 177, 178, 183, 187, 190, 197n, 200, 201, 202, 203, 206, 210, 212, 213, 225, 226, 229, 231, 233, 237, 240n
Peitchinis, J., 8
Perrewe, P. L., 141
Perry, D. G., 129
Plante, T. G., 105
Podolsky, D., 139
Polimeni, A., 137
Pollard, K., 123n
Ponterotto, J. G., 73, 120, 231, 234
Poortinga, Y. H., 15, 47, 200, 201
Pope-Davis, D. B., 51, 145
Porche-Burke, L., 226
Poston, W. S. C., 73, 122
Pugh, S. D., 121

Rasheed, S., 127
Rauscher, L., 144
Reasons, C. E., 128, 135, 149
Rector, J. M., 105
Reinhartz, J., 127
Rich, A., 86
Richards, P. S., 105
Ridley, C., 4, 43

Umemoto, D., 148
U. S. Census Bureau, 122, 127, 149, 150, 150n, 151, 154
U. S. Department of Justice, 136, 137
Utsey, S. O., 120

Van Langenhove, L., 224
VandenBos, G. R., 141
VanderStoep, S., 138
Van de Ven, P., 137
Vaslow, J. B., 121
Vasquez, M., 226
Vodanovich, S. J., 142
Vogel, S. R., 126
Vygotsky, L. S., 157

Wade, P., 189, 190
Waldrop, M. M., 224
Walsh, R., 20
Waterman, A. S., 109
Watkins, C. E., 126
Watson, J. C., 8
Wedding, D., 23, 24
Wegner, D. M., 10
Weidman, H. H., 51
Wei-Ming, T., 3
Weinberg, G., 136
Weinrach, S. G., 132

Weiss, L., 58
Weltman, S. F., 132
West, C., 23, 74, 120, 121
Whitley, B. E., 139
Wicker, L., 148
Wildavsky, A., 225
Wilson, W. J., 120
Wisch, A. F., 129
Wolf, C. T., 105
Wong, L. C. J., 14
Wong, P. T. P., 14
Wood, J. E., 131
World Health Organization, 127
Wrenn, G., 55, 93–94, 97, 99
Wright, L. W., 137
Wrightsman, L. S., 46, 127, 224
Wurf, E., 160

Yang, K. S., 14, 32, 34
Yoon, G., 25
Young, S., 186
Youngs, D. J., 194, 195
Yunger, J. L., 129

Zanna, M., 137
Zeichner, A., 137
Zenk, R., 72
Zinnbauer, B. J., 106, 107, 108

SUBJECT INDEX

American Counseling Association
(ACA)
  Advocacy Task Force of, 228
  on intersex procedures, 125
  legislative advocacy training from,
      230
American Psychological Association
  and reexamination of cultural bias,
      225
  Division 44 of (Society for the Psy-
      chological Study of Lesbian,
      Gay, and Bisexual Issues), 139
American School Counselor Associa-
  tion, 230
Analysis of Values Questionnaire, 189,
  190
Androcentrism, 126
Androgyny, 125, 129
Anthropology(ists)
  and cultural differences, 5
  relativist position of, 13
Anticlient and proclient model, 168
Anticounselor (TTM), 156, 161,
      162–163, 187, 189, 190–191,
      192, 194
Anti-Islamic oppression, 132
Anti-Semitism, 131–132
Appropriate interaction–intervention,
      54
Arbitration, as recovery skill, 182
Articulating of problem from client's
      perspective, 184–184
Asia, family styles in, 34
Asian psychologies vs. Western psy-
      chologies, 20. *See also* Chinese
      therapies; India; Japanese
      therapies
Association for Gay, Lesbian, and
      Bisexual Issues in Counseling,
      139
Assumptions, culturally learned, 54
Assumptions dominant in U.S. and
      European American context,
      77–78, 234
Assumptions behind inclusive cultural
      empathy, 54

1. on similarity and difference, 54,
      62–70
2. on culture as complex, 55, 70–76
3. on behavior and meaning, 55,
      76–80
4. on racism as unintentional, 55,
      80–91
5. on cultural encapsulation, 55,
      93–101
6. on inclusion and exclusion, 56,
      101–104
7. on spiritual resources, 56, 104–109
8. on ambiguity, 56, 109–112
Atheists, religious discrimination
      against, 133
Atman, 31
Attending, 171–173
  to cultural content, 231, 232
Awareness–knowledge–skill model,
      230–232
Awareness questions (self-assessment),
      238–239
Ayurvedic therapies from India, 37

Baker, Jean M., 139
Balance, 50–51, 178, 204–205
  achievement of in ICE, 51–53
  as goal, 179
  as multicultural counseling skill,
      206
  between positive and negative,
      207
Balance of power, in counseling, 202
Barriers
  in Alpha Culture, 243
  in Beta Culture, 245
  in Delta Culture, 247–248
  in Gamma Culture, 246
Behavior in Context (activity), 79
Behaviorism, and feelings, 170
Behaviors
  and expectations, 46
    culturally learned, 221
    in interpersonal cultural grid,
        211, 212, 213–214, 216,
        217, 219, 220, 237
  interpreting of, 155

and meaning, 55, 76–80, 185–186, 211

in synthetic cultures, 35–36

Beliefs, as influencing view of world, 111

Beta client

practicing inclusive cultural empathy with, 250–251

in reflection of feelings, 174

Beta Culture (strong uncertainty avoidance), 244–245

Bhagavad Gita, 37

Bias(es)

age-based, 142

cultural, 13

in psychology, 13

favoring Christians, 129, 131

gender, 127, 128

See also Discrimination; Prejudice

Bicultural model, 71

Bicultural contextualizer (BCC), 167–168

Biracial identity development model, 122

Bluest Eye, The (Morrison), 99

Bone: A Novel (Ng), 99

Both/and approach, 64–65

Boyd, Cyndy J., 139

Boy Scouts of America, gay scoutmaster expelled from, 138

Buddhism

and individual, 31

and mindfulness meditation, 157

Buddhist therapy, 37

Census Bureau, on race and ethnicity, 122–124

Challenging, as recovery skill, 182

Change, negative aspects of, 207

Changing the topic, as recovery skill, 182

Chaos theory, 224

Ch'i, 37

Chinese child-rearing practices, 33–34

Chinese philosophy, Tao in, 37, 50

Chinese revolution, 14

Chinese therapies, 37

Circuit, The: Stories From the Life of a Migrant Child (Jiménez), 99

Cisgendered, 128, 129

Clarifying Cultural Identity Variables (activity), 75

Classism, 148

Class status, 145, 148–151, 152–154

Client(s)

articulating problem from perspective of, 183

cultural context of, 4

increased diversity of, 14

Client advocacy, 228

Client resistance, recognizing of, 184–185

Client–student advocacy domain, 228–229

Client–student dimension, of counseling advocacy, 228–229

Client–student empowerment domain, 228

Clinton, Bill, 138

Cognitive balance, 50

Cognitive–Behaviour Modification, 176

Cognitive therapy, 160

Collective social perspective, 7

Collectivism (collectivist perspective), 25

and high-context perspective, 26–27

See also Non-Western collectivism

Common ground

and conflict management, 232, 237

in interpersonal cultural grid examples, 220

Community collaboration domain, 229

Complexity, 205–206

Complexity theory, 56, 224

Concha (case example), 63

Conflict

common ground in management of, 232, 237

gender role, 127

for high- vs. low-context perspectives, 26–27

and inclusive cultural empathy, 237
and interpersonal cultural grid, 213, 237
and orthogonal approach to individual identity, 71–72
Confucian perspective, and dependency, 34
Constructivism, and religion or spirituality, 107–108
Context
  and cultural variables, 119
  of experience, 67, 74
  See also High-context perspective;
    Low-context perspective
Convergence, 116, 151, 154
Convergent empathy, 4, 42
Council on American-Islamic Relations
    (CAIR), on attacks against
    Muslims, 132
Counseling
  and balance, 51
  balance of power in, 202
  culture as mediating, *xv*
  educational model of, 199–200
  empathy construction in, 43
  and formal vs. informal support
    systems, 16–20
  globalization of, 14–16
  and inclusive cultural empathy, 3
  multiculturalism excluded from,
    209–210
  from multicultural perspective,
    48–49
  relationship-centered models in,
    xvi
  relationship factors in, 4
  varying contexts of, *xv*
Counseling services
  formal, 17–19, 236
  informal, 17–19, 236
  nonformal, 17–19, 236
Counseling Technique Self-Report
    Inventory, 192
Counselor
  broad definition of, *xvii*
  cultural background of articulated,
    113

cultural sensitivity of, 72–73
multicultural competencies of,
    51–53
and objectivity, 48
Counselor Rating Form, 189
Counselor Rating Form—Short, 188
Counselor Technique Evaluation Scale,
    192
Countertransference, and ICE, 45
Critical-dialogic empathy, 24
Cross-cultural comparison, 6
Cross-Cultural Counseling Inventory,
    188–189
Cross-cultural research, and dilemma of
    cultural labeling, 216
Cultural assumptions of empathy, 12–14
Cultural beliefs, and mental illness diagnosis and treatment, 13
Cultural bias, 13
Cultural borderlands, 63, 65–66
  as connection points, 99
Cultural context of client, 4
  and ICE, 47
Cultural countertransference, 45
Cultural deficit model, 15
Cultural differences, 234
Cultural diversity, synthetic cultures as
    examples of, 34–36
Cultural empathy, 43, 44. *See also*
    Empathy
Cultural encapsulation, 55, 57, 93–101,
    206, 209–210
  combating vulnerability to, 98–100
  as common today, 97
    in mental health services, 13
  in ethical guidelines by professional
    counseling and human service
    associations, 235
  prevention of, 232, 234–235
Cultural grid, 233
  in Alpha Culture, 243
  in Beta Culture, 244
  in Delta Culture, 247
  in Gamma Culture, 246
  See also Interpersonal cultural grid;
    Intrapersonal cultural grid
Cultural identity constructs, 116

Professor–teaching assistant case study, and interpersonal cultural grid, 217–219

Psychoanalytic perspective, and feelings, 171

Psychologists, and cultural differences, 13

Psychology(ies)
    Asian and Western, 20
    cultural, 48
    and cultural differences, 5
    indigenous, 15
    international in scope, 23, 24
    paradigm shift in, 224
    and spirituality, 105 (*see also at* Spiritual)

Psychopathology, proper boundaries of, 20

Psychotherapy
    cultural assumptions underlying, 15
    globalization of, 14–16

Public arena dimension, of counseling advocacy, 230

Public information domain of advocacy competencies, 230

Race, 119–122
    and race census, 122–124
    salience of, 151

Race Census Discussion Questions, 124

Racial and Cultural Development model, 120

Racial identity development, 121–122

Racism
    anti-Semitism as, 131
    as unintentional, 55, 80–84, 121

Rating Sheet for Scoring Emotional Content of a Story and Emotions Felt While Telling a Story, 172

Rational emotive therapy (RET), and feelings, 170

Rationality, and intuition, 111

Reality therapy, and feelings, 171

Reasoning, and knowledge, 56–57, 206

Recategorization approach, 29

Recovery skills, 182–183, 208
    articulation of problem, 183–184
    overcoming defensiveness toward clients, 185–186
    recognizing client resistance, 184–185

Reductionism, 205, 224, 227

Referral, as recovery skill, 182

Reflection
    of feelings, 169–175
    of meanings, 175–177
    meanings and feelings combined for balance, 177–178

Refugees, 15

Rejectionism (toward religion and spirituality), 106–107

Relational meaning, 31

Relational needs, 58

Relational self, 20

Relationship factors, in counseling, 4

Relativism, and cultural encapsulation, 209

Religion, 104–109. *See also* Spiritual resources and spirituality

Religious differences, 129, 131–134

Religious privileges, 89

Research, intercultural, 208–209

Rituals, and cultural context, 77

Robinson, T. L., 117

Rogers, Carl, 7, 8–9, 11, 12, 176

Role reversal, as recovery skill, 182

Salience, 117–119
    of race, 151

Sandberg family (case example), 79–80

SAT scores, by income, 150

School–community dimension of counseling advocacy, 229

Sears, James T., 139

Self
    for collectivistic vs. individual cultures, 24
    contrasting perspectives on, 27, 29–31
    fundamentalist, 47
    as organization (Betz), 225
    relational, 20

Therapeutic relationship (alliance)
balance of power in, 202–204
in ICE perspective, 42
and diversity of clients vs. of
providers, 13–14
empathy in, 8
as emotional response, 9
and gender bias, 129
proper degree of influence in, 53
and similarities/differences, 63
See also Counseling
Therapies, non-Western, 37–39
Therapist's Notebook for Lesbian, Gay and Bisexual Clients (Whitman & Boyd), 139
There Are No Children Here: The Story of Two Boys Growing Up in the Other America (Kotlowitz), 99
Time, perspectives of, 66–67
Titchener, Edward, 8
Transgendered, 128
Transitional model, 71
Treatment of mental illness
and cultural beliefs, 13
Triad training model (TTM), 156, 161–164, 165–166, 186–195
debriefing for, 167
exercise on, 195–198
Truth
and cultural encapsulation, 94, 95
and exclusivism regarding religion, 107
TTM. *See* Triad training model

Uncertainty, positive, 109–110
debate activity on, 112
Unconditional regard, 9
Unintentional heterosexism, as straight privilege, 84–86
Unintentional oppression, 86–91
through religion in family life, 133–134
Unintentional racism, 55, 80–82
need to recognize, 121
as White privilege, 82–84

United Nations, on religious persecution and discrimination, 131
Universal design, 146–147
Universalist approach, 64
Unlearning, 99
U.S. Census Bureau, on race and ethnicity, 122–124

Validity, external, 13
Value expressive function, of homophobia, 136
Values, dimensions of, 34
Videotape, on culture-centered counseling competence, 231
Virtual client, 4–5
Vontress, Clemmont, 44
Vygotsky, L. S., 20

Web of inclusion, 49–50
Weinberg, George, 136
West, Cornel, 74, 120
Western, use of word, 7, 27
Western individualism
and non-Western collectivism, 15–16
See also Individualism
Western models of counseling,
among non-Western cultures, 14
Western perspective, 7–8
measurement scale for, 27, 30
and modernization, 207
Western psychologies, vs. Asian, 20
White privilege, 81
unintentional racism as, 82–84
White racial identity model, 122
Whitman, Joy S., 139
Williams, Walter, 139
Workplace, multicultural, 25

Yin/yang, 37, 51, 178
Yoga, 37

Zen Buddhism, 38

ABOUT THE AUTHORS

Paul B. Pedersen, PhD, received his PhD from Claremont Graduate School in Claremont, California. He is professor emeritus in the Department of Human Services at Syracuse University in Syracuse, New York, and visiting professor in the Department of Psychology at the University of Hawaii in Honolulu. His research interests include multicultural counseling and counselor education and training, international educational exchange and brain-drain issues, indigenous psychologies, alternative and complementary therapies, constructive conflict management in a cultural context, and intrapersonal (internal dialogue/self-talk) resources for mental health. He has taught at the University of Minnesota in Minneapolis, Syracuse University, and the University of Alabama at Birmingham. For 6 years he taught at universities in Taiwan, Malaysia, and Indonesia. He has authored, coauthored, or edited 40 books, 99 articles, and 72 chapters on aspects of multicultural counseling. He is a fellow of Divisions 9 (Society for the Psychological Study of Social Issues), 17 (Society of Counseling Psychology), 45 (Society for the Psychological Study of Ethnic Minority Issues), and 52 (International Psychology) of the American Psychological Association.

Hugh C. Crethar, PhD, is an assistant professor in the School Counseling and Guidance Program of the Department of Educational Psychology at the University of Arizona in Tucson. He is on the executive board of the National Institute for Multicultural Competence, has served in numerous positions within the American Counseling Association, and is the 2007–2008 president of Counselors for Social Justice. His work centers on promoting multicultural competence and advocacy competence in the field of counseling.

Jon Carlson, PsyD, EdD, ABPP, has earned doctorates in counseling and clinical psychology and also holds an advanced certificate in psychotherapy. He is a distinguished professor in the Division of Psychology and Counseling at Governors State University in University Park, Illinois, and director of the Lake Geneva Wellness Clinic in Lake Geneva, Wisconsin. He is a fellow of the American Psychological Association and holds a diplomate in family psychology from the American Board of Professional Psychology. He has authored more than 40 books and 150 professional articles and has developed over 200 commercial and professional videos. He is the founding editor of *The Family Journal* and past president of the International Association of Marriage and Family Counseling.